"DON'T SLEEP WITH STEVENS!"

New Perspectives on the History of the South

Florida A&M University, Tallahassee

Florida Atlantic University, Boca Raton

Florida Gulf Coast University, Ft. Myers

Florida International University, Miami

Florida State University, Tallahassee

University of Central Florida, Orlando

University of Florida, Gainesville

University of North Florida, Jacksonville

University of South Florida, Tampa

University of West Florida, Pensacola

New Perspectives on the History of the South   *Edited by John David Smith*

University Press of Florida

Gainesville/Tallahassee/Tampa/Boca Raton

Pensacola/Orlando/Miami/Jacksonville/Ft. Myers

Timothy J. Minchin

"DON'T SLEEP WITH STEVENS!"

THE J. P. STEVENS

CAMPAIGN AND

THE STRUGGLE TO

ORGANIZE THE

SOUTH, 1963–80

Foreword by John David Smith, Series Editor

Copyright 2005 by Timothy J. Minchin
Printed in the United States of America on recycled, acid-free paper

10 09 08 07 06 05   6 5 4 3 2 1

Library of Congress Cataloging-in-Publication Data
Minchin, Timothy J.
Don't sleep with Stevens!: The J.P. Stevens campaign and the
struggle to organize the South, 1963–80 / Timothy J. Minchin;
foreword by John David Smith.
p. cm.—(New perspectives on the history of the South)
Includes bibliographical references and index.
ISBN 0-8130-2810-8 (acid-free paper)
1. J.P. Stevens & Co.—History—20th century. 2. Labor unions—
Southern States—Organizing—History—20th century. 3. Textile
workers—Southern States—History—20th century. I. Title. II.
Series.
HD9859.S8M56 2005
331.88'177'00975—dc22

2004066119

The University Press of Florida is the scholarly publishing
agency for the State University System of Florida, comprising
Florida A&M University, Florida Atlantic University, Florida
Gulf Coast University, Florida International University, Florida
State University, University of Central Florida, University of
Florida, University of North Florida, University of South
Florida, and University of West Florida

University Press of Florida
15 Northwest 15th Street
Gainesville, FL 32611-2079
http://www.upf.com

For Olga

CONTENTS

FOREWORD

La Trobe University historian Timothy J. Minchin ranks
among the foremost exemplars of the "new" southern labor
history. Recent students of southern labor struggles examine microscopically the concerns of labor and management. They assess the broad implications of labor conflict
and contextualize them within the regional, national, and
international social and economic history of labor relations.

Minchin's *"Don't Sleep with Stevens!"* is the first book-
length examination of the seventeen-year fight between
organized labor and the giant textile company J. P. Stevens,
a corporation that operated more than seventy mills scattered in forty southern communities. During the 1970s the
highly publicized clash between J. P. Stevens and the Textile Workers Union of America (TWUA), later the Amalgamated Clothing and Textile Workers Union (ACTWU),
signified the use of new tactics by workers to unionize the
South's largest industry. It also signaled management's
fierce determination to resist organized labor.

Drawing upon a rich arsenal of primary sources, including much oral history testimony, Minchin uses the labor-
management struggle as a window to observe the obstacles
southern textile workers experienced, the limited gains of
their 1980 settlement, and how the North American Free
Trade Agreement ultimately had a devastating impact on
the South's textile industry. Dating back to the 1960s, labor
leaders targeted J. P. Stevens because of that firm's persistent and blatant violation of labor laws, including racial
and sexual discrimination. The company, according to
Minchin, "was a symbol of antiunionism." Determined to
kill labor organizing drives, J. P. Stevens employed the

tactic of selective discharges, cognizant that even if the National Labor Relations Board forced the firm to rehire fired employees, the union's organizing campaign would have collapsed by the time the laborers actually returned to work. Minchin points out that, under federal tax law, J. P. Stevens was entitled to deduct NLRB back pay awards from its taxes as legitimate business expenses.

To combat J. P. Stevens, union leaders employed several tactics. They sponsored a national boycott of J. P. Stevens's products, a strategy hindered by the fact that the company was large and diverse and its products were distributed under various brand names. The union also launched the first "corporate campaign," a weapon later adopted by other unions. The corporate campaign applied pressure on J. P. Stevens by forcing members of its board of directors to resign and by influencing financial and insurance companies to persuade J. P. Stevens's executives to bargain in good faith with the union.

ACTWU also conducted an extensive publicity campaign designed to pressure the company. The union's media campaign, according to Minchin, "portrayed the Stevens boycott as a fight for social justice against a lawless employer that had no respect for workers' rights." During the campaign, the union gained valuable support from liberal politicians, students, civil rights and women's organizations, and labor leaders in other unions both at home and abroad.

In response, J. P. Stevens launched a counterattack against ACTWU. The company, Minchin explains, "had a clear, centrally directed policy to defeat unionization at any cost." Flagrantly violating labor laws, J. P. Stevens fired many union supporters, spread rumors about organized labor, and linked unions with violence, corruption, economic decline, and racial equality. Antiunion workers across the South, convinced that the union's boycott threatened their job security, formed Employee Educational Committees. Such committees developed sophisticated direct mail techniques designed to convince southerners that J. P. Stevens, not ACTWU, represented their best interests.

After years of struggle, in which the union invested $30 million, in October 1980 J. P. Stevens finally recognized the union at those plants where they had won elections. Despite this apparent victory, the union never organized the vast majority of J. P. Stevens workers. To ward off the threat of unionization, J. P. Stevens had gradually improved its nonunionized employees' wages and benefits.

Despite the limitations of labor's victory, Minchin argues that ACTWU's triumph "still represented one of the biggest gains in the textile industry's history." Unionized workers in J. P. Stevens' plants eventually received better severance pay and a stronger seniority clause. While late-twentieth-century foreign competition decimated the South's textile industry, Minchin nevertheless underscores the importance of the J. P. Stevens campaign. During the long struggle, unionists squared off against a powerful and intransigent employer. And by forcing Stevens to accept a union presence in its plants, they won an important victory.

John David Smith
Series Editor

ACKNOWLEDGMENTS

This book would not have been possible without the help I received from skilled librarians and archivists in the United States. I am especially grateful to the staff at Cornell University's Kheel Center for Labor-Management Documentation and Archives. In particular, Patrizia Sione, Richard Strassbourg, and Melissa Holland helped navigate me through their massive collection of material on the J. P. Stevens campaign. Throughout my extended visits to Cornell, their help was vital. At the State Historical Society of Wisconsin, Harry Miller shared his unrivaled knowledge of the Society's holdings with me and also helped to make my trip fruitful. I owe thanks also to the staff at the Southern Labor Archives at Georgia State University, particularly Peter Roberts, Morna Gerrard, DeAnna Phillips, and Lauren Kata. The main collection that I used at Georgia State was unprocessed, and again capable archivists helped me to find the material that I needed.

I would also like to thank the Union of Needletrades, Industrial, and Textile Employees, who gave me permission to use their fine collection at Cornell. At UNITE's New York headquarters, Susan Cowell was helpful throughout, while in Roanoke Rapids, North Carolina, UNITE's representative Clyde Bush assisted me in locating former Stevens workers to interview.

The Philip Leverhulme Trust awarded me a research prize that I used to fund this project. I am very grateful to the Trust for their generous support of my work. In particular, it enabled me to make several much-needed extended research trips to the United States.

Academic colleagues have helped me a great deal. Over the years, I have profited enormously from the friendship and advice I have received from Bob Zieger and John Salmond. I have also received valuable support from my colleagues at La Trobe University.

To John David Smith, editor of the series that includes this book, I owe an enormous debt. From the start John David was unstinting in his encouragement and enthusiasm for this book. James A. Hodges and David A. Zonderman gave generous readings to the manuscript and offered constructive suggestions that undoubtedly strengthened it.

I would also like to thank all those who helped me at the University Press of Florida, particularly Meredith Morris-Babb, who was efficient, cheerful, and encouraging throughout. Both Meredith and John David Smith were particularly supportive as I relocated from Scotland to Australia in the middle of this project. On my travels in the United States, I was helped a great deal by my friends, particularly Chuck and Vonnie Spence, Richard Zieger, and Hatsy and Rick Nittoli.

I am also fortunate in having a supportive family who have consistently backed my work. In addition to young Sasha, who was cheerful throughout, this book is dedicated to my wife Olga, as without her understanding and love it would not have been completed.

INTRODUCTION

On November 30, 1978, thousands of people across the United States took part in Justice for J. P. Stevens' Workers Day. In seventy-four cities, activities such as rallies, marches, and press conferences, were held in protest against a giant textile company that had persistently shown its willingness to violate the law rather than recognize its workers' right to organize into unions. In New York City more than three thousand demonstrators marched in front of the company's midtown headquarters as part of a nationwide day of boycotting that was endorsed by Governor Hugh L. Carey and by the City Council. In Los Angeles hundreds of trade unionists and their supporters rallied in front of City Hall, while in Indianapolis protesters gathered at the local Hilton Hotel for a "hard times luncheon" of ham, beans, and bread. Finding that the hotel's tablecloths were made by Stevens, enraged protesters ripped them from the tables and dumped them in a pile on the floor. Activities were also held in many smaller cities; in Albany, New York, for example, a rally was addressed by Lieutenant Governor–elect Mario Cuomo, who told consumers to "shun the products of J. P. Stevens as you would shun the fruit of an unholy tree." Across the country, protesters carried signs urging consumers to steer clear of the company's sheets, a staple part of its textile business. Americans, they insisted, should not sleep in sheets made by a company that had repeatedly violated labor laws and was guilty of racial and sexual discrimination against its workers.[1]

The Justice Day protests typified the high profile of the J. P. Stevens campaign in 1970s America. The protests were coordinated in support of a major consumer boycott of Stevens products that the Amalgamated Clothing and Textile Workers Union (ACTWU), frustrated with Stevens's continued willingness to violate labor laws, had launched two years earlier in an effort to push the company to change its labor relations policies. In public relations terms, the boycott was a huge success. The effort was backed by a wide variety of supporters, including civil rights groups such as the National Association for the Advancement of Colored People (NAACP), the Southern Christian Leadership Conference, and the Congress of Racial Equality (CORE), women's organizations from the National Organization for Women (NOW) to the Council of Labor Union Women, and church groups such as the American Jewish Congress and the United Presbyterian Church. In addition, the boycott was endorsed by several U.S. governors, fifty-six U.S. representatives, and a range of senators. The Stevens struggle was also widely covered in the national press and even inspired Hollywood to produce *Norma Rae,* an Oscar-winning film based loosely on the story of a Stevens worker. In short, it was a major event of the 1970s.[2]

Although it is identified with the 1970s, the Stevens campaign began in the early 1960s. At the time, textiles was the only U.S. manufacturing industry that was not heavily unionized, and most mills were located in the historically antiunion southern states. Like Stevens, many companies had moved south in search of lower wage costs and weaker unions. By the early 1960s, textiles was by far the region's biggest employer, providing jobs to more than 600,000 southerners.[3] Leaders of the struggling Textile Workers Union of America argued that they had to organize a major company in order to make real inroads into the South. In the spring of 1963 they picked out Stevens, a well-known firm that employed some 36,000 people in the region. In selecting the company, TWUA strategists were assuming that a breakthrough at such a large employer would have a domino effect. "We felt," confirmed former TWUA president Sol Stetin, "that a breakthrough in Stevens, the second largest textile chain in the country, would, at long last, destroy the myth that southern textile workers could never organize."[4]

Union leaders calculated that CEO Robert Stevens, a former secretary of the army, would not be as antiunion as some of his counterparts. A figure who had held government office, they reasoned, would surely not violate the law. They could not have been more wrong. Resentful of being targeted, Stevens managers vigorously resisted the union, repeatedly firing and intimidating TWUA supporters. Again and again the company's activities were condemned by both the National Labor Relations Board and the federal courts. In 1967 NLRB trial examiner Horace Ruckel called Stevens "flagrantly guilty," asserting that the company had set out "to destroy the union root and branch by discharging its most active members." Federal judges agreed; in 1969 John Brown, chief judge of the Fifth Circuit Court, declared that Stevens had employed "a massive multi-state campaign to prevent unionization of its southern plants."[5] By 1975 Stevens had accumulated what trial examiner Marvin Roth called "an extraordinary history of unfair labor practice litigation before this Board and the courts."[6]

In the short term, the company's tactics worked. By the late 1960s the union's original organizing drives had collapsed, as few workers were willing to risk their livelihoods by supporting the TWUA. In the longer term, however, the company's harsh tactics helped the union, allowing it to mobilize an impressive range of allies to support its ongoing campaign. In 1976 the TWUA merged with the Amalgamated Clothing Workers of America (ACWA) specifically in order to create a bigger organization that could bring Stevens to its knees. Following the merger, the newly created ACTWU launched a major attack against Stevens, headed up by a "massive" consumer boycott. In addition, the union pumped its resources into a legal campaign, a well-funded publicity effort, and renewed organizing activities. The pressure eventually told, and in October 1980 the company finally recognized the union at those plants where it had won elections. The agreement led to ACTWU calling off its corporate campaign and boycott, although the legal campaign and organizing activities continued. The two sides reached a final truce three years later. In forcing the company to compromise, the union made an important breakthrough, especially as Stevens agreed to the automatic checkoff of union dues and the independent arbitration of grievances, terms that it had fervently resisted for many years.[7]

The union's willingness to conduct such a lengthy and costly campaign indicates the high priority that labor leaders attached to the fight with J. P. Stevens. Consistently arguing that the fall of Stevens would open up the South to unionization, labor leaders poured more than $30 million into their struggle with the textile giant. In March 1977 ACTWU president Murray H. Finley described the J. P. Stevens campaign as "the biggest labor struggle since the sitdown strikes in the breakthrough of auto and steel, the most important one that faces the American labor movement and the American people today—the battle to break through in the textile industry and in the South."[8] Harold McIver, who coordinated the union's organizing efforts against Stevens for nearly two decades, viewed the drive in similar terms. "The J. P. Stevens campaign," he wrote in 1978, "is the first priority of the labor movement and consumes a major portion of our resources." Labor leaders felt that Stevens could not be allowed to prove that it was possible to avoid unionization by openly breaking the law. As AFL-CIO official James Sala commented, "As long as we've got J. P. Stevens, we'll never really succeed in organizing the South. Not because of textiles, but because of the example it sets for this kind of resistance."[9]

Despite its prominence, the Stevens campaign has received little attention from historians. It has been largely bypassed in the recent upsurge in southern labor history, even though most studies have concentrated on textiles, the South's largest industry for most of the twentieth century.[10] At the time, the drive was well covered by writers in a range of journals, while investigative reporter Mimi Conway also produced an account based largely on interviews with workers at the company's plants in Roanoke Rapids, North Carolina.[11] In addition, some scholars have explored the story of Crystal Lee Sutton, the Roanoke Rapids worker whose story inspired *Norma Rae*.[12] The campaign has been nicely summarized in an overview article by James A. Hodges, and it is also covered in *Culture of Misfortune,* Clete Daniel's interpretive history of textile unionism. Utilizing newly available archival sources, it is now possible to write the first book-length account.[13]

Over the course of its long struggle with J. P. Stevens, the union ran an innovative campaign that forced the company to recognize it in those locations where it had won bargaining rights. This success, however, has to be set against its inability to organize the vast majority of the company's workers. The 1980 settlement in fact brought only around 7 percent of Stevens workers into the union fold. The failure of the union's organizing campaign has been generally associated with Stevens's lawlessness. In reality, however, the company's tactics shifted over time; in the early stages of the drive, Stevens did rely heavily on labor law violations to fend off the union, but by the late 1970s court orders had forced the company to moderate its stance. In the late 1970s the union was faced by a "new Stevens strategy" that caused it a range of unfamiliar problems. Instead of relying on supervisors to directly violate labor laws, the company proved increasingly adept at fighting the union through Employee Education Committees instead. Across the South, such groups effectively exploited workers' fears that the union boycott would cost them their jobs. The success of these committees highlighted how the Stevens campaign acted as a mobilizing tool not only for the union but for the company and its supporters as well. In the latter stages of its campaign, the failure of ACTWU's organizing efforts was also linked to an unsuccessful AFL-CIO effort to secure labor law reform, and to the company's ability to undercut the union's organizing appeal by matching its pay scales. Ironically, the threat of unionization forced the company to steadily improve working conditions, but this was of scant consolation to an organization that desperately needed new members.[14]

Race too played an underappreciated role in determining the fate of the union's efforts. Over the course of the campaign, the proportion of black workers in Stevens plants increased more than fivefold. Union strategists reasoned that African American workers, many of them radicalized by the civil rights movement, would be enthusiastic recruits to the cause. As the workforce integrated, the union drew a lot of support from African American workers because they faced continuing discrimination in the company's mills. As union leader Bruce Raynor recalled, "Stevens' mills were brutal on black people, they were kept down. People with education and degrees couldn't get good jobs, and they'd hire whites that couldn't read or write. . . . [A] big issue in the organizing was the promotions of blacks, the treatment of blacks."[15]

As the proportion of black workers increased, the union was pleased with their favorable response to its campaign. "It is encouraging to note," reported Sol Stetin in October 1979, ". . . that black employees in the textile industry and in the clothing industry as well in the South are willing to stand up to their employer and say they want a better way of life, want to engage in collective bargaining, want to go first class." Union leaders also asserted that a new generation of younger whites were more assertive than their forebears. They had a "national U.S. worker self-image" and were no longer willing to accept "second class" pay. "Their demands for personal recognition [and] civil liberties in the work place are demands which would not have occurred to anyone twenty years ago," asserted the union.[16]

At the same time, however, the influx of black workers caused problems that union leaders had not anticipated. In particular, these optimistic reports failed to take into account the continuing strength of racial division in the South. While African Americans did respond favorably to the union, their activism often made whites reluctant to join with them. Across the South, the union came to be seen as a "black union," ensuring that organizers could not attract the white majority that they needed to be successful. In May 1980, for instance, organizer Robert Ross typically complained from Walterboro, South Carolina: "After house calling about 25 new white employees I have been unable to get new committee members. . . . There is as usual a great deal of interest in organizing coming from blacks. Unless some of the whites that I have house called during the past couple of weeks decided to help, I do not see any use in starting a campaign in Walterboro at this point. I feel that many of the whites here still see this as a black campaign."[17]

The lengthy campaign to organize Stevens challenges conventional assumptions about the U.S. labor movement. In the affluent postwar era, unions have often been pictured as conservative and bureaucratic, more interested in servicing their members rather than in trying to reach out to the unorganized. Having achieved a commanding position in the central manufacturing industries, many unions showed little interest in organizing new members. As labor scholar Gilbert J. Gall has noted, "Through the postwar decades unions typically committed few resources to organizing." Longtime AFL-CIO leader George Meany was famously skeptical of mass organizing drives. Organizing efforts, he asserted, should be piecemeal and follow the path of least resistance—hardly the approach taken by the textile union in targeting J. P. Stevens. For seventeen years the TWUA and ACTWU conducted a major drive to organize the company, going into the red in the process. In the late 1970s the union's efforts diversified, yet organizing always remained at the heart of the campaign. At its peak, more than forty full-time organizers worked on the Stevens drive.[18]

Having failed to sign up a majority of textile workers in the 1930s and 1940s, the TWUA could not afford to sit back and concentrate on servicing its members. Throughout the postwar years, the steady movement of organized shops to the nonunion South undermined the union. Between 1950 and 1970, TWUA researchers estimated, their dues-paying membership in the New England cotton garment industry shrank from 132,000 to just 20,000. Many of these plants had moved south, where wage levels were consistently lower. In October 1976 the union calculated that the average textile wage in the northern "metropolitan area" was $5.00 an hour, compared to $3.85 in the South. For union leaders in the textile and apparel industries, organizing was simply a matter of institutional survival.[19]

In the 1960s and 1970s, textile mills dominated the southern economy, and union leaders put such effort into the Stevens campaign because they believed that cracking the industry was the key to organizing the entire Sun Belt region. Textile mills were, as a Heritage Foundation publication put it, "as much a part of Southern symbols as Baptist Churches, grits, and red-eyed gravy."[20] By the end of the twentieth century, the industry no longer held this position. Just as companies had previously moved south in search of lower wages, in the 1980s and 1990s many relocated to Asia or Latin America, where costs were lower still. They then imported their goods into the United States, undermining the economic viability of those factories that remained. The pace of job loss was especially rapid in the wake of the 1994 North American Free Trade Agreement (NAFTA), which led to many textile companies moving to Mexico. Between 1997 and 2002, 236 textile plants shut down in the Carolinas alone, with a loss of more than 75,000 jobs. Over the course of the 1980s and 1990s, economic decline had a devastating impact on the union, robbing it of the funding that it needed to carry on intensive organizing in the wake of the Stevens settlement.[21]

The Stevens campaign remains important, however, not least because of its impact on U.S. labor relations. In the late 1970s the AFL-CIO tried to use the case to secure labor law reform, but when its labor reform bill narrowly failed to become law, other firms were encouraged to copy Stevens's tactics. As Stephen H. Norwood's recent work has highlighted, since the early 1980s many employers have sought to openly resist unionization, often by deliberately violating labor laws. Just as Stevens executives had reasoned twenty years earlier, these firms calculated that they could effectively kill organizing drives by selective discharges, aware that even if fired employees were reinstated by the slow-moving NLRB, the campaign would have collapsed by the time they actually got back to work. Able to deduct NLRB back pay awards from their taxes as a legitimate business expense, some corporate executives even shrugged off the payouts as a "hunting license." In many ways, therefore, the Stevens campaign set the stage for the widespread union-busting of the post-1980 period. As AFL-CIO secretary-treasurer Richard Trumpka commented in 1999, "intimidation and interference by employers is such standard practice in today's workplaces that the freedom to form a union doesn't really exist at all."[22]

The Stevens campaign also showed that unions were still capable of fighting back against even the most hostile and powerful employers, and it offered important lessons on how they could effectively do so. Over the course of their twenty-year fight, union activists pioneered a range of new tactics, including the very first corporate campaign. In the 1980s and 1990s the corporate campaign became a common feature of labor struggles, with many efforts being headed by Ray Rogers, the maverick activist who came to prominence during the fight with Stevens. In the course of its battle with the textile giant, the union also linked up with allies in other countries, another tactic that became commonplace in subsequent struggles. Above all, the campaign highlighted what unions could achieve by moving beyond their traditional reliance on strikes and working with their allies in the community. Successfully turning their struggle into a cause célèbre, they forced a company that was a symbol of antiunionism to accept organized labor's presence in its southern plants.[23]

ONE

Selecting a Target

In the early spring of 1951, workers at Hockanum Mills in Rockville, Connecticut, walked out on strike after rejecting management demands for wholesale concessions. Rather than settling the strike, parent company J. P. Stevens unexpectedly sold the plant to a nontextile buyer. The workers' jobs were in fact already being performed by employees at a mill that Stevens had recently opened up in the southern states. During the labor shortage of World War II, unions had been able to organize five of Stevens's ten New England mills. In order to assure wartime production, the family firm reluctantly dealt with organized labor, but its executives were not pleased. Immediately after the war, they were keen to reassert control over their operations without "third party" interference. Between 1947 and 1963, the company closed four northern mills and established eight new plants in the South. As *Fortune* journalist Richard Whalen noted, by moving south Stevens had "said goodbye to the unions."[1]

As the company continued its closure of its northern plants, labor leaders complained that organized facilities were disproportionately targeted. In the 1950s and 1960s, Stevens certainly closed some big unionized mills. In 1957, for instance, the company threw nearly two thousand union members out of work when it shut a woolen plant in Garfield, New Jersey. In 1964 Stevens also closed a carpet mill in Freehold, New Jersey, the hometown of rock star Bruce Springsteen. On his hit record "My Hometown," a song that eloquently depicted the deindustrialization of the northern states, Springsteen later sang about witnessing the childhood closure of a local textile mill. Ultimately, both organized and unorganized shops were closed down by executives. Between 1951 and 1980, Stevens closed nineteen mills in New England and the mid-Atlantic states, of which eight were unionized. While the union had been able to organize the company's six largest northern mills, all of these factories were later closed by Stevens.[2]

Stevens's move south was typical of broader trends in the American textile industry. In the years immediately after World War II, many textile firms moved away from the industry's base in New England, where land and labor costs were high, to the cheaper southern states. So common was the shift that companies fleeing the north were termed "runaway shops" by frustrated union leaders. The economic advantages of moving south were clear: in 1946 southern textile wages were 12 percent lower than they were in the north, and over the next decade this gap widened further. In September 1953 the minimum wage at Stevens's New England woolen plants was $1.29 an hour, compared to $1.05 an hour in the South. The company's northern textile workers also received fringe benefits that were absent in the South, including paid holidays and retirement severance pay.[3]

Although the move of runaway shops into the South accelerated after World War II, it had been occurring for many years. Ever since the late nineteenth century, northern industrialists had moved south in search of cheaper wages and a union-free environment. In an industry where wages comsumed up to sixty cents of each sales dollar, the South had a major advantage. Because of the wage differential, Dixie's dominance gradually grew. In 1880 only 5 percent of cotton textile spindles were located in the South, but this increased steadily to 39 percent in 1910, 72 percent in 1937, and more than 90 percent in the early 1970s. As the South grew, the North declined. Between 1923 and 1933, 40 percent of New England's textile factories closed, with almost 100,000 workers losing their jobs. Over the same period, the percentage of textile workers based in the South rose from 46 to 68 percent. In the ensuing years, the trend continued. Between 1947 and 1957, New England witnessed a 50 percent decline in textile employment, the number of workers falling from 288,500 to 144,100.[4]

The TWUA was hit hard by these closures. Between 1954 and 1963, twenty-six organized mills shut down in New England. They included the American Wool Company in Lawrence, Massachusetts, which had employed more than seven thousand people in its sprawling complex. "In the

1950s and 1960s," reflected TWUA leader Sol Stetin, ". . . mill after mill was merged out of existence in the north and the work transferred to their southern operations, throwing workers out of work, destroying machinery and leaving communities in pretty bad shape." In 1948 the union had 347,000 members, but this fell dramatically to 135,000 in 1962. Battered by news of mill closings and layoffs, the mood among the union's leaders was understandably pessimistic. "There is no question," reflected research economist Sol Barkin in 1952, "but that the union will continue to contract and we will have to adjust to that."[5]

The economic decline of the northern textile industry meant that it was essential for the TWUA to make greater progress in the South. In the 1930s and 1940s the union had made great strides in organizing northern textile workers but had been unable to extend these gains to the South. In March 1964, confidential figures prepared by the TWUA's research department showed that there were 221,630 textile workers in North Carolina, of whom only 5 percent belonged to the TWUA. An even smaller number of Tar Heel textile workers belonged to the AFL's United Textile Workers (UTW). A similar picture prevailed in the other southern textile states. In South Carolina, for example, around 7 percent of textile workers belonged to the TWUA. In sharp contrast, 37 percent of New England textile workers were unionized, and the figure was even higher (46 percent) in the TWUA's Quin-State Region, which covered New Jersey, Pennsylvania, Delaware, Ohio, and Michigan. Over the United States as a whole, 22 percent of textile workers carried union cards.[6]

Prior to the Stevens campaign, southern textile workers had often tried to organize, but determined corporate opposition had made it very difficult to establish lasting unions. In 1929 a wave of strikes had rocked the industrial Piedmont, but they were bitterly repressed. As working conditions failed to improve, many workers continued to look to unions. Believing that the New Deal's National Industrial Recovery Act (NIRA) encouraged unionism, workers surged into the UTW in 1933–34. Feeling that the mill owners had failed to live up to the provisions of the NIRA, in September 1934 more than 170,000 southern mill hands took part in a general textile strike, the largest labor protest in the South's history. It was, claimed one participant, "the closest thing I've seen to a revolution in this country."[7] Again, the walkout was violently suppressed. In its aftermath, more than 75,000 union supporters were blacklisted, many of them ending up desperately searching for food and work. The scars left by such experiences were deep and lasting. "I'd about cry and get down on my knees to them begging for a job," recalled Roanoke Rapids worker Kasper Smith, "but they just strung you on and didn't say much of anything. I was seven or eight months out of work. I went to Danville, Burlington, and Durham looking for a job, but I couldn't find a thing."[8]

Following the 1934 strike, unions in the textile South continued to struggle. In 1937–38, the CIO's Textile Workers Organizing Committee (TWOC) worked hard to reestablish the credibility of unionism but made only limited gains. Established in 1939 in the wake of the TWOC drive, the TWUA made some gains during World War II, when the directives of the National War Labor Board forced employers to moderate their antiunionism, but a major organizing effort immediately after the war yielded disappointing results. In textiles the much-trumpeted Operation Dixie ran from 1946 until 1953 but netted the union only 11,000 extra members. Over the course of the campaign, antiunion mill owners violently opposed organizing efforts and refused to sign contracts even when their workers did vote for union representation.[9] As the union entered the 1950s, it endured a succession of humiliating defeats. In 1951 an attempted general strike collapsed, while five years later the Deering Milliken Company closed its mill in Darlington, South Carolina, after employees had voted for a union. In a widely publicized case, the company refused to reopen the plant even when workers agreed to recant their union membership, initiating a lengthy court battle that was still unresolved when the Stevens campaign began.[10]

Perhaps most damaging of all, in 1958–59 the union lost a lengthy strike at the Harriet-Henderson Mills in Henderson, North Carolina. As union members watched from the sidelines, the company recruited outside strike-breakers and imported them into the mills with the full backing of local and state authorities. As the dispute became increasingly violent, it received wide coverage in the southern press. Henderson was located at the heart of the textile Piedmont, and the strike frightened workers at many other mills. By the late 1950s, TWUA leaders argued that there was a "conspiracy" by the southern "power structure" to keep unions out of their region, a charge that they would repeat over the next two decades.[11]

The union's long history of defeat was a major obstacle for organizers to contend with as they headed south. The various setbacks undermined the confidence of both workers and organizers and gave extra ammunition to companies, who repeatedly associated unions with lost strikes. Sol Stetin later reflected that this legacy of defeat hurt the union in the South: "I've developed the belief that you're not going to make a breakthrough in the South until the labor movement is able to declare, and the people in the South accept, the idea of winning. Since that 1934 defeat of the textile workers . . . , there have been few victories in the South, real victories, where people can develop confidence. You know a success leads to a lack of fear. There is still too much fear on the part of the workers in the South."[12]

As Stevens moved south, managers took over mills that had previously been run by other firms. In several cases, workers had direct experience of union failure. At the large Patterson mill in Roanoke Rapids, the TWUA lost elections in both 1948 and 1959. At the Aragon plant in Rock Hill, it had failed in separate votes in 1939 and 1946. Even when the union had made gains, it had again struggled to establish a lasting presence. During World War II the TWUA had organized the Industrial Cotton Mills in Rock Hill, but after Stevens purchased the plant in 1947 the two sides were unable to agree on contract terms. When workers walked out in an effort to resist concessions, Stevens hired strikebreakers and destroyed the union.[13]

Structural obstacles also held back union efforts. As plant size in the textile industry was small, union leaders worried that companies would switch production away from any mills that they managed to organize. In July 1972 the TWUA's research department found that J. P. Stevens had seventy-three separate mills in the South, the largest of them employing barely more than a thousand employees. Any union faced a major organizing task in covering all these facilities, and no plant was big enough to have a real ripple effect on others.[14] Textile mills were also more likely to be located in small towns than in large urban areas. In 1967 only one in three textile workers worked in metropolitan conurbations (areas with a city of more than 50,000 people), compared to two out of three manufacturing workers as a whole. This complicated the organizer's job, as studies indicated that union membership levels were consistently higher in urban areas. In smaller towns, community opposition to organized labor tended to be more vocal, especially when there was one dominant employer.[15]

Stevens again epitomized this pattern, as most of the company's mills were located in small towns in the Carolinas where they were the major employer. By the mid-1960s Stevens ran twenty-five plants around the South Carolina Piedmont towns of Rock Hill, Spartanburg, and Greenville. In the mid-1950s the company had also bought the complex of mills in Roanoke Rapids, North Carolina. A small community in the eastern part of the state,

Roanoke Rapids was described by one journalist who visited it in 1979 as "90 miles from everywhere."[16]

Stevens's move south may have been part of a broader trend, yet it still represented a major change of direction for a textile company that had firm roots in the North. The family traced their lineage back to John Stevens, an Englishman who had emigrated to Andover, Massachusetts, in 1638. The firm itself dated back to 1813, when descendant Nathaniel Stevens had established a woolen mill in Massachusetts. Through Nathaniel's diligence the company survived and expanded. When he died in 1865, the business was taken over by his son Moses and changed its name to M. T. Stevens. Another family member, John P. Stevens, pioneered the company's moves into merchandising, and by World War I the J. P. Stevens Company was selling the output from nine cotton mills through its Manhattan office. In September 1946 the company went public, the selling house and mill company merging with eight other companies. Shortly afterwards, the firm began its aggressive acquisition of southern plants.[17]

Robert Ten Broeck Stevens epitomized the values of dedication, single-mindedness, and diligence that had turned a family-owned business into the second-largest textile firm in the United States. Stevens's life was in fact synonymous with the firm that he presided over. He was born in 1899, the same year that J. P. Stevens became an independent company, and from his earliest boyhood he was eager to head the family textile firm. After graduating from Phillips Andover, Stevens was persuaded by his father to go to Yale rather than enter the business right away. While he was at the Ivy League university, the United States entered the First World War. The young New Englander promptly joined up, completing his studies after serving as a second lieutenant in a Kentucky training camp. In 1921 he joined the company as a fledgling salesman, becoming president after the death of his father in 1929. In 1941 Stevens took a leave of absence to serve again in the army, rising to a position as deputy director of purchasing.[18]

After another spell working for the company, Stevens became secretary of the army in 1953. In this capacity he gained national prominence when he was grilled on national television by anticommunist senator Joseph McCarthy. For more than thirty-seven hours McCarthy interrogated Stevens about the record of the executive department he headed. Stevens emerged from the hearings with credit, being widely viewed as a determined but fair-minded man who had "stood up" to the bullying McCarthy. Censured by the Senate and stripped of most of his powers, McCarthy never recovered from the debacle of the army hearings. The textile firm was always Stevens's first love, however, and in 1955 he returned to oversee the firm's southern expansion. Famously working long hours, Stevens took the best interests of the company extremely seriously, and he strongly believed in management's right to have unilateral control over the running of its business.[19]

Throughout the company's growth, the Stevens family continued to be centrally involved in the business. Until 1969, when James D. Finley became CEO, an unbroken succession of family members headed the firm. Even after Finley's appointment, industry observers believed that Robert Stevens remained highly influential. "Even though Robert T. Stevens gives up the title of chief executive, retaining the post of chairman of the executive committee," noted the *Daily News Record,* the trade organ for apparel and textiles, "his strong grip on the company will remain." Following his official retirement in 1974, the obstinate septuagenarian still influenced the company's decision making. Unable to change the habits of a lifetime, he still faithfully worked a full day in Stevens Tower, the company's headquarters in New York City.[20]

By the early 1970s, J. P. Stevens employed over 46,000 people and made over $1.1 billion in sales.[21] Among textile companies, only the giant Burlington Industries was bigger. Stevens was the largest manufacturer of table linens for both commercial and home use, while sheets, pillowcases, and towels were also staple products. In addition, the company was a major manufacturer of apparel cloth, producing such popular items as denims and corduroys. A highly diversified firm, Stevens also manufactured carpets, ready-made draperies, industrial filter fabrics, leisure footwear, and tennis court surfaces.[22]

Well aware of the many obstacles that confronted them, union leaders nevertheless felt that they had to continue their efforts in the South. As a rising proportion of economic production was in the Sun Belt states, strategists reasoned that they had no choice but to organize the region. Between 1950 and 1975 the South's economy grew at an average annual rate of 4.4 percent, compared to 3.4 percent nationally, with every industry except coal mining performing better in Dixie than elsewhere. "The South," claimed TWUA organizer Robert Freeman in 1959, "is the most powerful and ruthless enemy organized labor has—it is weakening the Labor movement yearly by enticing organized industry to move South for cheap labor and taxes and guarantees immunity from unions."[23]

The roots of the Stevens campaign lay in a drive by the AFL-CIO's Industrial Union Department (IUD). Set up shortly after the 1955 merger of the AFL and CIO, the IUD aimed to ensure that international unions would tackle common problems together, overcoming the factionalism that had often afflicted the labor movement. Aiming to pool its resources in a "concentrated area," the campaign concentrated on the Greenville-Spartanburg area at the heart of South Carolina's growing industrial corridor. Initiated in February 1961, the drive was funded by a $4 million budget. Of this, $1 million came from the UAW, $1 million from the IUD itself, and the rest from other unions including the TWUA, the Steelworkers, the Machinists, and the Electrical Workers. According to *Textile Labor,* all of these unions "recognized the organizing challenge which faces the entire American labor movement and expressed a willingness to contribute both finances and manpower to the various campaigns." Apart from the South, the IUD also initiated drives in other areas where they hoped to establish a stronger presence, particularly greater metropolitan Los Angeles. James Pierce, an experienced staffer from the International Union of Electrical Workers, was appointed to head the southern campaign. Operating out of Greenville, Pierce supervised the efforts of fifteen staff.[24]

Over the course of a two-year drive, the IUD's southern organizers made a number of gains, but cracking the textile plants again proved to be impossible. By August 1962, coordinator Joseph Appelbaum listed eight companies where the IUD had won elections, but none of them were textile producers. At Wellington Mills in Anderson, South Carolina, managers fought off an intense organizing effort by discharging key supporters. Paul Swaity, a hard-working Canadian who served as the TWUA's organizing director for much of the Stevens campaign, later admitted his disappointment with the results of the IUD drive. "It was," he reflected, "a bust organizationally." TWUA organizers and leaders began to argue that they needed to take on a large chain company rather than a geographical area. "In trying to take on an area," reasoned Swaity, "even if we organize a small little plant here, it's marginal. . . . We can't get anywhere unless we get the chains." In January 1963 the union set up a committee to identify a chain company that they could focus their efforts upon.[25]

Headed by TWUA general secretary John Chupka, the committee quickly picked out J. P. Stevens. The giant employer was attractive partly because of its size: the TWUA wanted to organize a major, pattern-setting company, and Stevens was the second-largest chain in the industry. In the past, the union's organizing gains had tended to be confined to small companies, and activists felt that they had to break through at a major chain in order to significantly increase their presence in the South. Executive board member Joseph L. Hueter recalled: "since we had been organizing for the most part on the basis of small units in the past, it was determined that we should make efforts to organize a large chain." TWUA leaders reasoned, and would argue throughout their long campaign, that a breakthrough at Stevens would have a carryover effect. According to executive board member Wesley Cook, Stevens was picked out as an "organizing symbol"; he added: "The general feeling was that if you could crack any one of the top half dozen, it would result in making inroads in most of the rest of them." TWUA leaders modeled their thinking on the way the CIO had been able to organize the major mass-production industries in the 1930s by making breakthroughs at large pattern-setting companies. "The Labor Movement," Harold McIver noted, "recognizes that if significant breakthroughs are ever to be made in the South, the unorganized Textile Industry must be the first barrier to fall. As you are aware, history proves that the best way to crack an industry is by organizing a major chain and setting an industry-wide pattern for wages and benefits."[26]

The union also argued that it could use its resources particularly effectively against Stevens. Its efforts to organize Burlington Industries had achieved little, but Burlington's plants were scattered over a wide area, whereas Stevens's mills were clustered. As the committee reported, Stevens "is much more centralized than Burlington and operates larger units." In South Carolina the company had eleven plants in the Rock Hill area and a further fourteen in the Greenville-Spartanburg hub, while up in Roanoke Rapids the six Stevens mills employed more than 3,600 people. "With the same amount of manpower available," reported Chupka, "a larger part of Stevens, about 60%, can be tackled as against about 25% of Burlington." An analysis of the company's stockholder reports also indicated that Stevens had a good record of profitability, and this led union strategists to conclude that the firm was committed to expanding its southern operations.[27]

Within these clusters, the union picked out plants that were strategically important to Stevens. The Roanoke Rapids mills were described by research director George Perkel as "a natural target since they produce specialized products which are generally not duplicated in the rest of the chain." The Dunean mill in Greenville was selected because it was the company's largest synthetic weaving plant and was particularly important for Stevens's work on industrial and military fabrics. The union also noted that

Figure 1. Shift change in Roanoke Rapids, 1977. (Doug Magee/Kheel Center for Labor-Management Documentation and Archives, Cornell University.)

three mills in Great Falls, South Carolina, manufactured mill-finished fabrics that were rarely produced elsewhere. Above all, strategists sought to reduce the company's ability to force strikes and then source lost production from other facilities.[28]

The union also felt that its campaign would be well received by Stevens's workers. Leaders argued that the company's workers had a stronger desire for unionization than their counterparts at Burlington. In the fall of 1958, dissatisfied workers in Roanoke Rapids had begun an organizing campaign of their own. Led by two doffers, they had formed a Workers' Committee and published a notice in which they proclaimed that they were "sick and tired of stretch-out, pay-cut, personal abuse and demotions."[29] The TWUA had sent organizers to Roanoke Rapids and succeeded in signing up many workers. In 1959 they contested an election at the plants but went down to defeat. TWUA leaders blamed the loss on the bitter strike in nearby Henderson, which was still in progress when the election was held. In a vicious campaign, the company effectively linked the union to the violence. "The mills here were plastered with pictures of alleged bombings of cars and houses in Henderson," reported organizer Joe Pedigo. But by the early

1960s, with the Henderson dispute resolved, Chupka optimistically reasoned that the union would have a better chance. Encouraged by the fact that the TWUA had still received 35 percent of the vote, he argued that they should renew their organizing efforts.[30]

Despite the committee's recommendations, TWUA president William Pollock was initially reluctant to take on Stevens. "In developing the idea of a jointly financed southern textile organizing campaign with the IUD," he wrote Chupka, "I had in mind Burlington. I thought of that company feeling it may be more vulnerable—size—handsome profits—relationship to Kennedy administration." Burlington carried out a great deal of work for the federal government, and Pollock reasoned that the union could pressure federal agencies to cut off contracts if the firm violated labor laws. The TWUA president, however, quickly deferred to Chupka's recommendation that Stevens be selected instead—a deference that was influenced by internal political considerations. Pollock was then being challenged by a faction within the union who charged that he lacked dynamism and was too frugal. To hold on to his position, the embattled president relied heavily on the support of his experienced and respected secretary-treasurer. At such a time, the president was unlikely to go against the recommendations of Chupka's committee. Keen to prove that he could be a dynamic leader, Pollock decided to launch a bold campaign against Stevens.[31]

Pollock also liked the fact that the Stevens campaign was an IUD initiative. The TWUA chief felt that the IUD could bring fresh ideas about how to organize the South, and he reasoned that if the campaign failed, blame could be deflected away from his leadership. At the union's 1964 convention, a slate headed by Pollock and Chupka easily defeated their challengers. The fight was bitter and divisive, however, especially when former president Emil Rieve joined in the attack on Pollock. The fractious proceedings did little to help the union's image, particularly in the South. As Chupka commented, "If anyone thinks that this is going to help our union to organize . . . anyone down there, they are sadly mistaken." The resolution of the internal battle also had its benefits, especially as it allowed a united leadership to emerge. Pollock himself was energized by the fight, and in the later years of his presidency he showed a greater willingness to take risks. Becoming a more aggressive leader, he consistently backed the Stevens campaign and also came out against the Vietnam War in the AFL-CIO Executive Council. The fight was useful, remembered Sol Stetin, because "it provoked him [Pollock] into a greater degree of activity."[32]

In comparing Stevens with Burlington, union strategists also assumed that Stevens's managers would offer less resistance to an organizing campaign. Established in 1929, Burlington Mills was a native North Carolina corporation, and its top executives had always bitterly opposed unions. "The feeling was," recalled Swaity, "that Burlington was too vicious and too tough, and so Stevens looked like the second target and probably the best target, and that's how the choice was made." Stevens presented a sharp contrast to Burlington. "It was decided that Stevens was a good target for several reasons," said Swaity. "One, the feeling that this was a northern company, with Boston money. Boston money, and northern company, must have had some experience with unions. Stevens had plants organized in the north." Former TWUA southern director Scott Hoyman had similar recollections: "We had had a contractual relationship with Stevens under different initials, M. T. Stevens in New England, and so one thought was that, since they had bargained with the union, they wouldn't consider us as bad as a company that had never bargained with the union."[33]

In particular, union leaders reasoned that Robert Stevens's service as secretary of the army would work in their favor. "The other item was that there was some public exposure of Stevens," recalled Hoyman. "He was the secretary of the army at that time, so there was a hope by the union that they might be more temperate." Prior to the Stevens campaign, the union had lost several battles against native southern textile companies such as Burlington and Cannon Mills. A family-owned firm, Cannon had close control over a complex of mills in Kannapolis, a mill town near Charlotte. With many employees reluctant to challenge the company, organizing efforts had always collapsed. In comparison, Stevens did not have as harsh a reputation. Widely viewed as less belligerent than most southern textile executives, on the eve of the campaign Robert Stevens was described by *Fortune* as "quiet" and "mild-mannered" but "frankly sentimental about the company founded by his great-grandfather."[34]

Despite these perceived advantages, union leaders realized that they were unlikely to organize such a large employer quickly. "It was planned as a long-range approach," recalled Swaity. Still, the union clearly underestimated just how difficult it would be to organize Stevens. "In choosing J. P. Stevens as an organizing target thirteen years ago," wrote Stetin in 1976, "we never realized what tremendous obstacles would confront us."[35]

Strategists overlooked evidence of Stevens's vigorous opposition to organized labor, although it was clearly documented in their own files. In September 1953 a research department report had noted that "the company has succeeded in fighting off various organizational attempts at its southern plants." Another report claimed that Stevens's managers had a "bitter anti-union attitude" that had been illustrated well in the summer of 1951, when they had broken the strike at the Industrial Cotton Mills in Rock Hill. In the late 1950s the company had openly violated the National Labor Relations Act when its Roanoke Rapids workers had tried to organize. Passed in 1935, the NLRA had outlawed a wide range of "unfair labor practices," including discharging workers because of their union activity, threatening to close a plant if workers voted for union representation, and refusing to bargain. As would be the case in the 1960s, during the 1958–59 campaign the company initially used bulletin board notices to warn its Roanoke Rapids employees that joining the union would bring them "serious harm." Following this, managers fired key union activists and interrogated many of those who remained on their jobs. In particular, supervisors walked through the plants and threatened employees that the plants would close down if the union were voted in. Although the NLRB later found the company guilty of breaking the law, by this time the TWUA's campaign had petered out.[36]

In many ways, it was a lack of alternatives that pushed the union to take on Stevens. Previous efforts at Burlington and Cannon had collapsed, and Deering Milliken had killed organizing efforts by closing its Darlington mill. Although Stevens had resisted previous organizing efforts, the union had never attempted a sustained drive against the company. As unions had often been able to organize the southern branches of unionized northern firms, it was also understandable that TWUA leaders viewed Stevens as a promising target.[37]

As the union pointed out, working conditions in the southern textile industry were poor. Pay levels were the lowest of any manufacturing industry. In June 1969 the average factory wage was $3.02 an hour, but in the southern textile mills it was just $2.16. When the union began its campaign at Stevens, many employees earned less than $2.00 an hour, while some nonproduction workers took home just $1.25. Workers did not receive paid holidays or pensions, despite the fact that many toiled in the mills for their entire working lives. Arguing that the need to make production was all that mattered to the company, many complained about heavy workloads and poor safety standards. Roanoke Rapids worker Lucy Taylor told a congressional hearing that when a loom caught fire next to her, she had walked away because she was unable to breathe. "I went to the door and the bossman saw me," she explained. "I explained to him that I just couldn't get my breath, that I just had to breathe to live. He said, you will just have to go back on your job. The looms have to run. The machinery has to be taken care of. It costs money. But I can stand at the door and get all the help and the people that I want."[38]

As Taylor's story indicates, Stevens employees had little say over their working conditions. Lacking even an informal grievance procedure, many complained about overbearing supervisors who were able to harass them or give more favorable treatment to particular "brownnoses." "We didn't have no say-so with the bossman when anything would come up and we wanted to ask him a question about it," recalled worker Myrtle Cribbs. "He would listen to us but never nothing was done about it." Many consequently felt that only a union could improve their conditions. "A union's the only way you can get justice with a company like J. P. Stevens," declared Roanoke Rapids worker Lundee Cannon, who supported the TWUA from the start of its drive.[39]

Workers also complained about the company's attitudes to the sick and elderly. "They have no use for old people," claimed Stevens worker Maynard Lovell. "If you're old and you go to the hospital, they'll find some way to dismiss you. They want you to produce. If they think you're going to have hospital bills, they'll get you out." After a lifetime of laboring in dusty mills, some older workers developed byssinosis. Commonly known as brown lung disease, byssinosis was endemic in the southern textile industry. A chronic condition, it killed many by gradually reducing their breathing capacity. Although the British government recognized the condition as early as 1940, in the United States resistance from industry groups ensured that no constructive action was taken until the 1970s, when the campaign against Stevens helped to spur a major effort to secure compensation and clean up the mills.[40]

Like many low-paying industries, textiles had a long tradition of female employment. Women were in fact more likely to work in textiles than in other manufacturing industry; in 1966, for instance, 45 percent of textile workers were female, compared to 27 percent of employees in manufacturing as a whole. For decades, textile mill owners had used female labor as a way of depressing wage rates, and in the South mill hands had traditionally been recruited on a family labor system that required both men and women to work. By offering low wages, mill owners pushed family members to work alongside each other in their plants.[41]

At the time of the Stevens campaign, around 40 percent of the firm's employees were women. As was the case across the textile industry, women workers at J. P. Stevens found it difficult to secure the higher-paying jobs. Many charged that the company ignored their qualifications or experience when it made promotions. "We're supposed to get jobs according to seniority," noted Nadine Buckner. "But its just a joke. There's no way I'll get ahead unless we get organized." Others resented the fact that the company's low wages forced them to work in the mills. Said Dorothy Varnadore: "I work because I have to make a living—you can't make it at Stevens on one person's pay."[42]

The company's black workers also found it difficult to secure access to the better-paying jobs. The southern textile industry had a long record of discrimination against blacks, and as late as 1960 they comprised only 3.3 percent of its workers. In contrast, 7.6 percent of all manufacturing employees were African American. In the years immediately after the Civil War, the first mills had been promoted as a way of providing employment for the region's poor whites. As the industry employed large numbers of white women, social taboos prevented the hiring of large numbers of black men. In South Carolina, where Stevens ran many of its plants, the 1915 Segregation Act made it illegal for anyone "engaged in the business of cotton textile manufacturing . . . to allow . . . operatives . . . of different races to labor and work together within the same room." The law, which stayed on the books until 1960, had a separate clause that excluded many nonproduction jobs, establishing a tradition of black employment in these positions. Social custom ensured that other southern states followed a pattern similar to the Palmetto State's.[43]

Prior to the 1960s, African Americans comprised less than 5 percent of Stevens workers. Only black men were hired, and they were confined to a small range of menial, nonproduction jobs. "Let's go back to the fifties when I worked there," said Jettie Purnell from Roanoke Rapids. "At first all the black did was scrub floors, worked out there opening cotton, you know, inhaling cotton, wasn't no blacks in the mills, didn't have any black women. . . . The only thing they would hire you for was to clean, work out in the yard, cleaning up the yards. The mill company controlled everything then, the hospital, the country club." Some African American men also worked as truck drivers, but they were not allowed to make long-distance deliveries. A few black cleaners did enter the production areas, but they were strictly barred from operating the machinery. In the 1950s Sammy Alston worked as a janitor in the Roanoke Rapids mills. "I used to work up there at that mill," he recalled. "What I was doing was putting in spit trays, putting sawdust in it, and I was cleaning bathrooms. . . . They had some little spit trays, what they used to spit in, you put sawdust in it . . . keeps them from spitting on the floor. . . . I would always get them up, put new ones down, and I had bathrooms I had to clean up. Weren't black people working there and I was the only one to come through there, and it would be nothing in that card room but white people."[44]

Until the 1960s, mill managers fought to maintain the racial status quo. Most commonly, executives argued that they had to operate their mills in accordance with "local custom," asserting that their white workers would walk out if more blacks were hired. In addition, many claimed that blacks were not as qualified as whites. Outspoken African Americans did try to challenge the color line, but they achieved little before the civil rights legislation of the 1960s mandated changes. A civil rights leader in Roanoke Rapids, Joe P. Moody, recalled that when blacks tried to secure nontraditional jobs at Stevens plants, the company "always had some kind of excuse."[45]

In the 1960s, civil rights laws finally began to force the southern textile companies to hire greater numbers of African Americans. In particular, Title VII of the Civil Rights Act of 1964, which abolished discrimination in employment, had a major impact on the South's largest industry. Over the next fifteen years, the industry would integrate at a rapid pace, the proportion of black workers increasing from less than 5 percent to around 25 percent. Anticipating the influx of greater numbers of blacks into the industry, TWUA leaders were optimistic. For decades they had struggled to organize a predominantly white workforce, but now they reasoned that a new generation of black workers would prove more responsive to their appeals. Although they were being hired in greater numbers, blacks were still more likely to be confined to lower-paying jobs, and many looked to the union as a way of tackling these inequities. Locked out of the best jobs, many African American workers felt that they had less to lose by joining the union. As Sammy Alston recalled, "I don't think we had nothing to lose because the only thing he could do was fired you, that's all, and you couldn't have went no lower because you was working at the last level right there, and they constantly come and hired people over the top of you, come in there and create jobs for people."[46]

The progress of the civil rights movement clearly influenced the launching of the Stevens campaign. In July 1963 the union's reasons for initiating the drive were laid out in "America's Stake in the South." In this widely cir-

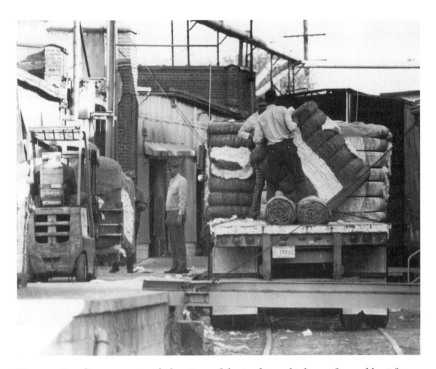

Figure 2. Loading raw cotton bales. One of the traditional jobs performed by African American men in the southern textile industry was handling raw cotton bales at the start of the production process. Here, three men work on a loading platform at the Stevens complex in Roanoke Rapids. (Frank Blechman Jr./Kheel Center for Labor-Management Documentation and Archives, Cornell University.)

culated pamphlet, TWUA leaders insisted that the time was right for a major onslaught on Dixie. The previous month, President Kennedy had introduced his civil rights bill, sounding the death knell for de jure segregation in the South. His speech marked a major breakthrough for the civil rights movement, as for the first time Kennedy had described civil rights as a moral issue. The union noted that change was at hand in the region; the "barriers to meaningful civil rights" were being lifted, and southern blacks were emerging as a powerful political force. As more industry moved in and a two-party system emerged, TWUA leaders argued that it would now be easier for them to sign up new members.[47]

The union also promoted its drive by arguing that it was in the broader national interest to organize the South. "America's Stake in the South" documented that pay and fringe benefits lagged behind in Dixie. In terms of average hourly pay, there was a regional differential of around 25 percent.

With fringe benefits taken into account, the gap was even wider. The union calculated that if the pay gap between the South and the rest of the country were closed, the economy would be enriched by $46 billion a year. Thus all Americans would benefit if southerners were paid more.[48]

For TWUA leaders, increasing union membership in the region was also intended to aid the passage of progressive legislation at the national level. The union outlined how conservative southern congressmen had traditionally blocked liberal legislation. "In other words," it asserted, "successful political efforts in other parts of the country are either cancelled out or diluted because sufficient inroads have not been made in the strength of reactionary forces in the South." TWUA leaders argued that if there were more union voters in the South, they could undermine conservative politicians. "It is in areas where unions are weak, where repressive labor laws prevent workers from organizing, that the seeds of reaction exist," declared William Pollock. "How much progressive legislation have we seen blocked by the Dixiecrat-GOP coalition in Congress?"[49]

"America's Stake in the South" was an effort to build support for the Stevens campaign, and it was circulated to a range of politicians, community leaders, and labor activists. In general, however, the drive to organize J. P. Stevens was launched without the fanfare that had accompanied Operation Dixie. Back in 1946, union leaders had claimed that they were embarking on a "holy crusade" that would sweep through the South and "organize everything in sight." Such rhetoric, strategists reasoned, had only encouraged corporate resistance. As organizers headed South to begin this campaign, they hoped that a more understated approach would yield better results.[50]

TWO

Persistent Unremedied Violations

In the early summer of 1963, twenty-four organizers headed south to work on the Stevens campaign. Any organizer venturing into the textile South knew that such efforts were likely to meet stiff opposition, and most were aware that a company as large as Stevens would not be organized quickly. Few, however, anticipated the ferocity of Stevens's response. Sol Stetin later reflected, "Very truthfully, I never imagined that the company would carry on the way it has."[1] It was in these opening exchanges that the company relied heavily on openly violating labor laws in order to deter unionization. Across the region, supervisors interrogated or dismissed union supporters, particularly on the eve of elections. As NLRB trial examiner Horace A. Ruckel noted, the company had embarked on a "systematic attempt to rid itself of union adherents." Stevens, added trial examiner Thomas Ricci, had committed "massive and deliberate" unfair labor practices in order to crush the organizing drive.[2] In the first round of Stevens cases, the NLRB found the giant textile maker guilty in twenty-one of twenty-two decisions, but even this did little to cow recalcitrant executives. According to the union, the company's fierce opening represented "an anti-union campaign unparalleled in modern American labor history."[3]

In order to crush the union's efforts, Stevens managers fired many of the TWUA's leading supporters. In all, the NLRB found Stevens guilty of illegally discharging sixty-nine employees during the initial stages of the drive. By removing the most prominent union activists, the company was able to send a clear message to the rest of the workforce that open support of the union would not be tolerated. In addition, company officials used many other tactics to intimidate those who remained on the job. They spread negative rumors about organized labor, repeatedly linking unions with violence, corruption, and economic decline. They recruited the highest-paid production workers and encouraged them to disseminate this propaganda. On some occasions, managers also tried to use the race issue to undermine the union. The initial organizing efforts took place at the height of the civil rights movement, and company officials seized on the chance to weaken the union by telling their predominantly white workforce about organized labor's support of the civil rights movement. And, across the South, Stevens's efforts drew on a great deal of community support, which helped managers to effectively isolate union supporters.[4]

The lengthy NLRB cases show that J. P. Stevens had a clear, centrally directed policy to defeat unionization at any cost. They establish that, although the company's plants were spread out across the South, plant managers communicated regularly with one another and with the firm's legal department, which gave overall instructions on how to oppose the campaign.[5] In the first group of cases, which became known as Stevens I, Ruckel commented on the company's unity. "The record," he noted, "shows close cooperation and a unity of action between the top management at all Respondent's plants, even to the extent of identical posted notices to its employees, identical reply letters to the Union, and the posting of copies on the bulletin boards." Reviewing Stevens's continuing violations, trial examiner Boyd Leedom blamed top executives for the extensive labor-law violations. "Substantially all of the law violation of the Respondent . . . must stem from the decision of one man or a very few men at the top of the management structure," he concluded.[6] After sitting through many weeks of drawn-out hearings, Leedom concluded that the company's witnesses were following "a policy" that had been set out by high-level managers. It was designed, he explained, "to defeat this Union's organizational effort at the cost, if necessary, of committing unfair labor practices and then denying the unlawful acts in the process." These officials were engaged in a joint "crusade" to eradicate unionism that caused them to participate in and tolerate actions that they would not have supported individually.[7]

The company's response reflected top executives' dislike of being singled out for a major union drive. Feeling that they had been underestimated, Stevens's executives were determined to prove the union wrong. Hal Addis, vice president for industrial relations, insisted in 1980 that the union had made a tactical mistake when it selected the company in 1963. "They thought J. P. Stevens would fall quickly," he asserted. This feeling was shared by other managers. "The union did not believe we would stand up to protect the rights of the employees," insisted Hampton Shuping, a corporate vice president.[8] Another company executive remembered that Robert Stevens, who had come south in search of lower costs, made up his mind "to fight like hell. . . . he was upset that the union thought he was a patsy . . . and now he decided to prove himself."[9]

Stevens's management also believed that unionism would undermine their economic viability. They repeatedly pointed out that the textile industry was highly competitive, with small profit margins. They pictured union leaders as greedy and power-grabbing autocrats who failed to appreciate the company's economic position. According to company officials, submitting to union demands could lead to bankruptcy. Power-hungry union leaders would not stop until their power "would dominate not merely employers— but even more truly, employees—and beyond employers and employees, the whole American people."[10]

Robert Stevens himself was reluctant to comment publicly on the union campaign, although the *Daily News Record* did obtain an exclusive interview with the taciturn executive in the summer of 1967. In it he stated his core belief that there was no need for a "third party" to interfere between the company's workers and management. "A third party," he claimed, "can serve no useful purpose, and a majority of our employees evidently feel the same way." Stevens vigorously defended his company's record, insisting that he paid "top wages and benefits in the industry" and that his workers were "happy." He linked unions with "liquidations, strikes [and] hard feelings," asserting that they had little to offer. He also particularly disliked the TWUA's efforts to portray his firm as an outlaw. "You know," he fumed, "we haven't existed in this country and this industry, and made progress, for 154 years by being lawbreakers, despite what some people would have you think."[11]

In the interview, Robert Stevens confirmed that he had been angered by the union's decision to "target" his company.[12] By being singled out, the quiet executive had clearly been changed. As *Fortune* journalist Walter Guzzardi Jr. put it, "the thought of union organizers at the company gates turned mild-mannered Robert Stevens into Fighting Bob, and management decided to do battle." Union strategists were caught off guard. As staffer

Bert Beck later admitted, they had expected the northern-based company to "fight like hell but fight fairly."[13]

At the start of their campaigns, organizers found that they made good progress, confirming their belief that many of the company's workers wanted a union. In plants around Greenville, Great Falls, and Roanoke Rapids, they proceeded in the conventional fashion of approaching workers and persuading them to sign union cards. In June 1963, South Carolina–based organizer Lawrence Gore reported: "Leaflet distribution at Stevens plants 1 and 2 in Great Falls, S.C. Had enough help to complete both plants and reception was excellent." More than a hundred workers soon returned cards to Gore, many doing so at the plant gates on their way to and from work.[14]

Once the union had recruited a solid core of supporters, however, the company had the targets that it needed to launch its program of mass discharges. In a vain effort to protect its members from being fired, organizers followed an agreed policy of sending the company the names of all those who had signed cards. Managers, they argued, would not be so bold as to dismiss those who were publicly identified as union members. In fact, Stevens seized upon the lists as their opportunity to fire the most active and outspoken activists. Some union leaders later questioned the wisdom of mailing these lists to the company; in doing so, they asserted, the union had played into Stevens's hands. In November 1963, TWUA executive council member Mike Botelho claimed that the union's open identification of its members was "like a red flag goading the bull." The lists certainly aided the company's campaign, yet in most locations managers already knew who had joined the TWUA anyway. Most of the company's plants were located in small towns, and there was little anonymity for those who had signed union cards.[15]

Organizers reported that their task became a lot more difficult once the company received the membership lists. From Great Falls one wrote simply: "Names sent to employer . . . eight of these fired. . . . 6 of 8 asked before fired: want to change your mind? Will you stool?" In Roanoke Rapids a rash of early discharges took their toll on the drive. "Had more than 100 on committee; now 30—and they are furtive," wrote an organizer." By November 1963 the TWUA's executive council noted that the drive was faltering "because the people are afraid of being fired."[16]

Most of those who were fired were initially watched more closely in the plant, as supervisors searched for a pretext to issue them with a "write-up" and remove them. Once the company received the names of those who had joined the union, they also posted these names on plant bulletin boards, ensuring that the entire workforce would be aware that union members were being scrutinized. "Ever since our names went on the board," commented Greenville worker James Rosemond, "they have been watching our every move, trying to get something on us." Another Stevens worker from Greenville, Garvis Powers, claimed that he overheard foreman Ross Griffin discussing the names on the board with two newly hired workers: "I saw Mr. Griffin point to our names on the board as union men, and I heard him say, 'We are going to get rid of these guys and replace them with new men.' The new guys started laughing and Mr. Griffin looked down to where I was."[17]

Across the South, union activists complained that the company's attitude to them changed dramatically once it found out that they had joined the TWUA. Talmadge Clearly had worked at the company's Dunean mill since 1939 and had never received a personnel action report. He said he had even been complimented on his work by company officials. But after he joined the union, Clearly asserted, his supervisor warned him that his "days were numbered." Shortly after this, the veteran twister tender was discharged for listening to the radio during working hours, even though by his account this was a common practice in the plant.[18] Roanoke Rapids worker Herbert King, who had held his job for thirteen years, also testified that his supervisor had previously complimented him on his performance. He described how, once he joined the union, the same boss began watching him closely, even hiding behind spinning frames and then appearing with complaints. King was later dismissed for not performing his work on schedule. Ollie Varnadore, a Stevens employee since 1943, similarly related that supervisors would hang around in the alleys close to her work area after she joined the union. "[I]t got on my nerves so bad," she testified, "that I had to go to the doctor." Like many activists, Vernadore was later fired for unsatisfactory work.[19]

Individual discharges illustrate well just how far the company was willing to go in its drive to wipe out the union's presence. At the Victor plant, one union activist was removed after thirty-three years of commended service, receiving his first write-up a week after his supervisor had first questioned him about the TWUA's campaign. The veteran employee was fired on the grounds that he refused to sign the write-up that the company had produced. At one of its plants in Whitmire, South Carolina, the company discharged Jess Cudd, a sixty-three-year-old worker who had first gone to work in a textile mill when he was nine years old. In all his years of holding down the same job, Cudd had never before received a write-up. "It's mighty funny they took fifty years to find he wasn't no good as a spinnin' doffer," commented Cudd's wife. Cudd related that his supervisor, apparently feeling some remorse about his action, had advised Cudd to adopt his son's children (the son was also fired). "Your Social Security will help you get just about as much as you was making up here," explained the company official.[20]

Similar stories came in from across Stevens's plants. Amos E. Fendley was a model employee who had worked at the Dunean mill since World War II. Leedom noted that Fendley "was not only a satisfactory employee, but had been recognized as one of such capability that he was on occasion out on jobs requiring special attention, and had been complimented by his supervisors for the quality of his work." Once he became active in the union, the company began to make complaints about Fendley's work. He was finally fired for not locking a switch, even though supervisors testified that they had never heard of anybody else being dismissed for this reason. It was, concluded Leedom, merely a pretext thought up by managers "looking for an excuse to get rid of Fendley."[21]

At all of its plants, one of the company's main aims was to eliminate strong union activists who were capable of influencing those around them. At the Rosemary plant in Roanoke Rapids, managers were especially keen to remove Horace Spence. Unlike many union activists, Spence had worked for Stevens only for a year and a half, but in this time he had already received two promotions and was widely regarded as a good worker. In May 1963 Spence joined the union and was quickly able to sign up many of his immediate coworkers. Following this, the company fired him for making seconds. In reality, as Ruckel noted, seconds were "constantly resulting" and were normally tolerated by managers. "I conclude," wrote Ruckel, "that Respondent did not discharge Spence for the reasons which it alleges, but because of his activity in the Union."[22]

Collaborating with antiunion workers, supervisors sometimes hatched crude plots to remove union activists. At the Dunean plant, managers were particularly determined to eliminate Rev. G. W. Dennis, one of the first African Americans to join the union. An influential preacher, Dennis was nevertheless unable to secure more than a menial janitorial position at the mill. In August 1963, managers fired Dennis because he had allegedly knocked over another worker with a small "hand truck" that he pushed around the plant. Dennis, who earned $1.24 an hour, used the truck to transport cleaning supplies between the plant's restrooms. He denied that he had hit anybody with his truck, and asked to talk to the person who had made the charge so that he could "pray a special prayer for them." His supervisor initially refused this request, telling Dennis that "you will have plenty of time to pray." The janitor insisted on talking to the man he was supposed to have knocked down, and the company eventually allowed him to do so. The uncomfortable accomplice, enlisted by supervisors as part of a plan to discharge Dennis, admitted that he had not been run over but claimed that Dennis had "liked to" knock him down. After this, the janitor was dismissed, even though he too had never been reprimanded before.[23]

Many of those who were discharged openly disputed the reasons that the company gave for their removal. Some union activists were fired on the grounds that they had engaged in horseplay, yet they claimed that the company had turned a blind eye to such behavior in the past. "Everybody did it," claimed Joseph K. Williams. "If there was—during the two years that I was employed there if they had a fired everyone who was engaged in horseplay they would have fired the whole card room." Other evidence established that company officials had traditionally given workers a certain amount of leeway, provided that they performed their jobs satisfactorily. In one case a Roanoke Rapids worker was discharged for taking too long to fetch himself a soft drink. A month earlier the same man had fought a coworker in the plant, a clear violation of company rules, but he had not been dismissed because he was a "good" worker.[24]

In the light of this testimony, company officials struggled to respond to the charge that they had harassed or simply fired union activists in order to stall organizing. Throughout the long parade of Stevens cases before the NLRB, company witnesses were frequently evasive and unconvincing. Accusing them of lying under oath, Leedom concluded that the case highlighted the "importance of the simple principle that those who take an oath to tell the truth should do so." Despite all the evidence to the contrary, company officials sometimes tried to flatly deny that they had committed unfair labor practices, occasionally putting forth unlikely explanations in an effort to cover their tracks. On one occasion, a supervisor even testified that he had accidentally driven past a union meeting while looking for somewhere to buy an ice cream. He added that he had not seen a worker whom he later discharged because he did not know him by sight, despite the fact that the fired activist had been employed at the plant for more than seventeen years. Not surprisingly, the NLRB refused to credit this testimony.[25]

More senior managers frequently argued that the discharges were part of a broader effort to increase efficiency. Leland Burns, the assistant general manager of the company's Rock Hill mills, tried to defend the discharge of several union supporters on these grounds. "We were having considerable trouble," he asserted, "and there was a lot of slackness, and a lot of things wrong in the plant, and we were making an all-out effort to correct the situation. . . . there was an intense drive in all areas of the plant to stop mistakes." Burns added that the union's presence had distracted employees and caused problems in the plant. "Well, when this union campaign started," he asserted, "and there was more inattention, there was more distraction, more talking, and that kind of thing, than we've ever seen before, and that resulted in some write-ups." Some union activists, Burns added, were neglecting their jobs and acting in an arrogant manner. "It was brought to my attention on many occasions that people were making it clear that they had rights, and we couldn't do this, and we couldn't do that, and they were being obnoxious on the job, and there were violations of rules, and there was some discontented talking, and that kind of thing, while this campaign was going on."[26]

In responding to charges that they had closely watched union supporters in order to find a pretext to fire them, supervisors often asserted that they were just carrying out their jobs. William Broughton denied harassing union supporter Billy Pressley in Great Falls. "My job is supervisor," he asserted, "which requires a lot of following up, and I don't think I watched him any closer than I did anyone else." Many again insisted that they watched workers only because they were striving to improve efficiency in the plants. "I know of no instance," claimed assistant superintendent W. E. Lindsay, "where I have watched anybody because of their name being on the board; I have watched jobs and machinery and personnel because of trouble they were giving us." The NLRB found these claims generally not credible, as most discharges were clearly related to union activity.[27]

While company witnesses tried to argue that they had legitimate motives for the dismissals, some testimony provided clear evidence to the contrary. In Roanoke Rapids, former foreman John Robert Pitt testified that discharges for bad work were unknown in the past, as "you are going to make bad work, so much of it." Pitt also explained that, once the union campaign began, supervisors were gathered by their superiors and ordered to find out who had joined the TWUA. "I was to tell on anybody that belonged to the Union," he noted candidly. This information would be passed up the management chain and leading activists "would be fired." Pitt also confirmed the company's intention to close any mills that the union organized. "It boiled down to the fact that if the Union won they were going to shut these Mills down," he stated.[28]

Pitt's motives for testifying are not clear, although he claimed that he was not willing to lie for the company. His testimony was certainly corroborated by others. Joseph Carlton Britton, another Roanoke Rapids foreman, was told by his overseer to report the names of any workers under his supervision who had joined the TWUA. At some plants, workers who were subpoenaed also outlined how the company was determined to eliminate union supporters. At a Greenville area mill, worker Ronnie A. McClain testified that he had seen assistant overseer Charles Harrison harass sweeper Alvin Baker, a union supporter who was subsequently discharged. "I saw him [Harrison] in several different places; either always behind him or right in front of him," said McClain. The supervisor followed Baker around the mill and made him pick up small pieces of "white waste" or string roving. In revealing testimony, McClain explained that sweepers had never previously been required to separate the roving from the rest of the trash.[29]

From the company's viewpoint, the firing of union supporters was particularly effective because it took so long for them to be reinstated by the NLRB and the courts. Once activists were dismissed, most workers hung back, waiting to see if they would get their jobs back. As time went by and discharged activists were not put back to work, campaigns fell apart. In Great Falls, Lawrence Gore's optimism proved to be short-lived.[30] After signing up a core of workers, the union followed its standard procedure of mailing their membership list to the company. Nine union supporters were quickly fired, and the whole tone of Gore's reports changed. "We have nine fired," he reported in August 1963, "and eight of those were ones that mailed names in to company as committee people. . . . If we can get these people back I believe we will have a chance, otherwise no." As the discharges continued, other workers became afraid to sign up. "The signing is slow," reported Gore in February 1964. "Most all say they want to see what the Gov't. does in the discharges."[31] The delay in reinstating the fired workers gradually wore down the veteran organizer's morale. He wrote in March 1964 that "everybody is so tired of waiting. Eight months now since first discharge and we talk about the speedy NLRB." Shortly before leaving Great Falls after a draining campaign, a dispirited Gore noted glumly, "Everybody we contact says they will sign when the fired go back to work. This may take two years if ever. Our activity now is of not much good."[32]

As time went on, union organizers took to checking into the financial condition of discharged workers who were unable to find employment at other local mills. Their suffering was witnessed by others and served as a public reminder of the dangers of joining the union. Organizer J. D. Goad tried to help Jess Cudd, the veteran worker from Whitmire who had been fired in January 1964. Two and a half years later, Cudd was still waiting to be reinstated and was reported to be "in poor financial condition." As the winter of 1966–67 began, Goad wrote that he was very concerned about Cudd. "Went to Whitmire, S.C," he noted, "to look in to the condition of Jess Cudd found him out of food and fuel reported to Al Motley. Will follow up on this."[33]

The discharges also hurt the union's organizing campaign in other ways. Rather than signing up new members, staffers had to spend a great proportion of their time preparing the union's case before the NLRB. The first round of field hearings took more than six months, as 384 witnesses together compiled more than 12,000 pages of testimony. Not surprisingly, they were the longest hearings ever held by the board. The reports of southern director Scott Hoyman indicate that he spent the bulk of his time locating witnesses and preparing the union's case. "Worked in Charlotte IUD office on complaints to be presented to NLRB," he noted typically in August 1963. The problem was not restricted to campaign directors; organizers too had to keep a close written record of the company's alleged violations in order to build an effective case before the labor board.[34]

After just a few months of organizing, the union's lawyers realized that Stevens's lawlessness had destroyed their campaign. As early as November 1963, assistant general counsel Edward Wynne complained that the company's "persistent unremedied violations will inevitably lead the Stevens employees to conclude that the protections offered by the Act are a sham and a fraud."[35] By the time discharged workers were actually reinstated, the union's campaign had completely collapsed. In fact, it was December 1967, almost five years after the start of the campaign, before Stevens asked the sixty-nine illegally dismissed workers to return. The move came after the Supreme Court decided on December 11, 1967, not to hear an appeal of a lower court's order that the company reinstate those who had been illegally discharged. Those affected received back pay and 6 percent interest, which for some totaled as much as $30,000. Stevens was unlikely to be deterred, especially as it was able to save around $350,000 by deducting the back pay as a business expense. In a statement, the company claimed that it would abide by the decision but added that it was confident that its employees would "continue to prefer dealing with us in a direct and personal relationship rather than through an outside organization."[36]

The union's problems were compounded by the fact that Stevens did not simply rely on the discharge of union activists to achieve its goals. In addition, supervisors and antiunion workers made their opposition to unions very clear to the rest of the workforce. In order to undermine the TWUA's efforts, Stevens frequently used its loom fixers to convey an antiunion message in the plants. Working through loom fixers possessed a number of advantages for the company. They were the highest-paid workers in the mill, and the job carried considerable prestige in textile communities. Although they were still paid hourly, the fixers enjoyed a variety of privileges not shared by regular production employees. Many had access to supervisors' offices, where they were allowed to order extra materials and to use the telephone. In the course of their work, loom fixers moved around the mill, so they were well placed to spread an antiunion message. Loom fixers also acted as intermediaries between management and workers, conveying management orders and reporting back to supervisors about particular employees. They cherished their extra privileges and were anxious to distinguish themselves from the production employees. While the latter usually wore denim to work, for instance, loom fixers proudly sported formal shirts and dress pants.[37]

Many loom fixers hoped to progress into management positions, making them keen to carry out the company's bidding. On some occasions the fixers did carry out limited supervision while regular overseers were away. As they were hourly paid, however, Stevens could distance itself from their actions. As the company put it, loom fixers were employees with "no supervisory status above the lowest level of authority." As such, any statements they made about the union were simply their personal opinions.[38]

Both company officials and loom fixers used their authority to influence workers against the union. From the start of the campaign, they repeatedly linked unions with violence and strikes. At the Dunean plant, the company posted pictures of dynamited homes on plant bulletin boards, claiming that the homes had been damaged during the bitter Henderson strike. Captions placed underneath the pictures read: "The people at Henderson, N.C. Have no pay check while their on strike" and "Don't let this happen to your house." The pictures were not removed until after the election.[39] Loom fixer Lonnie Edwards also walked through the mill showing workers a clipping from a business publication about the Henderson strike. "If I owned J. P. Stevens and the union entered my plant," he proffered, "things like this would happen and I would close it down." The article again included pictures of bombed-out houses. Edwards, according to worker Gail Phillips, "turned the pages and showed us the worst pictures in the book. After he showed us the book, he said the book would be in Mr. Larson Hall's office if we wanted to read it."[40]

Similar tactics were used at other plants. At the Republic mill in Great Falls, union activist William C. Aldridge was targeted by loom fixer Frank Hancock. Hancock, who had free access to the department office, called Aldridge there and told him to leave the union while he was still able to do so. He warned Aldridge that he should not "lose what he was making," referring specifically to the 1951 strike in nearby Rock Hill. At a range of plants, both supervisors and loom fixers also reminded employees of the 1934 strike, stressing that the union had struggled to feed the strikers. From the company's plant in Watts, South Carolina, an organizer noted "supervisors threatening hunger if unionization—remember 1934."[41]

The company linked unions with plant closures, particularly in the northern states. Again, workers were sent the message that the union threatened their economic security. At the start of every organizing drive, the company posted a notice that was drafted by Whiteford Blakeney, a notoriously anti-union attorney who was hired by Stevens to fight the campaign. In it, the company claimed that "if this Union were to get in here, it would not work to your benefit but, in the long run, would itself operate to your serious harm." Within the mills, company officials freely expressed their view that the TWUA's wage demands had caused the economic decline of the New England textile industry. At the Dunean plant, for example, worker Bob F. Spoon complained that his shift overseer "told me that he understood up north that a union was causing them to go bankrupted and out of business."[42]

Ominous references were made to the plant in Darlington, South Carolina, that the Deering Milliken Corporation had closed after its workers had voted for the TWUA. Supervisors suggested to their employees that Stevens would likewise shut its mills rather than deal with the TWUA. Albert Sanders stated that he was told by a supervisor that if the union was voted in at the Dunean plant, "they will close it down just like they did at Darlington, Stephens has too much money." Claiming to have management's ear, loom fixers repeated these warnings. In Apalache, South Carolina, MacDonald

Lindsey recalled that one respected fixer told workers that "the Company could shut the doors and make a warehouse out of the plant if the Union came in."[43]

Company officials also tried to associate unions with organized crime and corruption. In the 1950s and 1960s, government probes into the financial mismanagement of the International Brotherhood of Teamsters gained national news coverage. Although most unions never suffered financial scandals, labor's opponents used the stories to tarnish the entire union movement.[44] In Roanoke Rapids, supervisors told workers to stay well clear of an organization that was "nothing but a bunch of gangsters." At a Greenville area plant, company officials similarly spread rumors that union organizers were "just racketeers." Although anticommunist sentiment had subsided since the mid-1950s, when McCarthyism lost credibility, some loom fixers also tried to link unions with communism. Dunean worker Ethel Blakely, for example, stated that a loom fixer told her that "there is a lot of Communism in organized labor."[45]

Both supervisors and loom fixers also spread propaganda that directly appealed to white fears that they could be replaced on their jobs by blacks. In many ways, the first phase of the Stevens campaign occurred at the perfect time for the company to use such material. The southern textile workforce was still overwhelmingly white, but white southerners had witnessed more than a decade of civil rights activism that had resulted in much greater rights for African Americans. After the passage of the 1964 Civil Rights Act, white textile workers knew that greater job integration was bound to occur. While frequently failing to challenge segregation on the ground in the South, many unions had supported the civil rights movement at the national level, providing funding to leading organizations such as the NAACP. Labor leaders such as Walter Reuther, president of the United Automobile Workers (UAW), had stood beside civil rights activists during high-profile protests, including the 1965 Selma-Montgomery march. The company was thus able to tell its overwhelmingly white workforce that unions supported integration.[46]

In May 1965 the union contested an election at the company's Dunean plant. At this time Stevens was just beginning to integrate its mills. In the Dunean plant, only a tiny number of African Americans had secured production jobs; in September 1964, for example, only two blacks worked in the weave room on the third shift, and they were still required to use a distant "colored" bathroom. With Title VII about to become effective, Dunean workers knew that this was likely to change. As a result, both loom fixers and supervisors warned workers about organized labor's support for the civil rights movement, adding that the union would support extensive job integration. Loom fixer Harold Du Bose told Ethel Blakely that "if the union got in, they would pull the niggers in on us, and they would take our jobs." She added, "That's just the way he said it—niggers." DuBose traveled freely through the mill with a clipping that highlighted how unions had supported the recent Selma-Montgomery march. Keeping the clipping in his top pocket, he was able to easily show it to workers. "I had to carry it somewhere, didn't I?" he quipped. Following these efforts, Du Bose was promoted to a management position.[47]

Workers had a mixed reaction to Du Bose's efforts. After being shown the Selma clipping, at least one employee said that she wanted to stay away from the union. But other workers complained that Du Bose was interfering with their work. The racial views of these workers are not known, but it is likely that they did not want Du Bose to bother them because they knew that he was trying to undermine the union.[48] While Du Bose was apparently the most active in using racial material, he was not alone. During the same campaign, head warp man Wilson McCraw circulated pictures of Martin Luther King standing next to Walter Reuther. The UAW leader was described to workers as "a head man of the union" and the man that they would be "working for."[49]

When election time came, the company made an all-out effort to use the race issue. Before the vote at both its Dunean and Estes plants, managers assembled employees and showed them the pictures of Reuther and King. Stating that the images had been taken in Selma, managers explained that the Selma-Montgomery march had been partly financed by the AFL-CIO. They also stated that the UAW had given $25,000 to the NAACP and that unions had paid $160,000 to bail out civil rights workers in another town. They then asked their workers: "Do you want your money sent down to Alabama to help support Martin Luther King, help get these niggers out of jail? When the union members told Walter Reuther they don't want their money sent to help the niggers he told them to shut up. . . . Do you want your money to go to Selma, Ala., to help support these niggers and Communists and goons and beatniks?" The union later cited the company's injection of the race issue as a major cause of their heavy election defeats at Dunean and Estes. At the time, southern director Scott Hoyman also complained privately about these tactics. "In captive audience speech," he wrote in his weekly report, "Co. raised race issue. This is tough here."[50]

Although union supporters were forbidden to talk about the union while they were clocked in, antiunion employees were often encouraged to fight the TWUA on company time, especially if they could persuade card signers to change their minds. As individuals agreed to withdraw, supervisors would cross out their names from the posted membership lists, publicly undermining the union's support. At the Watts plant, the company received the names of forty-six workers who had signed TWUA cards. Supervisors quickly responded by distributing slips that allowed workers to revoke their cards. These were printed in a company office and given to nonunion employees to freely circulate in the plant. The company, as the NLRB noted, even "furnished antiunion employees the services of its typewriters and Mimeograph machine, and the services of an employee to reproduce withdrawal announcements which were then distributed among the employees for signing and mailing to the Union." Through these tactics, the company and its supporters managed to secure the withdrawal of forty-two of the forty-six union members. "The Union in the Watts plant was wiped out," concluded NLRB trial examiner Horace Ruckel.[51]

The company's fierce antiunionism was backed by local community leaders, ensuring that TWUA activists felt just as isolated outside the plants as they did on their jobs. In Great Falls, a town of little more than three thousand people, the local police repeatedly harassed union supporters. Like many other members of the community, police officers feared that the union would only bring economic devastation to their town, especially if the company shut the mills rather than deal with the TWUA. Discharged worker William Sibley claimed that when he was distributing leaflets with organizer Lawrence Gore, the chief of police came by and told Gore to "wipe his ass with them." The law enforcement official then allegedly turned to Sibley and warned him, "You'll starve yourself, family, me and half of Great Falls to death fooling with that Union, if you'll leave that Union alone you might get your job back." Not surprisingly, Great Falls workers who did join the union found that they enjoyed little anonymity. A resident of the town, assistant general manager Leland Burns admitted that it was impossible not to know workers' allegiances in such a small community: "we live in a town of 3500 people down there, and we have got 100 to 125 supervisors, and we got all these people giving out leaflets; somebody always sees them;

'so-and-so gave out leaflets today' or 'so-and-so gave them out yesterday'; they all pass that information on to me."[52]

In the Greenville area too, the company received a great deal of community support. In the tiny textile community of Slater, local professionals even became involved in placing pressure on TWUA supporters such as David Collins, an outspoken activist who had succeeded in signing up many of his coworkers. Everywhere Collins went, community leaders pressured him to change his mind. He claimed, for example, that a local lawyer told him that if the workers organized, "you'll be out on the street and the Government won't back the union." While Collins was being examined by the company doctor, the medic wasted no time in telling his patient to leave the union. "He said," related Collins, "I should go to the management and tell them I had done the wrong thing in joining the Union, because Slater was good to its employees and gave them plenty of work to do. He said that if I lost the job, he knew I had a bunch of children, and this Union wouldn't feed my children." Despite this pressure, Collins still decided to "stick with the union."[53]

Other community institutions also opposed the union. The local press consistently backed Stevens. During the campaign at the Estes mill, for instance, the *Saluda Valley Record* printed an antiunion letter but refused to publish a reply from a TWUA supporter. The union responded by printing the letter in one of its leaflets, but its author was then harassed and later discharged. In both Greenville and Roanoke Rapids, the local papers also remained largely supportive of Stevens. In some cases, even local universities and colleges played their part in supporting the giant textile maker. Several examples vividly spotlighted the communications between company officials and civic leaders, and their shared desire to keep unions out of their communities.[54]

These links are highlighted well by the case of Greenville worker Roger D. Foster. Foster was a strong union supporter who was enrolled in part-time courses at Bob Jones University, an institution well known for its conservative ethos. In NLRB hearings, Foster testified that he was repeatedly called by the university's business manager, who told him that an anonymous "friend" of the university had informed college president Dr. Bob Jones Sr. of his union involvement. The university, Foster was told, "did not approve of some of the communistic activities connected with unions," and they consequently advised him to "get out of this union thing." Shortly after he refused to do so, Foster was fired by the company. Another part-time student,

Ralph Moore, was pressured to leave the TWUA by officials of the Holmes Theological Seminary. A leading seminary administrator in fact wrote Moore that he "cannot be a Christian and belong to a union." Although their student did not agree with this statement, the college upped the pressure by telling him that he would be dismissed if he did not "get out of the union completely." Citing his long-term desire to become a missionary, Moore withdrew from the union.[55]

Facing an opponent that was more than willing to violate labor laws, the union found little joy in trips to the polls. In May 1965 the TWUA lost the Dunean election by a vote of 871–679. The NLRB later upheld the union's objections to the company's conduct but, following the vote, workers remained afraid to support the TWUA, and the union lost a second election by a bigger margin—a result again set aside by the NLRB. In the spring of 1965 the union also lost a vote at the Roanoke Rapids complex, by a margin of 1,684 to 1,186. "A solid union majority of the company's 3000 employees in Roanoke Rapids, N.C., was destroyed by company violations," charged William Pollock. "The union lost an election that should have been won and the employees are without the representation a majority of them clearly indicated they wanted." Finding the company guilty of a range of unfair labor practices, including the unfair discharge of seventeen key activists, the NLRB set aside the Roanoke Rapids election. In this case, union leaders did not try to contest another vote because they reasoned that the company would only break the law if they did so.[56]

By the end of 1965, the union's organizing campaign against Stevens was on the verge of collapse. Although some staff insisted that workers still desired outside representation, any organizing campaign ultimately needed election victories in order to continue. The results certainly emboldened Stevens's officials, who began to make their first public statements about the drive. In 1965 Stevens publicized the TWUA's defeats in its annual report and thanked its employees. The following year, top executives similarly noted with satisfaction that organizing efforts had "diminished" following these setbacks.[57] Officials argued that their employees did not want a union and were better off dealing directly with them. The 1967 Annual Report stated that "the vast majority of employees in your Company's manufacturing plants have not indicated a desire to be represented by a union." Although some executives argued that the campaign had distracted its workers, Stevens continued to expand in the South. Between 1963 and 1966, in fact, the company reported record sales.[58]

As an NLRB official put it, by the summer of 1965 the Stevens case had already become "a major controversy." Reflecting on their efforts, union chiefs declared that they had been the victims of "a huge, well-organized, cold-blooded campaign on the part of this Company to stamp out an organizing drive at a number of the Company's mills in North and South Carolina." The union felt that it could not walk away from the campaign at this point; to do so would only reaffirm that Stevens's lawlessness had worked. Although it had been bruised and weakened, the union was determined to expose Stevens' harsh tactics to a broader audience.[59]

THREE

Changing Gears, 1966–1969

In June 1966, TWUA leaders publicly acknowledged that their "major drive" at J. P. Stevens had "not yet produced any victories." Having been soundly defeated in every election that it had contested, the union could easily have called off its campaign. Despite this, TWUA leaders wanted to fight on. Taking heart from the positive publicity that the case had generated, particularly in the national press, they claimed that the Stevens case had "focused national attention upon the southern anti-union conspiracy" and had graphically illustrated the need for labor law reform. Campaign strategists also continued to believe that Stevens workers desired union representation and would vote for the TWUA in fair elections.[1]

In the late 1960s, the focus of the union's energies increasingly switched away from a heavy reliance on organizing. Instead, activists tried to bring pressure against the giant textile firm through other means. Leaders endeavored, for instance, to stop the awarding of lucrative government contracts to Stevens. The union also used the Stevens case as part of its effort to strengthen workers' legal right to organize; in 1967 several fired workers traveled to Washington to give testimony before congressional committees. And, not least, the union initiated a publicity campaign designed to bring pressure on the company, recruiting support from liberal politicians, students, and labor leaders. With their emphasis on publicity, these efforts anticipated the boycott and corporate campaign that ACTWU would later launch against the company.

In this period the union did not abandon organizing at Stevens plants, but it no longer conducted a full-scale assault. In particular, organizers now tackled smaller plants rather than the major "clusters" they had previously focused on. The company resisted just as vigorously as ever. Stevens managers were determined to ensure that the union did not gain any foothold, no matter how small, in its southern plants. As they suffered repeated election defeats, union officials argued that it was impossible to hold a fair vote at a Stevens plant. By the end of the 1960s, the organizing drive at Stevens had almost completely collapsed.

After losing four major elections in 1965–66, neither TWUA nor IUD leaders were willing to continue organizing efforts on the same scale. By May 1967 the TWUA's organizing department reported that "the campaign against 25 plants of J. P. Stevens, which began in the Spring of 1963, has been curtailed in recent months." At this time only four organizers were still working on the Stevens drive.[2] Not until the mid-1970s, when the union won a major election in Roanoke Rapids, would organizers make another large-scale assault on Stevens's southern plants. "We had just a few staff left," recalled Paul Swaity. "We maintained a few organizers, and we were kind of searching around, and we had elections during all that period, but there was really no intensive drive until after the Roanoke Rapids victory."[3]

Swaity wanted to assign more personnel to the Stevens campaign, but in the late 1960s the majority of his southern staff were sidelined in what the union called "holding operations." Reflecting the prevailing corporate resistance to unions in the region, these were chiefly cases where the TWUA had won elections but had been unable to secure contracts. Organizers had to stay on the ground and try to hold together their members' morale. By June 1969 seven southern organizers were tied up in such situations, causing staff shortages that frustrated Swaity.[4] With an organizing record that was "far below standard," Swaity was desperate to start some new campaigns, yet he was unable to do so.[5]

Having scaled back the number of organizers, the union now increasingly used the Stevens case to try to secure labor law reform. In the spring of 1967 the union launched Operation Focus. According to staffers, this campaign was designed "to help bring public attention to the southern conspiracy," particularly "the ineffectiveness of the law to protect workers' right to organize."[6] As part of Operation Focus, the union produced "The Hollow Promise," a special booklet on the Stevens campaign that succinctly summarized the case for labor law reform. In all, the TWUA's publicity department distributed nine thousand copies of the report to "opinion molders in the principal walks of life," including members of Congress, religious leaders, and major newspaper editors. A complementary booklet entitled "Conspiracy in Southern Textiles" drew heavily on the Stevens case, again asserting that only a change in the law could quell the vicious antiunionism that prevailed in the South.[7]

Union leaders viewed Stevens as the key player in the "southern conspiracy." Within the TWUA, the company had already become a pariah, a symbol of southern employers' hatred of organized labor. At the union's 1968 convention in Washington, D.C., delegates spontaneously pulled off tablecloths after a representative from Maine found that they were made by J. P. Stevens. As the *New York Times* reported, "Ashtrays, water glasses and other articles on the tables crashed to the floor when many of the 1200 delegates of the Textile Workers Union of America pulled off the tablecloths." Some delegates suggested burning the cloths in a massive bonfire, but this idea was vetoed by the traditionally cautious William Pollock, who was determined to see that the impromptu protest did not get out of hand. The union did, however, finish its convention with delegates sitting at bare tables rather than using cloths made by Stevens. And it made a formal protest to the Hilton hotel chain about its use of the company's products.[8]

The TWUA's leaders also took their case to Washington. TWUA representatives told the House's labor subcommittee in 1967 that half a million southern textile workers faced "a conspiracy" to keep them nonunion. When workers tried to organize, claimed Pollock, "The power structure of the community is mobilized against the union: Anti-union 'citizens' committees are formed, enlisting merchants, clergy, professional men. . . . Workers are denied a place to hold union meetings." To be sure, these dark claims of a conspiracy were in many ways exaggerated. They pictured southern companies as monolithically nonunion, overlooking the fact that the attitudes of executives to organized labor did vary. Some companies, such as Dan River Mills and Crown Mills, had established stable relationships with the union that dated back to the 1940s. But if the union was guilty of overstating its case, it was clear that its experience with Stevens was representative of broader trends.[9] The union's organizing efforts had, in fact, often been savagely opposed by both corporate officials and community leaders. In the 1960s many firms were willing to break the law in order to deter unionization, and Stevens's harsh tactics failed to draw criticism from other industrialists, particularly in the South. Shortly before the launching of the campaign, an IUD effort to organize Wellington Mills in Anderson, South Carolina, was similarly thwarted by the firing of union supporters. As was the case at Stevens, the NLRB found that Wellington had committed unfair labor practices, but the company appealed the decision and the drive ran out of steam. In 1965 a TWUA effort to organize Schneider Mills in Taylorsville, North Carolina, was also met with mass firings. Swaity reported in January 1966 that Schneider was conducting a "vicious campaign to destroy [the] union." The organizer involved, he explained, was "having a very difficult time and is quite concerned whether he can maintain a strong situation for another four months waiting on Washington decision." The union's files documented many other organizing drives in the South that were crushed by employers' lawlessness. In 1969 Pollock himself claimed that his union faced "the same tactics of discharge and opposition . . . almost invariably in the south."[10]

In the late 1960s the TWUA also worked with the AFL-CIO in an effort to stop J. P. Stevens from receiving government business. In the third quarter of 1965, the union federation estimated, Stevens received more than $21.5 million in contracts from the Pentagon. In May 1966, AFL-CIO president George Meany wrote President Lyndon Johnson urging him to cut off all defense contracts to Stevens, a proposal that a company spokesperson termed "a ruthless retaliatory move." Meany received a reply that there was nothing in the law to compel the Department of Defense to pay attention to the findings of the NLRB. Johnson's advisers recommended maintaining the status quo, especially as Stevens was "the sole supplier of some textiles." The Department of Defense, they explained, "would be hurt if it had to quit doing business with Stevens." At the height of the Vietnam War, a conflict on which Johnson had staked his reputation, the administration was reluctant to jeopardize supplies from a key company. In addition, presidential advisers argued that social policy questions should not influence the procurement of defense supplies, and that the union's complaints against Stevens should be addressed purely through the NLRB. Throughout his term in office, Johnson rebuffed AFL-CIO demands to issue an executive order that would deny government work to persistent labor law violators.[11]

The Stevens campaign also stimulated political debate. In April 1966 the NLRB had found Stevens guilty of "massive unfair labor practices" and had ordered some unusual remedies in an effort to change the firm's behavior. In particular, company officials had to gather all of their workers together and inform them that they would stop violating the law. Angered by the move, four southern congressmen sprang to the textile maker's defense. South Carolina's L. Mendel Rivers, John L. McMillan, and William Jennings Bryan Dorn, together with Georgia's Phillip M. Landrum, insisted that the remedies went too far. The NLRB, they insisted, was wrongly "setting itself up as a 'policy-making' body." Rivers and Dorn also attacked union efforts to bar labor law violators from receiving government contracts. "We have a serious uniform shortage now," claimed Rivers, "and such an executive order would aggravate it further."[12]

The four Democrats' willingness to publicly stand behind Stevens underlined the close links that existed between the South's political and economic elites. Many leading southern Democrats viewed unions as unwanted intruders into their region. One of the most influential politicians in the region, North Carolina's senior senator Sam Ervin, acted as legal counsel for Deering Milliken during the lengthy legal proceedings that followed the closure of the Darlington mill. In 1967 the TWUA also complained that both Ervin and fellow Tar Heel senator B. Everett Jordan wanted to ensure that a vacancy on the U.S. Court of Appeals was filled by a representative who would support "textile owners' conduct in labor relations."[13]

While Stevens was backed by southern political leaders, the union's case was supported by liberal northerners. These regional divisions anticipated the way that the case would polarize public opinion a decade later. In the late 1960s the union's supporters were led by New Jersey congressman Frank Thompson Jr. A strong believer in unions, Thompson argued that labor laws were far too lax to deter companies such as Stevens. "The J. P. Stevens Co.," he insisted, "has so far lost all the battles but has won the war. It has achieved its objective—to keep the union out. Its violations of the law, assuming the reviewing court upholds the Labor Board, will be punished by a wrist-slapping. The contest between the J. P. Stevens Co. and the U.S. Government is unequal." Angered by the Stevens case, Thompson and other northern Democrats tried unsuccessfully to strengthen workers' right to organize.[14]

Congressional hearings offered the union the opportunity to communicate its case against Stevens to a broader audience. In the summer of 1967, several of the company's workers gave vivid testimony to the U.S. House Select Subcommittee on Labor, which was chaired by Thompson. Shirley Hobbs from Roanoke Rapids explained how both she and her husband were discharged by Stevens after they joined the TWUA. "Lincoln freed the slaves," she noted, "but J. P. Stevens enslaves his workers with fear, blackballing and work overloads." Another Roanoke Rapids worker explained how she was fired after she took a leaflet from a TWUA organizer. "I haven't worked since," she noted bluntly.[15] Doris J. Hicklin, a discharged worker from Rock Hill, South Carolina, cried on the stand as she explained how she had been dismissed for wearing a union button in the plant. "I wouldn't take it off," she noted defiantly. Asserting that the committee was prolabor and would not allow them to present their side of the story fairly, company officials refused to respond to these allegations.[16]

As the hearings highlighted, a core of workers refused to be cowed by Stevens's tactics. In them, the union did have a base of support to build on, and organizers insisted that they stood a good chance of winning any free vote. Some activists were truly fearless. In Roanoke Rapids, John Love attended all the union meetings and helped in handing out literature. He also drove around the small mill town with a two-by-five-foot sign on the back of his truck that read "For the future of yourself and your family, help support the union." Lloyd A. Boyd, another Roanoke Rapids worker, responded to the company's harassment by taking two witnesses into his supervisor's office and reading out a written declaration. "I prepared a statement," he related, "telling Fowler that I was definitely—definitely believed in organized labor and that I was going to do my utmost to organize the mill."[17] At the Dunean plant, meanwhile, union supporter William Lee came to work with up to seven union buttons on.[18] Others spoke out in support of union claims that the company had scared workers into voting against the TWUA. Dunean worker Jimmy C. Riddle took the brave step of giving a public statement to the union in the wake of its failed campaign. "I am giving this statement," he explained, "because I believe in freedom and what is right, I witnessed things in the plant which were stepping stones to Distatorship. They took the peoples freedom away from them. It was not a free election. The company won there fear."[19]

By the late 1960s the union had also tapped the support of other groups. Although the campaign had not achieved the high profile that it would later on, some concerned citizens were already criticizing Stevens. Students from several colleges protested in 1967 against the company's unfair labor practices. In May of that year, students and faculty members held a conference in Greensboro, North Carolina, to explore textile workers' rights. Richard Horne, a senior from nearby Guilford College, explained that students were supporting textile workers because "many look upon the mill situation in the south as an immoral situation." Another student similarly spoke of his "moral and Christian concern" for southern textile workers. The Stevens campaign, claimed *Textile Labor*, was mobilizing "the conscience of the community."[20]

Others also attacked Stevens's antiunionism. In the spring of 1967, Stevens was forced to drop plans for its top directors to attend a banquet in Charlotte because they feared that the visit would lead to demonstrations by former employees, college students, and union members. Instead, the firm's executives stayed in New York City.[21] Even in the Big Apple, the company was attracting some protest. In December 1967 the local chapter of the Socialist Party organized a demonstration of union members outside the company's midtown headquarters. Similarly outraged by the firm's anti-unionism, members of the New York–based Drug and Hospital Workers' Union, who were themselves trying to organize in the South, also protested outside Stevens Tower. Appalled by the company's labor policies, a range of unions continued to fund the IUD's faltering organizing drive.[22]

The national press proved to be another ally for the union in these difficult years. In the summer of 1967, *New York Times* reporter Walter Rugaber wrote a detailed article on the campaign following a visit to a Stevens plant in Greenville, South Carolina. The article exposed the poor working conditions in the mill, with employees having no regular rest periods, lunch hours, or smoking breaks. Workers complained about low pay and heavy workloads, although many reasoned that protesting about their conditions was futile. "I can't afford to get messed up in this union business," commented one apprehensive worker. "They've fired a bunch of them who did and they'd fire me." Quoting extensively from the NLRB's damning decisions, Rugaber detailed Stevens's repeated violations of labor laws. The article certainly did Stevens few favors, and a *Times* editorial further questioned the firm's conduct. While many Americans believed that unions were too strong, it noted, the Stevens story suggested otherwise. In fact, although the U.S. Court of Appeals for the Second Circuit had recently found Stevens guilty of engaging in "a major campaign of illegal anti-union activity," there was still "no break in the militance of its resistance."[23]

The article caused Robert T. Stevens, who was generally tight-lipped about the dispute, to write a letter of complaint. The indignant CEO insisted that Rugaber had given a "twisted presentation" of the facts. "Unfortunately, no employes opposed to the union were quoted in the article," he charged. "Your reporter was welcomed into our plant, and given unsupervised opportunity to talk privately to any employe he chose to interview."

Stevens insisted that his employees had repeatedly rejected the need for outside representation, but that power-hungry labor leaders had refused to respect their wishes. He also claimed that labor laws were "the subject of continuous reinterpretation" and that his company would "obey the courts when these finally state the law in the issues brought against us."[24]

Aware that the company's antiunionism was being directed from the top, TWUA leaders tried to privately influence leading executives to change tack. In the spring of 1967 William Pollock made a personal appeal to the "conscience" of the Stevens directors. It was, he claimed, time for a "signal from the top." If this was not forthcoming, he warned, the union would not back down. He claimed that the company's "ruthless policy" was "now a major concern of the entire trade union movement. . . . No trade union will turn away from the challenge J. P. Stevens and Co. has flung down to working people and to the Government itself." Refusing to respond privately, Stevens instead published an open letter in the industry press in which it confirmed its determination to fight on. Attempts to "loudly denounce" the company would not cause its top officials to "surrender our convictions and welcome the union into our plants."[25]

The results of this defiance were apparent when the union did try to organize Stevens facilities. In the summer of 1967 the TWUA launched a new organizing campaign at Stevens's Black Hawk cotton warehouse in Greenville. The warehouse had a small workforce, around fifty people, but it was also very important to the company's operations because it supplied some twenty southern plants with unprocessed cotton. At the time of the organizing effort, jobs at the facility were still completely segregated: blacks worked in the warehouse proper, whites in the facility's machine-repair shop. Laboring in hot and dusty conditions, the warehouse workers moved raw cotton around by hand. When the union began its campaign, it quickly attracted more support from these workers than from whites. Early meetings drew as many as twenty warehouse laborers, but only one white shop employee was willing to attend. The union was confronting a problem—the reluctance of whites to organize with blacks—that it would come up against repeatedly in subsequent campaigns.[26]

Stevens countered the union's success in recruiting African American employees by reducing the amount of cotton that was shipped to the Black Hawk facility, transferring the work to outlying warehouses. By doing so, Stevens was able to lay off seventeen black employees on the eve of the election, claiming that the move was necessitated by reduced demand. The

NLRB, however, concluded that the company had acted to undermine support for the union. "The layoffs," it noted, "were designed to dissipate the Union's strength, and were made because the employees had demonstrated their support of the Union." Stevens had implemented, it added, "a preconceived plan to defeat the Union in the election."[27]

The company's continuing willingness to violate labor laws was also evident elsewhere. In August 1967 the TWUA began a campaign at Stevens plants in Dublin, Georgia, after workers showed a strong interest in organizing. The company responded by firing the six employees who had initiated the drive. Then the management gathered the employees and threatened to close the Dublin plants if they voted the union in. According to NLRB records, one overseer told employees "about the coal mines in North America that had shut down and gone out of business on account of a union and pointed out that 'they might be killing the goose that laid the golden egg' and could be making a coal mine town out of the city of Dublin, and the government would have to feed the people. . . . He also stated that during a slack period with a union the Company could just continuously lay the employees off one at a time and not call them back, until the whole mill was shut down."[28] In a similar vein, supervisors warned workers that the company was considering a move to South America, especially if the TWUA did organize the mill. In order to drive the point home, Dublin employees were reminded that none of Stevens's seventy-four southern plants were organized. Although the company was found guilty of committing unfair labor practices and the fired union activists were eventually rehired, the TWUA never succeeded in even contesting an election in Dublin.[29]

In election campaigns, Stevens also mixed its harsh tactics with economic incentives. In the spring of 1969, the general manager of the company's plants in Shelby, North Carolina, granted all of his employees a wage hike and an additional paid holiday. The NLRB found that both moves were designed to deter unionization. As trial examiner James T. Barker concluded, the company "sought to gain maximum impact" from the move "by joining their announcement in a preelection, antiunion speech." In this speech, general manager James Sheppard also mentioned the "disruptive effect" of strikes, citing two local examples as evidence.[30] In finding the company guilty of committing unfair labor practices, the NLRB explained that Stevens had used a blend of incentives and threats to defeat the TWUA.[31]

The company's antiunionism continued to be directed by top officials. In the spring of 1969, Stevens director Robert Froeber visited the firm's plant in Hickory, North Carolina, shortly after the TWUA had started an organizing campaign. Meeting with supervisors, the hosiery division president decreed that the union must be defeated. Local managers were pressured to ensure that the union did not gain its first foothold in the firm's southern operations, as Froeber told them that the union was moving too fast and that he would "be damned if [this plant is] going to be the first one organized." He blamed his subordinates for allowing the TWUA to make progress, telling them that union advocates had to be stopped and could be fired on a pretext. After this, plant manager William Thor met with his supervisors and informed them: "We've got to get rid of these kind of people regardless of what it takes, no matter what it takes." Not surprisingly, the company then rapidly discharged several union activists. Although the NLRB found that Stevens had committed unfair labor practices, Froeber had ensured that the Hickory mills remained nonunion.[32]

The company's desire to remain union-free also continued to be enthusiastically embraced by local community leaders in the South. In January 1968 the TWUA began an organizing campaign in the small Georgia town of Statesboro, fifty miles west of Savannah. Workers responded well to the drive, and organizers were soon able to petition for an election. On the eve of the vote, the company committed a number of unfair labor practices that wiped out the TWUA's majority. Supervisors threatened workers, telling them that the plant would close if the union was voted in. "J. P. Stevens," claimed supervisor Bob Stepto, "will throw away this plant just like I am throwing away that nickel." Workers were again reminded that none of the company's seventy-four southern mills were unionized and that the Statesboro mill was "too small . . . and too new, to carry a Union." The plant had only been built in 1964, and community leaders worried that a union would drive the firm away. Even Mayor William Bowen became involved, warning one employee: "We don't need it [the union] and if it comes to town the plant will close, and I know what I am talking about."[33]

Workers remembered that these tactics were very effective. Home to Georgia Southern University, the small town had few other industries that could provide work for local people. "Statesboro is a college town," explained union supporter Myrtle Cribbs. "It's a farming community, too, and a lot of people that worked in there had never had jobs that paid any money. They were sharecroppers and they didn't have hardly anything to live off. They were buying better furniture and buying cars to have better transportation. When the people went around and knocked on doors and said, 'If you vote the union in, they're going to close the plant,' naturally it put fear in them because some of them couldn't read or write. It put fear in their soul and I feel we really didn't lose the election to Stevens because people were still strong for it until these fellows did go around and start knocking on doors."[34]

At the same time, the company effectively undermined support for the union by directly addressing workers' grievances. On the eve of the election, they granted all mill employees their first lunch break. While the break was only eighteen minutes long, it helped to dissipate workers' complaints about having to work right through the middle of the day without any stop at all. During the eighteen-minute period, workers could shut off their machines and were allowed to go and sit at chairs and tables that had been specially provided for the purpose. Line managers also made other changes in order to address specific grievances. During rainy weather, workers were allowed to use passageways through the plant so that they could reach the parking lot without getting wet. In addition, managers extended workers' smoking periods and installed more soda and snack vending machines. All of these moves suggested that managers recognized the need to make constructive changes in order to deter unionization.[35]

The Statesboro case offers a classic example of how Stevens's preelection tactics could wipe out the union's majority. On the eve of the vote, the union claimed that 80 percent of the workers had signed cards, yet it ended up losing by a margin of 198–110. In a subsequent decision, the NLRB set aside the election without a hearing, finding the company guilty of a wide variety of unfair labor practices. Company officials had unlawfully fired several union supporters and had altered working conditions in order to discourage union organization.[36] The campaign, noted the board, had been marked by Stevens's "extensive and egregious unfair labor practices in an effort to thwart the Union's organizational drive." Relying on the union's card majority, the NLRB ordered Stevens to recognize and bargain with the TWUA.[37]

Stevens refused. Following the election, the company continued to make changes in wage rates and workloads without consulting the union. Executives argued that they had no duty to bargain with the TWUA until the case was decided by the U.S. Court of Appeals, though the NLRB subsequently ruled that Stevens needed to comply with its earlier finding. On March 22, 1971, the Court of Appeals for the Fifth Circuit also found that the TWUA was the bargaining agent and enforced the NLRB order that required the company to bargain with the union.[38]

This decision failed to fundamentally alter Stevens's unwillingness to bargain. Although company representatives finally sat down with the union, negotiations got nowhere. Particular sticking points were the company's refusal to agree to a checkoff of union dues, which it argued would require additional administrative costs, and its opposition to binding arbitration, which it insisted was unnecessary because the union retained the right to strike. Both of these items were regarded by the union as central to any contract; the checkoff was needed to ensure a local union's financial viability, and arbitration provided workers with an alternative method of settling disputes without resorting to strikes. Stevens officials even encouraged TWUA leaders to call a strike, well aware that they could easily switch production to other mills or import nonunion labor into the idle plant.[39]

Coming on the back of its earlier defeats, the union's continuing failure to win an election at any of Stevens's southern plants was a real blow. At the same time, union leaders were determined to continue the campaign, and they found reasons to remain optimistic. In particular, they insisted that Stevens workers wanted a union. Refuting the company's claims that its employees were contented, many workers did continue to show an interest in organizing. In March 1968 a former union staffer from Montgomery, Alabama, reported that workers at the local Stevens mill were eager to be organized. TWUA leaders looked into the situation, but it would be eight years before they began an intensive drive at the Montgomery plant.[40] In October 1969 plant worker David C. Johnson similarly urged the union to begin an organizing campaign at the company's mill in Wallace, South Carolina. "As you probably already know," he wrote Pollock, "they frown upon any connection with labor unions, but I feel that with the right information and someone with the ability to organize and influence people this plant could be organized for T.W.U.A." With only a small number of organizers available, the TWUA did not begin a campaign in Wallace until the fall of 1972.[41]

In the late 1960s, working conditions in Stevens's plants remained poor, and employees certainly had no shortage of grievances. Many complained about heavy workloads and overbearing, unsympathetic supervisors. In 1968, Press Associates journalist Ruth Stack visited the Carolinas and found that many of the firm's workers were willing to complain off the record. "You can go eight hours without a trip to the water house," explained one. "If you make two trips, the supervisor will call you and give you a talking about it." "We don't eat lunch at any particular time," complained another. "You just grab a sandwich and then a loom stops, so you put it down on the loom and run around and start it up again. But then you forget about the sandwich and don't come back until it's all dried out anyhow."[42]

Still, most workers were afraid to come out in the open and take on the company. Although they had legitimate complaints, many reasoned that it was pointless to support the union because the company would never recognize it. In 1967 an elderly female spinner at one of the company's South Carolina plants complained that her workloads were constantly increasing. Like many veteran employees, the anonymous worker had spent her entire working life in the mills but had little job security. At the age of sixty-one, after forty-three years of continuous service, she took home just $57 a week. Despite her low pay, the worker was afraid to support the union. "They'll close this plant down before they'll do that," she insisted. "They're so hard-headed they're going to win or stop one. They're not going to let nobody tell them what to do, not the Government or nobody. You don't know J. P. Stevens." Similar sentiments were easy to find, showing how Stevens's harsh tactics had produced a feeling of powerlessness among its southern employees.[43]

By the end of the 1960s, the Stevens campaign had emerged as a test case for TWUA leaders. They took pride in their fight against such a vicious opponent of unionism, believing that it would benefit the whole labor movement. Despite the lack of organizing success, union leaders also insisted that the strongly worded NLRB decisions were boosting their drive for labor law reform. The high-profile case had certainly helped the TWUA to publicize the vehement opposition that it frequently confronted in the South. As the union noted in 1968, the Stevens campaign was "an extremely useful tool in focusing national attention upon the outrageous deprivation of the right of textile workers to organize."[44]

The union also argued that the organizing climate in the South was improving. In the 1950s and 1960s the South's economy grew at a faster rate than the national average. While the growth of the nonunion South often worried labor leaders, TWUA strategists argued that industrialization would improve the organizing climate. In 1966 the union asserted that the "migration of modern industries" into the region was making textile workers more aware of their low wages and was creating a labor shortage that increased their bargaining power so that, in this period of economic growth, many were throwing off "the shackles of employer-inspired fear" and demanding better pay and conditions. While the union's optimism was partly justified, strategists overlooked the fact that many dissatisfied textile workers were leaving the industry altogether rather than turning to unions.[45]

Figure 3. Back pay award. The union proudly publicized the cases of Stevens workers who were reinstated with back pay, such as Rock Hill worker Doris Hicklin, who won $15,691 through the NLRB in 1968. She was pictured in *Textile Labor* with her husband. (UNITE/Kheel Center for Labor-Management Documentation and Archives, Cornell University.)

During the winter of 1967–68, TWUA leaders were also encouraged by the reinstatement of the sixty-nine employees who had been unfairly discharged. William Pollock claimed that the news had proved "once and for all that the law is much bigger than J. P. Stevens or any other textile corporation. The union is confident, now that the highest court in the land has ordered J. P. Stevens to cease its five-year campaign of terror and coercion and its flagrant disregard of the National Labor Relations Act, that the Stevens workers will no longer be cowed and intimidated and will resume their efforts to build a union." Following the decision, TWUA and IUD leaders met in Charlotte and promised a renewed effort to unionize J. P. Stevens. "We'll organize J. P. Stevens," they pledged, "no matter what it takes."[46]

Over the next two years, other TWUA leaders expressed their commitment to continue the Stevens fight. In July 1968, Sol Stetin addressed a union rally in Atlantic City and promised to carry on the campaign. Eighteen months later Scott Hoyman termed the Stevens drive "unfinished business . . . high on the agenda." In 1970 the TWUA's convention also unanimously approved a resolution that called for the organization of the South. The resolution proudly noted that Stevens's conduct had been slammed by both the NLRB and the courts. It also asserted that the TWUA had made a breakthrough by being certified as a bargaining agent in Statesboro. "In our six-year struggle with J. P. Stevens we have established a beachhead," it claimed. Despite its failure to win any elections, as the 1970s began the TWUA was pledged to continue its long-running campaign against J. P. Stevens.[47]

FOUR

Saving the Campaign, 1970–1974

In the early 1970s the TWUA's efforts to organize J. P. Stevens mills continued to fail. Following its defeat in Shelby, the union did not contest another election at a Stevens plant until 1972, when it lost a vote in Turnersburg, North Carolina. The following year was a disaster for the union, as it suffered further conclusive defeats at Stevens mills in Walterboro, South Carolina, and Aberdeen, North Carolina. In addition, the company easily defeated an organizing campaign in Wallace, South Carolina, partly by stooping to a new low in dirty tricks. These setbacks tested the leadership's resolve to continue the Stevens campaign. Some suggested calling off the effort, although others insisted that the union had invested too much in the struggle to turn back.[1]

Other factors encouraged the union's decision makers to continue the campaign. The increasing proportion of African American workers was widely viewed as a particularly positive development. For years organizers had struggled to organize the South's white textile workers, and they hoped that blacks would be more responsive. Between 1960 and 1969, black employment in textiles increased four times faster than the national average for all manufacturing. Driven both by a labor shortage and by Title VII of the 1964 Civil Rights Act, executives began to hire African Americans in a wide range of production jobs. In South Carolina, where many Stevens plants were located, the proportion of black mill workers increased from less than 5 percent in 1964 to around 30 percent in 1976. By the mid-1970s, African

Americans made up roughly a quarter of the workforce in the other southern textile states.[2]

Observing these changes, TWUA leaders repeatedly argued that African American workers would respond enthusiastically to the union's campaign. They would be supported, according to optimistic union accounts, by a new generation of whites who had grown accustomed to integration and were more willing than their predecessors to unite with blacks. Buoyed by these hopes, in 1973 the union decided to make one final attempt to organize Stevens's major complex in Roanoke Rapids. The plants were located in a part of eastern North Carolina that was around 40 percent black, and for years local African American leaders had complained about the company's refusal to hire blacks in production jobs. Between 1970 and 1975, however, the proportion of blacks in the workforce increased from 19.4 percent to 37.1 percent. Throughout an extensive drive, organizers drew heavily on support from these workers and were able to secure an historic election victory. This breakthrough saved the campaign, providing TWUA leaders with the confidence to escalate their fight against the company. It was a crucial turning point that paved the way for the launching of the corporate campaign and boycott.[3]

Prior to this breakthrough, union leaders had little to cheer. As organizers continued their efforts, they found that the Statesboro case was a major obstacle. In the early 1970s Stevens began to reduce employment at the plant, citing declining demand for the type of yarn produced there. At the time of the 1968 election, 330 employees worked at the mill, but this fell to 220 in 1972 and just 135 by the fall of 1974. In May 1975 all production was stopped and the entire workforce promptly laid off. The company also closed two other southern plants in the early 1970s, though both were later reopened with new product lines. What was significant about Statesboro was the company's reluctance to reinvest in a mill that it had owned for less than a decade. Exchanges between the two sides became bitter, as the union accused managers of refusing to furnish the information it needed to investigate company claims that the plant was unprofitable. Convinced of his opponent's bad intentions, Scott Hoyman asserted that Statesboro plant manager Billy Smith would provide only "unsupported generalized statements" about the mill. For its part, the company claimed that it had provided "detailed factual information" to the NLRB about its reasons for closing the plant—a decision based purely on economic grounds.[4]

Despite these assertions, Stevens made considerable use of the Statesboro situation to hold back the union's organizing efforts. The union claimed that Stevens was using Statesboro as a "dreadful example." "In various representation elections held since the bargaining order at Statesboro," it explained, "the Company has pointed out the decline in production and the unused machines there to influence Stevens workers in other plants to vote against representation by TWUA." On the eve of the 1972 election in Turnersburg, a letter sent by the company to the local workforce noted that in Statesboro, the only mill in the chain where the union had won bargaining rights, "a large portion of the machinery and equipment . . . has been standing and out of operation for the last two years. Likewise, the people in that plant frequently have only worked four days a week."[5] The company also posted a notice in the plant that publicized the fate of the Statesboro mill. Harold McIver, who headed the Turnersburg drive, later blamed these threats of plant closure as the "chief reason" for the TWUA's defeat. Before the elections in Aberdeen and Walterboro, managers also told employees about the declining employment levels at Statesboro.[6]

Across the South, company officials used captive-audience speeches to intimidate and frighten workers on the eve of elections. At the compulsory meetings, plant managers bombarded their workers with negative information about unions. Union officials privately admitted that the company was very adept at using these gatherings to undermine their support. In January 1974, TWUA representative John Weiser wrote Swaity that the preelection speech given by plant manager Jack McGill in Walterboro was "a masterpiece in the art of propaganda." Following a familiar formula, McGill's speech destroyed the image of the international union by arguing that it was interested only in enriching itself by collecting dues. He then proceeded to instill fear in his audience by linking unions with strikes, violence, bitterness, and plant closings. Nobody could remain neutral when faced by this threat, asserted McGill, because it promised to take away workers' individual freedom and would lead to economic disaster for themselves and their families. McGill warned his employees: "This Textile Workers AFL-CIO Union can take you down a road that you will not want to travel, the road to strikes and long and bitter violence. This has been its record at many places. . . . There are many incidents in which the people have voted for the Union and soon after they have voted it in, they were out on strike. And while they were out on the picket line, other people came and took their jobs." McGill backed up these claims by running through a range of strikes that the TWUA had lost, working back to the Harriet-Henderson dispute.[7]

Following this speech, the union ended up losing the election by a vote of 499 to 166. They filed objections to the company's conduct, many of which focused on the speech. In addition, Stevens was accused of denying overtime to pro-union workers, threatening those who wore union buttons, and discharging a union activist. In this case the NLRB dismissed the union's objections, finding insufficient evidence of many charges and ruling that McGill's speech constituted "permissible campaign propaganda" that workers "could evaluate for themselves."[8]

The effectiveness of these preelection addresses led union activists in Wallace to try to disrupt the speech given to them on the eve of their 1973 election. On September 17, two days before the scheduled vote, the company held a series of employee meetings. Following the standard pattern, managers stopped all work in the mills and ordered employees to hear the speeches. During the first-shift gathering, three workers got up and asked questions while the general manager was trying to give his address. One employee asked the manager if he intended to close the plant if the union came in, while another brazenly asserted that he had a right to talk. All three employees continued to stand throughout the speech, throwing the stunned executive off guard and distracting the audience from what he was saying.[9]

When it was time for the second- and third-shift speeches, company officials anticipated that they would be heckled. As pro-union employees stood up and asked questions, managers refused to answer them and quickly adjourned the meetings. Following this, the workers in question were fired for refusing to obey orders. Determined to crush the union, the company discharged twenty-two of its most prominent activists. Not surprisingly, TWUA leaders filed unfair labor practice charges, and the NLRB immediately postponed the election until the charges could be investigated. Although the union argued that its supporters had been unfairly dismissed, the NLRB dismissed these complaints, arguing that "the interruption of the meetings was a concerted act of the prounion employees."[10]

The actions of the twenty-two Wallace employees again highlight the bravery of some Stevens workers. Like others who openly fought for union rights, these workers were fully aware of the company's record of violating labor laws. Yet they directly confronted company officials, asking them why they would not engage in a full debate about what union membership would mean to its employees. Worker Thomas Cassidy recalled that he "asked how much they paid their lawyers to write that speech, and then we had kind of a little debate, and they told me to sit down." Asserting that they had 65 percent of the workers signed up before the addresses, the union claimed that the company's tactics had destroyed their campaign. In response, Stevens insisted that its workers themselves recognized that they did not want to be represented by the TWUA. "It appears that there has been a strong trend developing among the employes against the union," blasted company spokesperson Paul Barrett. "It seems very likely that these incidents were planned in order that the resulting terminations would give the union an excuse to file charges with the labor board . . . thereby blocking the holding of an election."[11]

During the Wallace campaign, the company closely followed the movements of union organizer Al Motley. In the 1960s, company officials had often kept close tabs on what organizers were doing, but in Wallace they took their surveillance to a new level. In October 1972 Motley had checked into the Wallace Motel, which was directly across the street from Stevens's plants. A small town located near the North Carolina state line, Wallace was economically dependent on the mills. Most of the motel's guests were either visiting company officials or engineers who were working on temporary contracts at the mills. When he arrived in town, Motley was able to secure a room and go about his job with little apparent harassment. Using the room as a base, the veteran organizer regularly met workers there, spending the rest of his time traveling door-to-door or contacting prospective members by telephone. Three months into the campaign, Motley discovered that his motel telephone would not work. When the phone was opened by a Southern Bell repairman, he found that a bugging device had been installed. The device had turned the telephone's mouthpiece into an "open mike" capable of picking up all conversations in the room where Motley had held union meetings. The bug had also deactivated the switch that turns off the circuit when the phone is on the hook, ensuring that anyone on the other end of the line could hear what was going on in the room even when the phone was not in use.[12]

The device had been installed with the full knowledge of both the motel management and Wallace plant manager Harold Guerry. With the cooperation of the motel switchboard operator, who was married to a mill supervisor, the buggers had rented another room and had monitored union meetings through a phone that was permanently connected to Motley's room. Company officials, now knowing who supported the union, were able to direct their supervisors to harass or observe these employees accordingly. Later on, officials were also able to fire the union's most effective leaders.[13]

The Wallace case exemplified how local business leaders in the South wholeheartedly supported Stevens in its fight with the union. Like the switchboard operator, Motel owner Della Richardson had close links with the giant textile maker. Her business was dependent on custom generated by the mills, and the town had prospered since Stevens moved in. "The J. P. Stevens Company is her livelihood," claimed Assistant U.S. Attorney Marvin Smith during the legal proceedings that arose out of the case. "Without J. P. Stevens's cooperation, without their friendliness, she is dead. Her business is gone; she has got an empty motel. So she has a reason and a motive to cooperate with anyone from the Stevens plant who wants her cooperation." When Motley first complained that his phone did not work, the motel staff even called Guerry to alert him to the problem. The call, he testified, "scared the daylights" out of him. The panicky mill manager contacted Southern Bell and urged them not to open the telephone receiver. The repairman knew Guerry and initially agreed, but a service foreman at the phone company was determined to inspect the receiver himself. When he did so, he discovered a bug that was, in the words of one expert witness, "crude but very, very effective."[14]

The FBI investigated the bugging in Wallace, singling out both Guerry and Larry Emerson Burroughs, another Stevens manager. On December 14, 1973, the two men were found guilty by a federal jury of bugging Motley's phone, although a U.S. District Court judge later overturned the conviction on the grounds that they had been indicted under the wrong section of the relevant federal statute. In addition, the court held that the prosecution had not submitted enough evidence to prove that the phone company was a common carrier engaged in interstate commerce. Finding these technical errors, the court ruled that it was unnecessary to express an opinion on the guilt or innocence of the two men. Independently of the criminal action, the TWUA also filed a civil suit to recover damages caused by the surveillance. The company later settled this suit with a payment of $50,000 to the plaintiffs and their attorneys. Following the dismissal of its NLRB charges, however, the union was unable to rebuild its campaign in Wallace.[15]

The NLRB's failure to force Stevens to moderate its antiunionism horrified the leaders of the AFL-CIO. At a time when they worried about increasing resistance to unionization, the federation saw Stevens's behavior as very disturbing. The company, they noted, "constantly thwarts the wishes of their employes . . . [and] thumbs its nose at the national policy and explicit legislation with respect to union organization and the concept of collective bargaining."[16] By the early 1970s, federation leaders insisted that Stevens's defiance was an open challenge to the entire labor movement. In February 1973 the AFL-CIO's executive council issued a statement condemning the company's conduct and calling for the NLRB to seek stronger remedies, including a broad bargaining order. The federation felt that federal officials had not done enough to curb Stevens's lawlessness. "In a society struggling to obtain justice, law, and order for all of its citizens," it noted, "governmental tolerance of brazen and consistent law violations by a J. P. Stevens, because it is wealthy and powerful, is intolerable." The AFL-CIO's interest in the case paved the way for the full backing it would give to the boycott campaign a few years later.[17]

Despite being criticized by the AFL-CIO, the top brass of J. P. Stevens remained in no mood to compromise. In 1969 Robert T. Stevens had been replaced as CEO by James D. Finley, leading labor leaders to hope that the company's attitude to unions might soften a little. Robert Stevens, after all, had clearly taken strong personal offense at the way that his company had been selected as an organizing target, whereas his successor had less invested in the bitter battle with the TWUA. In addition, the new CEO was the first to come from outside the Stevens dynasty. Such hopes overlooked the fact that Finley was widely viewed as Robert Stevens's handpicked successor, and he inherited his mentor's fierce independence. As the *Daily News Record* put it, "Finley is described by some as a man who is strong-minded in the Stevens tradition." Stevens board member David W. Mitchell also described Finley as "a very strong-minded individual who, when he believes in something, sticks by it—he runs his business that way."[18] Like Robert Stevens, Finley exerted a strong control over his subordinates and decreed that there should be no change in the firm's labor relations approach. Thomas Macioce, the president of one of Stevens's main customers, privately told union officials that Finley was "a rigid doctrinaire person who, besides calling all the shots at Stevens, will fight to the death." As long as Finley remained at the helm, a change in the company line was unthinkable.[19]

Finley was the first southerner to head the historic textile firm. He grew up in the small central Georgia town of Jackson, where his family were farmers, going on to study engineering at Georgia Tech. When World War II broke out, Finley entered the army and served under Stevens, who was a colonel at the time. Stevens liked his young lieutenant and asked him to come and work in the family textile firm. In 1945 Finley began a long career with J. P. Stevens, rising through a series of positions to eventually become CEO. It was this shared military background that bonded Finley and Robert Stevens. Both had firm mindsets and felt that their authority should be respected by their subordinates. Although Finley had replaced Stevens as CEO, the former chief continued to influence company policy behind the scenes.[20]

Following the setbacks in Turnersburg, Walterboro, Aberdeen, and Wallace, the TWUA's leaders realized that the Stevens campaign stood at a crossroads. Although they had secured a great deal of publicity and support, the constant election defeats led some to privately doubt the wisdom of continuing. "There was no question," recalled Paul Swaity, "that in the early seventies, because there had been no results, the opposition to continue with Stevens was strong within TWUA. . . . There was strong opposition from various regional directors saying that we're pissing money away, let's put the money where we've got joint boards, we've got established bases, et cetera." The lack of success took its toll on union leaders, causing some to argue that it would be better to concentrate their resources outside the South. Research director George Perkel also recalled the opposition to continuing the Stevens campaign: "There started to be serious concern that we were barking up the wrong tree, [that] it was a no-win situation."[21]

Despite these concerns, the bulk of the TWUA's leaders realized that they had to continue trying to organize in the South, where the vast majority of the industry was located. Having invested so much in the Stevens fight, many activists were also reluctant to abandon it. As organizing director, Swaity was particularly keen to continue the campaign. He insisted that the union had at least established a base of unfair labor practices that it could use to publicize the case. He also rejected the idea of initiating a campaign against another southern textile company, pointing out that such an effort was unlikely to secure quick results.[22]

New TWUA president Sol Stetin was an important figure in keeping the Stevens campaign going. A small-framed man, he was a committed and determined union activist who argued that it was vital for the TWUA to try to organize the South. Born in Poland in 1910, Stetin had emigrated with his family to New Jersey when he was eleven years old. As a young man, he went to work in a local textile dye mill, becoming active in the Dyers Federation. Stetin's determination and ability saw him rise quickly through the ranks of the union. In 1941 he was appointed manager of the South Jersey Joint Board, becoming New Jersey regional director two years later. In

1968 he was elected TWUA general secretary-treasurer, going on to become president between 1972 and 1976.[23]

Following the Walterboro and Aberdeen debacles, even Stetin privately pondered the future of the Stevens campaign. The Roanoke Rapids election was clearly a watershed; as Stetin himself commented in 1973, if the union did not win in the North Carolina town, it should consider whether to continue with the entire Stevens project. The new TWUA leader knew that he would have to make difficult choices in order to ensure the organization's survival. In January 1973 he called his staff together to discuss the way forward. He did not pull any punches. "Let's face it," he told those assembled. "We are weaker today than we were ten years ago." Reeling off a list of recent northern plant closures, Stetin informed his staff that the union's membership was continuing to fall. The need to organize the South was more acute than ever, yet the region was home to a "vicious anti-union conspiracy" that repeatedly frustrated their best efforts. Stetin called on his staff not to be despondent but to draw inspiration from the "commitment and idealism" of the union's early leaders.[24]

Even at the start of 1973, Stetin was already thinking about joining with another union in order to create a bigger and more powerful organization. Small companies were increasingly merging, and the new TWUA leader felt that unions had to follow their example if they were to be effective. "Is there anything holy or even logical about continuing to operate the labor movement with 135 international unions, each going its own way?" he asked. Stetin also called for the union to become more responsive to the needs of black workers. "The ranks of black workers in the textile industry is growing daily," he declared, "and we must not let them down in their fight for economic and social justice. . . . Black workers are on the move and we must move with them."[25]

As African Americans surged into a wider range of southern textile jobs, TWUA leaders argued that they would break up the region's antiunionism. As early as 1970 Swaity had told the union's convention, "The organizing climate in the South is improving. . . . Black employment is increasing and the black workers are generally more anxious to join the union than are the whites." Other leaders noted that African Americans possessed an understanding of the need for collective action that had been forged in the civil rights struggle. "The new Black workers," claimed a 1972 report, "have brought with them an awareness of the need for cohesive group activity to protect their interests." At the same time, the union argued that younger workers were more willing to stand up to the mill owners. As other industries increasingly moved into the region, textile workers would realize that they were poorly paid and would demand better wages and working conditions. "The sense of dependency upon the employer which had pervaded many southern mill towns has been breaking down as new industries have moved in," asserted the union.[26]

While they hoped to capitalize on the influx of African Americans into the industry, the TWUA itself had a mixed civil rights record. In the South, white workers dominated leadership positions within local unions. In 1973 Bruce Raynor began working for the union's education department in the South. Looking back, he remembered that white union officials often resisted the entry of blacks into leadership roles. "The textile union in 1973 in the South was a heavily white-led union," he reflected in 1995, "and the locals were led by whites, even though by that time there were lots of blacks in the plants. . . . There was huge resistance on the part of the older white leadership. Some of our staff resisted the change; the staff was almost totally white, in many cases fairly conservative on the race issue. There was almost no black staff. And so that's the way the union looked."[27]

At the national level, leadership positions were also dominated by whites. When the TWUA began the Stevens campaign, no African American had ever sat on its executive council. In 1964, Chicago representative Edward Todd became the first African American to be elected to the council, but the TWUA's leaders remained overwhelmingly white and male. In the late 1970s all of the union's joint board managers and regional directors were white men. In an interview for the union's oral history project, Todd pointed out the continued failings of both the TWUA and ACTWU when it came to promoting blacks and women to leadership positions, although he ensured that his comments remained restricted until after his own retirement. "This is my position, the way I think and the way I'm operating," he reflected in 1978. "Our union . . . the textile workers' union, the ACTWU, is guilty of the same things that they are charging J. P. Stevens. Namely, they do not have an affirmative action program; they do not have blacks or minorities or women in a policymaking position; they do not have a program to recruit and to train for that position. Consequently they are as guilty on all of those counts as they are charging J. P. Stevens."[28]

It was only in the mid-1980s, after the conclusion of the Stevens campaign, that ACTWU began to make significant progress in recruiting women and minorities into leadership positions. In 1987 the union set up a top-level civil rights committee to try to "meet the challenge of developing the best Civil Rights programs for our members." At the same time, a new generation of union leaders proved more responsive to black demands for equal rights.[29]

Despite its own mixed record, union leaders were right to sense that the influx of African American workers offered an opportunity for them to revitalize their campaign. In particular, the company's record of racial inequality provided the union with another means of attacking Stevens. By the late 1960s, charges of racial discrimination were already putting the firm onto the defensive, exposing it to negative publicity that helped the union's cause. In 1969 the Department of Defense had held up contracts to the nation's three largest textile firms—Burlington Industries, J. P. Stevens, and Dan River Mills—on the grounds that they had not done enough to hire and promote black workers. In order to receive lucrative contracts, the textile makers were pushed to implement affirmative action programs, although their halfhearted efforts failed to address most black workers' grievances.[30]

Many turned to filing complaints with the EEOC, created to monitor compliance with Title VII of the 1964 Civil Rights Act. By August 1975 the commission had received some 178 charges of Title VII violations against J. P. Stevens alone. As the EEOC's efforts frequently failed to produce voluntary compliance, many black workers exercised their right to bring civil action under Title VII. Between 1970 and 1973, Stevens was hit with three major class-action suits in the Carolinas alone. The company tried to downplay the litigation, calling it "normal" for such a large employer. Despite these claims, the lawsuits illustrated that many of the firm's employees were not as satisfied as executives liked to assert they were.[31]

Shortly after Stetin became TWUA president, he and Swaity decided to relaunch the organizing campaign in Roanoke Rapids. Both men viewed the North Carolina town as one of their promising locations. It was home to a cluster of mills that together employed more than three thousand people, ensuring that the union could establish an important stronghold if it were successful. In addition, staff had maintained contact with a core of union supporters since they had lost the election in 1965. Most important, African Americans now made up a good third of the workers, and TWUA leaders argued that they would make the difference in a new campaign.[32]

Although the union emphasized positive changes, much remained the same in Roanoke Rapids. The mills still dominated the small community and many residents feared that Stevens would leave town rather than recognize the union. As a result, the TWUA continued to face considerable community opposition. During the campaign, union supporters complained that banks and finance companies denied them new loans. The local radio station also refused to accept union advertizing, and several ministers preached against the TWUA.[33]

The workers were able to draw on strong support from many of the allies that the TWUA had mobilized over the previous decade. Several prominent Democratic politicians backed the union's campaign, including senator and ex–vice president Hubert H. Humphrey. A former aide to Martin Luther King, Georgia congressman Andrew Young, asserted publicly: "Unionization is a matter of life and health and happiness and a way for J. P. Stevens workers in Roanoke Rapids to achieve it is to give full support to the organizing efforts of the Textile Workers Union of America."[34]

As they had predicted, union leaders found that some of their strongest support in Roanoke Rapids came from African Americans. In August 1974 the notes from one organizing committee meeting recorded this clearly: ""Attendance at 8/14 shift mtgs: 50-100-50, with 60–70% black." Black workers' support for the union was a reflection of how they continued to be disproportionately assigned to lower-paid jobs. At the Roanoke Rapids mills, African Americans had made progress into production jobs but whites resisted their entry into higher-paying positions. In 1969, just 2.9 percent of skilled craft jobs at the complex were held by African American men, even though they held more than 30 percent of semiskilled operative positions. As late as December 1980, a white man with a tenth-grade education made forty-nine cents an hour more than a black male with the same qualifications. Consigned to lower-paid positions, African Americans felt that they had less to lose by supporting the union.[35]

Like their counterparts in other plants, disgruntled African Americans in Roanoke Rapids turned increasingly to filing charges with the EEOC. Charge forms vividly record black workers' frustrations. Cromwell Faulcon typically complained on his form that job opportunities at the plant were unequal. "There are some white men," he noted, "that can't count over one hundred and no high school education, but still they are puting them on job that they want put a colored man on with a high school education." Summing up how many felt, Mable Moody Miles similarly charged in 1972 that "I and other Negro employees with qualifications equal or better than those of Caucasian employees are limited to certain job classifications."[36]

Union leaders were encouraged by the response of blacks to their efforts, but they soon worried that white employees were much less enthusiastic. Unlike many blacks, who had only recently entered the mills, most whites remembered how the company had crushed the 1965 drive. The reinstatement of those who had been fired in the earlier campaign failed to assuage the fears of many employees. Monopolizing the better-paying positions, whites also had more to lose by joining the union. "The first meetings," recalled Swaity, "were almost totally all black people, who would come out to meetings."[37]

During the organizing drive, the company also made an effort to undermine black support for the union. In May 1973, Stevens mailed a letter to all its workers that made a "special" appeal to blacks. Noting that the union was making "intensive" efforts to sign up blacks, the company insisted that its own civil rights record was improving: "These Plants of our Company here at Roanoke Rapids are now furnishing hundreds, and many hundreds, of jobs to black employees. The level of your jobs and rates of pay and benefits are steadily rising. A great deal is being achieved by you and in your behalf." Black workers were advised not to be "impatient" with a company that was striving to improve equal employment opportunities. The letter backfired on Stevens. Swaity reported that "a number of black workers brought the attached letter to my attention and indicated they resented Stevens' reference to how much the company is doing for black workers. Some of them said the company would not hire black workers for years; they have a lot of gall talking about what they've done for black workers!"[38]

The company also tried to encourage whites to steer clear of the union. Stevens told its employees that if blacks joined the union en masse, they could "dominate it and control it in this Plant." Shortly before the election, the company's supervisors posted a gruesome photograph of a white man who had been killed in a racially motivated murder. They also posted photographs of the black suspects, writing underneath, "Would you want this to happen here?" African American worker Bennett Taylor recalled that managers tried hard to divide the workforce along racial lines. "They did use that kind of propaganda," he recalled, "saying that if you vote the union in, they tell the whites it's going to be all-black union." James Boone, another African American worker, recalled that Stevens supervisors made special appeals to white employees: "They had management go round to the whites houses and just talk with them about not voting for the union."[39]

The union was ultimately able to get enough white support to win the election largely because many whites were dissatisfied with the performance of the company's profit-sharing plan. In the early 1970s the U.S. economy faltered and the stock market performed poorly. At the time of the Roanoke Rapids campaign, Stevens's profit-sharing plan, which had been established in 1965, offered workers no protection against such fluctuations, and many became concerned when their monthly statements indicated decreases. Union attorney Henry Woicik later wrote that "a major reason for the TWUA Roanoke Rapids election success appears to have been worker dissatisfaction due to erosion that took place in such Trust Fund by reason of the stock market's decline." On the ground in Roanoke Rapids, TWUA representative Clyde Bush also felt that the drop in the profit-sharing plan was crucial to the TWUA's victory. "In seventy-four when we won the election," he later recalled, "I think one of the big factors [was] . . . the way the company was taking the profit-sharing money, and they knew that once they took it, it wasn't going to be brought back."[40]

Older white workers were particularly affected by this dip. In general, this group held stable, good-paying jobs in the mills and were among the least likely to join the union. Now, however, they had a strong economic motivation to vote for the TWUA. Bennett Taylor remembered how this

Figure 4. Roanoke Rapids workers celebrating their 1974 election victory. (Kheel Center for Labor-Management Documentation and Archives, Cornell University.)

economic issue did help to bridge the racial divide that the company tried to widen between the workers, and added, "but what the company didn't realize, that if you and I work side by side, when they hit you in the pocketbook as well as they hit me in the pocketbook, that makes you realize that, hey, the company don't care no more about you than it does me. Back then we had what you call a profit-sharing plan, and a lot of the older workers . . . some of them had been in there so long until it had got to a point that every year that they got their statement it was a decrease. . . . The older white workers couldn't understand, whether it was black or white that just came into the plant, they couldn't understand how do my statements show up a decrease. . . . I was in-plant organizer in my plant, which is Roanoke Fabricating Plant, and I started using it to our advantage. I said, 'Look . . . once we vote the union in, negotiate a contract, we're going to negotiate a pension plan that the company contribute to that is going to show an increase every year.' . . . When you start talking facts like that, whether you're black or white, you know, people understand when you start taking my money."[41]

Other factors helped to pave the way for the election success. Although many workers continued to fear that Stevens would never recognize the union, organizers insisted that the reinstatement of fired activists did show that the union could offer some protection to its members. More important, once these workers were back on the job, they once again headed efforts to sign up their coworkers. The fact that Albemarle Paper Company was organized also helped to break down antiunion prejudice, especially as many of Stevens's workers were related to paper mill employees. Union activist Crystal Lee Sutton, for instance, was first exposed to unions through her ex-husband Larry "Cookie" Jordan, who earned considerably more at Albemarle than she did at Stevens.[42]

On August 28, 1974, the TWUA won the Roanoke Rapids election by a vote of 1,685 to 1,448. Union leaders were elated. By making a breakthrough in a key Stevens "cluster," they argued, they were on the way to opening up the South to unionism. Walter Hobby, the president of the North Carolina AFL-CIO, claimed that the victory signaled "a new day in Dixie," and added, "J. P. first, the textile industry second, and then the whole South." The victory clearly spurred TWUA leaders to fight on with renewed vigor. As the union's executive council report put it, the victory brought "new hope" to the Stevens struggle. The campaign would now move into a new phase, as Stevens fought bitterly to keep its southern plants unorganized, while the TWUA strove to capitalize on its vital breakthrough.[43]

FIVE

Planning a Boycott

In the immediate aftermath of the Roanoke Rapids election, some observers wondered whether Stevens would promptly abandon its fierce opposition to unionism. "Now that the union has demonstrated by its success at a seven plant Stevens complex in North Carolina that it can win a Government-supervised election," suggested the *New York Times* in a Labor Day editorial, "perhaps the company will turn away from the illegal tactics that have already cost it well over $1 million in back pay to workers who have suffered from discrimination because of union activities." Over the next few months, the company's conduct showed that it had no intention of changing course. In a subsequent organizing campaign at its plant in Wallace, North Carolina, executives launched a vicious preelection attack. At the same time, managers in Roanoke Rapids resolutely refused to sign a contract, staggering union representatives with their intransigence. The union charged that Stevens was refusing to bargain in good faith, a complaint that was later upheld by the NLRB. Negotiations quickly stalled, and the union realized that it was in danger of losing momentum unless it could exert additional pressure on the company.[1]

By now, union leaders were aware that NLRB decisions could not bring about a change in Stevens's attitude. Instead, activists realized, they had to find new ways of pushing the company to change course. Prior to the election they began to explore how they could achieve this, and they developed their ideas in earnest after their victory at the polls. In the process they identified many of the issues, including the company's lawlessness and its record of racial and sexual discrimination, that they would utilize so effectively later on. In addition, staffers explored Stevens's poor health-and-safety record, realizing that this too could be used as a mobilizing tool. Arguing that a strike was unlikely to succeed, strategists decided that a consumer boycott would be the best way of attacking Stevens. Union researchers investigated the risks that a boycott entailed, ultimately reasoning that the prospect of organizing such a large employer justified the move. In order to make their boycott as effective as possible, in June 1976 the TWUA merged with the much bigger Amalgamated Clothing Workers of America, a union that had just conducted a boycott against the Farah Manufacturing Company. They also secured the full backing of the AFL-CIO for their escalated campaign.[2]

In addition to preparing for a boycott, the union continued its organizing efforts. Looking to capitalize on their breakthrough, TWUA leaders quickly began a fresh campaign at Stevens's plant in Wallace, North Carolina (more than a hundred miles from Wallace, South Carolina, where Stevens also owned a mill). Like Roanoke Rapids, Wallace was a small community in eastern North Carolina, and African Americans had made steady progress into a range of production jobs over the previous decade. Again, union strategists reasoned that they could base a successful campaign around these new recruits. In Wallace, however, Stevens showed that it had learned from its defeat in Roanoke Rapids, and the union was unable to repeat its success.[3]

The company's conduct confirmed that the Roanoke Rapids loss had not cowed it in any way. In Wallace, wrote Sol Stetin, the company's "brutal and unlawful tactics were again brought into full play." The TWUA president felt that Stevens was so disturbed by its Roanoke Rapids defeat that it "threw the book" at the union in Wallace.[4] On the eve of a February 1975 election, managers mailed to all of their employees a seven-page letter that linked unions with violence and division. In particular, the document publicized the cases of southern textile workers who had lost their jobs after taking part in strikes. "It should not be overlooked or forgotten," it noted, "that WHERE UNIONS ARE IS WHERE STRIKES GENERALLY OCCUR. Everybody knows that! And everybody knows that strikes mean strife and strain, tension and turmoil—often destruction, violence and bloodshed—and bitterness and misery, debt and regret." The letter also suggested that the plant could close if workers voted for the TWUA. "Of what value," it asked, "are so-called high Union contract rates in plants that are shut down and not paying anything to anybody?" The TWUA subsequently lost the Wallace election by a vote of 540 to 404. Complaining that the company had harassed union supporters and threatened to close the plant, organizers quickly filed charges with the NLRB.[5]

Given the viciousness of the company's onslaught, Stetin argued that the union had done well to gain more than 40 percent of the vote. "In view of the pre-election intimidation practiced by Stevens in this campaign," he wrote, "the wonder is so many of these workers had the courage to vote for the union." The veteran activist insisted that many southern textile workers wanted to be represented by a union. In November 1974 the TWUA had also contested an election at Cannon Mills in Kannapolis, North Carolina. Cannon dominated the town of Kannapolis, and TWUA leaders took pride in just securing an election in the "giant anti-union fortress." Although it lost, the union was able to obtain 45 percent of the vote, which Stetin interpreted as another encouraging sign. The result, he wrote, "augurs well for the future."[6]

Although union leaders publicly blamed Stevens's onslaught for the defeat in Wallace, privately they acknowledged that other problems had also played a part. In retrospect, organizing director Paul Swaity felt that the union should have done more to prepare the Wallace workers for such an attack, and the campaign was certainly not as well planned as the Roanoke Rapids drive had been. After the euphoria of their first victory, perhaps union leaders also felt that the company would not fight them as hard again.[7]

In Wallace, Stevens also used economic incentives to undermine the TWUA's appeal. In February 1975 the company announced that it would support and maintain the full value of all the payments it had made into the employee profit-sharing plan. Aware that worker dissatisfaction with the erosion in the trust fund was a major cause of its defeat in Roanoke Rapids, the company acted to prevent the union from using this issue again. TWUA strategists realized this, especially as the move was widely publicized just before the Wallace vote. "The purpose of the announcement," wrote attorney Henry Woicik, "virtually on the eve of the Wallace election, was to thwart TWUA's organizing of the Stevens chain."[8]

Although the union had won the Roanoke Rapids election, by the time of the Wallace vote six months later it had made little progress toward securing a contract. As a result, Wallace workers wondered whether the union had the power to actually deliver the benefits that it promised. From the start of negotiations, company officials were determined to prevent their opponents from gaining a strong contract. Acting under clear orders from above, branch managers quickly revealed their opposition to any form of arbitration, well aware that it was a key union demand. Independent arbitration would give the union a means of addressing their members' complaints, and it was particularly disliked by company officials who felt that they should have unilateral control over the running of the plants. Conscious of the difficulty of winning strikes in the South, the union was sensitive to company taunts that it could solve grievances through walkouts instead.[9] "Without arbitration," said Stetin, "no agreement is worth the paper it is written on. . . . They say to us, 'Well, you can strike.' Sure, they would like us to strike Roanoke Rapids with 3600 people, while all other plants are operating. The nerve of this corporation."[10]

The company was also unwilling to grant wage and benefit increases that would have given the Roanoke Rapids workers an economic edge over their nonunion counterparts. Acutely aware of how this first contract would influence the union's organizing efforts, Stevens wanted to be able to argue that its workers had nothing to gain from voting for the TWUA. Until the company finally signed a contract in October 1980, in fact, Roanoke Rapids workers failed to receive the annual wage increases that the company awarded to its nonunion employees. Thus Stevens tried to use its Roanoke Rapids employees as an example to those in its other plants.[11]

While Stevens was clearly reluctant to compromise, the union was also partly responsible for the slow pace of the negotiations. As TWUA leaders were simultaneously trying to organize other company facilities, they were also eager to secure a strong contract that they could hold up to nonunion workers. In October 1974, Paul Swaity urged TWUA negotiators to increase their demands. "We must keep in mind," he warned, "we have a continuous organizing campaign in other Stevens plants and the company will use what we say, and do, in Roanoke Rapids on us as they did in regard to Statesboro." With both sides reluctant to compromise, negotiations got nowhere. Within two years of the election, the two sides had met on at least fifty-seven occasions but had failed to make any real progress.[12] As late as June 1977, union negotiator Jack Sheinkman reported that the two teams were "still far away from a contract."[13]

The automatic checkoff of union dues proved to be a particular stumbling block. As had been the case in Statesboro, the company remained fundamentally opposed to an automatic checkoff, yet the union saw the clause as essential. The TWUA had accepted many contracts in the past without a checkoff, forcing them to rely on workers to voluntarily pay their union dues. In most cases this had resulted in a fall in the number of dues-paying members. This was a particular problem in the South, where right-to-work laws made union membership voluntary. Savvy employees took advantage of these laws to enjoy benefits negotiated for the entire bargaining unit without paying dues; southern locals, complained a frustrated Swaity, were "plagued with free riders."[14] In January 1968, one TWUA study of its southern local unions found that only 66 percent of potential members were actually paying dues. Five years later, another internal investigation found that only 53 percent were paying. In North Carolina there were some locations where only a quarter of eligible workers actually paid dues. By the early 1970s, TWUA leaders consequently argued that all new contracts should include an automatic checkoff.[15]

In other ways the Roanoke Rapids situation typified the union's broader experiences in the South. After election victories in the region, the TWUA had frequently struggled to secure contracts. "Our major organizing problem in the south is our inability to get contracts after we win certification," noted Swaity in 1969. This problem had dogged the union throughout the postwar period. In January 1955 a report by the union's research department found that there were thirty-one cases where the TWUA was "technically" the bargaining agent but had never secured a labor agreement. Many of these situations were in the South, and some even dated back to World War II, when antiunion managers had reluctantly agreed to recognize the TWUA during exceptional wartime conditions.[16] The issues that held up the Roanoke Rapids contract—the checkoff and arbitration—were also typical stumbling blocks. In the decade immediately following World War II, the union had struck many firms after they refused to agree to these terms.[17]

While negotiations dragged on, the union faced the difficult task of trying to maintain the support of its members on the ground. In the past, workers had often drifted away from the TWUA when it had been unable to secure a labor agreement. Stevens certainly banked on this happening in Roanoke Rapids, and it tried its best to erode the union's support in the mills. Staffers complained that the company was victimizing union activists on the job, sending out a clear message that TWUA membership brought no special privileges. "Following the election in Roanoke Rapids on August 29, 1974," charged union attorney Henry J. Patterson Jr., "the company made unfavorable changes in work conditions in certain departments where visible union support was the strongest and in some cases altered the working conditions of particular employees in reprisal for vocal union support." In addition, the TWUA claimed that Stevens had unfairly fired three of their leading committee members.[18]

Although it had not been able to secure a labor agreement, the local union in Roanoke Rapids was able to represent workers. Seeking to build support, international representative Clyde Bush worked to develop programs that involved the rank and file as much as possible. In particular, he quickly established an informal grievance procedure that was popular with many workers. The union also picked up support from workers who had previously feared that the company would shut the mills if the TWUA won an election. In addition, it gained backing by promising to end the company's unpopular policy of putting injured employees on sick leave rather than giving them unemployment pay, a practice that saved Stevens money. Heading off company charges that they were interested only in collecting dues, the union did not take any money from the Roanoke Rapids group. As a result, it is impossible to definitely state whether the TWUA's support declined in the years after the election, although its leaders insisted that they maintained the backing of the majority of those in the bargaining unit. Union leaders were certainly proud that they were able to keep the Roanoke Rapids local going for so long without either dues payments or a contract.[19]

Although it had secured enough white support to win the election, a disproportionate amount of the union's backing continued to come from African Americans. In 1976 a visiting PBS film crew captured this, as several black workers eloquently explained their reasons for supporting the union. "I just want, if my son decides not to go to college, I want to make sure it's better for him if he wants to work at the mill," claimed James Boone, now a shop steward in his department. "I want it so he can go in there, won't breathe cotton dust, he'll go in there and won't slip, grease on the floor, water on the floor. I want him so that he can go in there and hold his head up and give the man eight hours a day of work—that's all I'm asking. And to respect him and pay him a decent salary. And the only way we're going to do that is by letting the Union represent us." Other African Americans argued that their wages were inadequate to properly support their families. Clara Williams complained that the company's workers had no choice but to buy on credit, trapping many in debt. "If we could make a decent living, we could go like other Americans and shop and pay cash for what we get," she explained, "but here you can't do it; at $3.40 an hour, it's just me and my husband. He works and I work, and we don't even make enough to pay the bills and have fun. You either have fun or you pay bills; there's not enough money left over for both."[20]

Supporting its claims that a new generation of textile workers were more willing to speak out, the union also gained support from the young. Youthful pro-union worker Danny Blackwell maintained that his generation were less fearful than their elders. "I'd say the majority of the older whites are more afraid to stand up for their rights," he claimed, "because they are older and they're afraid if they do lose their job they won't be able to find another one. And the younger whites, they're not as much afraid because they feel like they're young and they can always look out for another job." As the South's economy diversified, younger workers were clearly best placed to take advantage of new opportunities. Like African Americans, many were also dissatisfied because they were more likely to be confined to undesirable shift assignments.[21]

Despite its ability to build support inside the plants, the union struggled to secure acceptance in the broader community. The small town was located in a rural area where many residents had eked out a living from sharecropping before the plants were built. By the mid-1970s it had become, in the words of a PBS journalist, a "fairly prosperous community" with "its share of new homes and suburban shopping plazas." The textile mills were, as businessman Howard Bloom put it, "the pivot of the community," and entrepreneurs worried that a union would cause Stevens to up and leave. In particular, they fretted that a boycott would hurt an economy that was dependent on textiles. "When employment goes down one percent in this city, it's tough," he noted. The business community were also concerned that local workers were not receiving the same pay increases as the firm's unorganized employees, with most viewing this as an indication of the economic damage that unions could cause.[22]

As negotiations stalled, TWUA leaders realized that they had to find other ways of exerting pressure on the company. In December 1974 research director George Perkel noted in a confidential memo to Stetin that, although the union had obtained bargaining rights at two locations and had secured "heightened public awareness of the company's anti-labor record," there was still no sign that the firm would actually deal with it. "Management is adamant," noted the native New Yorker. "It refuses to bargain in good faith. It fights every organizing attempt with ruthless attacks. The only hope of changing management's course is to increase the pressure."[23]

Led by staffers in the research and legal departments, TWUA strategists explored several ways of turning the screws on Stevens. The term "corporate campaign" had not yet been coined, but union leaders identified many of the central ideas that Ray Rogers would later develop, classifying their thoughts as a "campaign of pressure." An important figure in this change of strategy was general counsel Joel Ax. An astute lawyer, Ax forcefully argued that the union needed to move beyond its reliance on NLRB charges and exploit Stevens's willingness to violate other laws. The company, he pointed out, was willing to break civil rights laws and had a poor health and safety record. He asserted that the union should exploit these two issues by filing civil rights charges on behalf of "affected" employees and requesting plant inspections under the 1970 Occupational Safety and Health Act. "It appears to me," he concluded, "that we will have a greater chance of conquering the Stevens chain if we can create this kind of massive activity in every area of their operation. We must make it costly enough and hot enough for them to cease their illegal labor activities and sit down at the bargaining tables with us."[24]

The union's subsequent tactic of putting pressure on Stevens's directors was previewed as early as September 1972, when Perkel explored the way many of these executives sat on the boards of other companies. The long-serving research director also explored Stevens's overseas holdings, anticipating the links that ACTWU would later make with unions at these facilities.[25] In addition, he began to explore the possibilities of using shareholders to exert pressure on the company's directors, pondering whether to launch a stockholders' suit against management. Such a suit, he argued, could be brought on the basis that the company was wasting money on its long-running fight with organized labor. Perkel and union attorney Henry Woicik also bought shares in the company and attended the 1975 stockholders' meeting. They did not ask any questions, but were there to judge whether union delegates could participate "actively" in future meetings.[26]

It was a wide-ranging consumer boycott, however, that union leaders envisaged as their central method for bringing outside pressure to bear on Stevens. In the wake of the election, Perkel extensively researched the company's product lines and recommended to his superiors that a boycott offered the most effective means of curbing Stevens's antiunionism. "A substantial portion of the company's products is sold on a name-brand basis," he asserted. "An effective boycott could hurt the company."[27]

The success of recent boycotts encouraged TWUA leaders to use the tactic. In the 1960s and early 1970s, the boycott emerged as a weapon capable of exerting real economic leverage against companies that otherwise refused to recognize organized labor. In a long struggle to organize a union at the Farah Manufacturing Company, a garment maker based in Texas, the ACWA had used a boycott to bring the company to the table. An ACWA leader later claimed that the Farah boycott was "without [a] doubt, the most successful such campaign in American labor history." This was not an empty boast: the ACWA boycott clearly did affect the company's profits, contributing to the $8.3 million loss that Farah suffered in 1972. By early 1974 the apparel maker had been forced to shut two plants and was running a three-day week at its other factories. Shortly afterwards, its managers signed a contract with the union.[28] TWUA leaders were impressed by the Farah boycott, and in the mid-1970s they held "in-depth meetings" with ACWA officials in an attempt to copy their tactics.[29]

In the 1960s a mass boycott of table grapes by the United Farmworkers had also successfully attracted support from many liberals who had otherwise grown disillusioned with the labor movement. Reflecting on this effort, TWUA leaders sensed that a boycott could mobilize a broad range of public opinion. They were also encouraged by their own experience of running a successful boycott against Oneita Knitting Mills. A northern company, Oneita had moved south to escape unionization, setting up two textile plants in a rural part of eastern South Carolina. Following a union election victory in 1971, managers refused to sign a contract, pushing the union to launch a simultaneous strike and boycott. A majority of the Oneita workers were African American women, and the union was able to mobilize support from both feminists and civil rights groups. In the summer of 1973, the Oneita campaign was successfully resolved when the company agreed to sign a contract, a real achievement in the textile South. The Oneita boycott was, reflected Stetin, "one of our brighter moments."[30]

Union strategists reasoned that a boycott of J. P. Stevens could attract even more support than their Oneita effort had. Both black and female employees claimed that the company discriminated against them, and the firm also had a poor health and safety record. Campaign leaders Harold McIver and Nick Zonarich recommended to Stetin that the union make particular use of the brown lung issue as "an organizing tactic." In addition, many Americans were already aware of Stevens's record of labor law violations.[31]

Another major factor in the union's decision to launch the boycott was its recognition that it could not successfully strike against a company as large as

Stevens. It had won the Roanoke Rapids election with only 54 percent of the vote, and in the mid-1970s the nationwide recession had led to widespread unemployment across North Carolina. At such a time, leaders reasoned, the company could easily recruit strikebreakers if it needed to. Past experience supported this judgment. Since the 1930s, many TWUA strikes had been broken as companies had imported replacement labor, a move that was usually fully supported by local community leaders. Scott Hoyman remembered that Stevens officials even goaded him to call a strike: "Stevens had kept saying, 'Why don't you strike, Mr. Hoyman?' We said, 'We don't want a strike.' . . . They had thirty-five thousand people. They would have loved it if we had gone out on strike."[32]

Union staffers did explore the option of striking Stevens, but they soon ruled it out. "The union recognized that a strike, labor's traditional weapon, could not succeed in achieving its goals in the circumstances encountered here," noted one key document. "The company has too many unorganized plants which it could use to perform the work normally done at the organized plants. Instead, we launched a nationwide consumer boycott in 1976 to hit the company where it could not evade the impact of our concerted activity."[33] Justifying the move to another union leader, Stetin explained that his staff had exhausted other alternatives. In particular, they had tried to work through a number of undisclosed "third parties" in an effort to persuade "top management" to compromise, but these efforts had been rebuffed. "Since the company violations and campaign to destroy the union toehold continue," wrote Stetin, "we have no alternative but to try to find a more effective means of bringing them around. Strike action in 7 out of 85 plants would be ineffective. It appears our only real alternative is a massive national boycott."[34]

As part of their preparations for such a large undertaking, union leaders explored the risks. Even in the planning stages, they were particularly conscious that a boycott could hurt their efforts to build support among Stevens workers. Strategists were very aware of the contradiction of asking for workers' support while also conducting a boycott that could eliminate their jobs. In addition, no union had ever attempted a boycott against a company as large and diverse as Stevens. Leaders also fretted about the "potential effectiveness" of a boycott, as investigations into the firm's operations quickly established that the company made a wide range of products, many of which were not sold directly to the consumer.[35] The TWUA was "putting itself on the line," noted Scott Hoyman, and if its effort failed to produce obvious results, the company's hand would be strengthened. The costs of funding a boycott were "staggering," and there were considerable legal risks as well.[36]

Boycotting activities could in fact easily breach various sections of the NLRA, especially if union agents themselves put pressure on companies not to buy Stevens products. In the closing days of the Farah boycott, NLRB general counsel Peter Nash was proposing to issue a complaint and seek a federal court injunction against the ACWA on the grounds that visits by union agents to retail stores constituted a violation. This would also have exposed the union to a damage suit, although in the event Farah settled before this action occurred.[37]

Overall, union strategists reasoned that they could overcome or minimize many of these problems. Doubts about the boycott's effectiveness were addressed by reasoning that the union could concentrate its effort on the company's home furnishings, as these were sold direct to the consumer. According to the union, this alone would be enough to force a change in policy. "A small percentage drop in overall sales is enough to affect a company significantly," asserted Hoyman. In addition, union leaders argued that the boycott campaign would produce negative publicity for Stevens, and that this too could force a change in the firm's labor relations stance.[38] Worries about the impact of the boycott on Stevens's workers were also assuaged, as leaders argued that employees could be educated that the firm's intransigence made the move necessary. Workers would be told that they had to make short-term sacrifices in order to secure a better long-term future for themselves and their families. Aware of the restrictions on boycotting, the union aimed to concentrate on activities with less legal risk, such as media publicity, handbilling to consumers of the company's products, and "non-coercive appeals" to retailers.[39]

Other factors also pushed the union to embark on such a costly and risky strategy. Philip W. Moore, a corporate lawyer hired by the TWUA to explore whether they should launch a full-scale campaign against Stevens, argued that the potential benefits of organizing such a large employer justified the commitment. Again, the union's view of the company as the key to organizing the entire South pushed them to dig even deeper. "There is no question," wrote Moore, "that the future of the Textile Workers Union of America will ultimately depend on its survival in the South. Purely in terms of money, a victory at Stevens is worth possibly $500,000.00 per month. A victory at Stevens is potentially worth some 700,000 workers or nearly two million dollars per month. The potential income alone justifies what appears to be inordinate expenditure of funds in order to win the battle." Union leaders concurred with this assessment. Scott Hoyman noted in December 1976: "Stevens is an exceedingly important company in the industry, and it would be very significant if it were organized. It has become a symbol."[40] At the time, Stetin himself predicted that the decline of the northern textile industry would continue; the South was undoubtedly "the most important place" for the union. The struggle had also assumed a symbolic importance for the diminutive but determined TWUA leader, who had taken a close interest in it since the early 1960s. The fight against J. P. Stevens, he told his colleagues, had become "a crusade for the whole American labor movement."[41]

Following its breakthrough in Roanoke Rapids, the U.S. labor movement stood ready to help the TWUA. Now that the union had proved its claim that Stevens's workers wanted union representation, AFL-CIO leaders were determined to break the textile giant's resistance. In August 1975, AFL-CIO president George Meany gave a special message to Stevens workers, declaring that in "their struggle" they had "the full support of the AFL-CIO and its 14 million members." The 1975 AFL-CIO convention passed a resolution of support for the J. P. Stevens struggle and urged "consideration to the development of a boycott of J. P. Stevens products if such action proves necessary." Meany appointed a special committee to mobilize the labor movement behind the Stevens campaign.[42] In February 1976, a statement by the AFL-CIO's executive council branded Stevens "the nation's number one scofflaw" and reaffirmed the "all-out support" of the federation to the Stevens campaign. Although he had often been suspicious of ambitious organizing efforts, Meany was piqued by Stevens's refusal to bargain and threw his personal authority behind the TWUA's fight. "J. P. Stevens," he wrote in June 1976, "didn't just take on its employees or their union when it chose its lawless path to labor relations. J. P. Stevens took on the entire labor movement."[43]

Like TWUA leaders, AFL-CIO chiefs soon took pride in their high-profile fight with Stevens. The boycott, noted federation strategist Thomas R. Donahue, was "one of the biggest and most ambitious boycott efforts ever undertaken." AFL-CIO leaders viewed Stevens as a symbol of corporate resistance to unionism and felt that the credibility of the labor movement rested on its ability to curb the company's arrogance and make it bargain in good faith. Also like TWUA leaders, AFL-CIO chiefs reasoned that only by organizing a large pattern-setting company in the region's largest industry could labor unions ever make significant progress in the South.[44]

In order for the ambitious boycott to have a chance of success, TWUA leaders realized that their own union needed more resources and power. Thus they were keen to merge with the larger ACWA. The Stevens campaign was a central reason for the move. As Bruce Raynor recalled, "The TWUA merged with the Amalgamated in 1976 because we needed the resources to win the Stevens battle. See, the TWUA was a great little union, it just didn't have the resources to beat these textile companies." With more than 350,000 members, the ACWA was twice as large as the TWUA, and its varied assets included the nation's only union-owned bank.[45]

It was Stetin who initiated talks with ACWA leaders, and he remained a strong supporter of the merger throughout lengthy discussions. Stetin advocated the merger even though he knew that it would require him to play a subordinate role in the new organization and to give up his seat on the AFL-CIO executive council. He was willing to do this if the new union agreed to fight to the finish with J. P. Stevens. Although the TWUA was considerably smaller than the ACWA, Stetin got his way. In joining together, the leaders of the two unions agreed to launch a "vigorous consumer boycott" against Stevens. At the merger convention, the new union passed a resolution that pledged its commitment to the "showdown with J. P. Stevens," while the merger agreement itself stipulated that ACTWU would work by every available means to ensure the company's subjugation.[46]

While the Stevens campaign was central, the merger was also driven by other factors. The two unions had many similarities. The bulk of their members were in the South, and both had been hurt by the flight of organized northern firms to the region. In addition, the textile and apparel industries were closely related, and 40,000 ACWA members were employed by firms with textile subsidiaries. Both unions were also increasingly being hurt by overseas imports, which were already causing layoffs and plant closures, particularly in the apparel sector. In joining with the ACWA, TWUA leaders initially hoped that apparel workers could refuse to handle Stevens cloth, although they later found out that this would have entailed an illegal secondary boycott.[47]

Remembering the cost of the Farah boycott, some members of the ACWA's executive council were reluctant to become involved in an even bigger campaign. They were convinced by their new leaders, however, that they confronted a unique opportunity to create a "more outstanding" organization. Between 1946 and 1972 the ACWA had been led by Jacob Potofsky, an ageing functionary who had become increasingly reluctant to take risks.

When he retired, a more youthful and militant leadership took over. Barely fifty years old when he was elected president, Murray Finley was typical of a new breed of college-educated labor leaders. After completing degrees at the University of Michigan and Northwestern University, he had risen rapidly through the ranks in the union's midwestern region. A lawyer by background, he was well placed to head the Stevens campaign. At the same time, the union was reinvigorated by the election of Jacob Sheinkman as secretary-treasurer. The son of Ukrainian immigrants, Sheinkman was educated at Cornell and won praise for his vigorous performance as the ACWA's general counsel.[48] Following the merger, Finley described the new union as "totally committed" to the Stevens campaign, while Sheinkman told ACTWU's executive board that "the J. P. Stevens undertaking was not only a commitment that was made as a result of a piece of paper and a merger but is an opportunity. A failure for this union would be disastrous."[49]

The new ACTWU president was also keen to initiate more organizing in the South, particularly at Stevens plants. On the eve of the merger, Finley argued that the Stevens campaign would help efforts to organize the southern apparel industry. "If we want to open up the South and the Southwest to organizing the unorganized in the apparel industry," he explained to one journalist, "we must help them [textile workers] also organize the unorganized at Stevens, Burlington Mills and others." Finley was very aware that the flight of organized shops to the nonunion South had gravely weakened both the ACWA and the TWUA. "The real thing that hurt our industry and our members was the non-union growth in the south and southwest," he admitted after the merger. "There are a million textile workers in our jurisdiction and about 500,000 in men's apparel."[50]

In the fall of 1976 the new union hired the staff that it would need in order to conduct an effective nationwide boycott. In all, thirty-one paid personnel were brought on board. Five were based at boycott headquarters in New York, the rest in various cities across the nation.[51] By January 1977 ACTWU had established field offices in twenty-seven U.S. cities. Staff in these centers began to build support for their efforts by enlisting the help of both individuals and organizations. In particular, they set up boycott committees staffed by activists from a wide range of supportive organizations. These committees helped to organize community outreach events, as well as carrying out leafleting, petitioning, and store visits.[52]

In the closing months of 1976, ACTWU's leaders were cautiously optimistic. They had a nationwide staff in place, and they were launching a boycott in what they hoped was a more favorable national political climate. Although the AFL-CIO failed to give strong backing to moderate Democrat Jimmy Carter, ACTWU was one of a number of unions that enthusiastically backed the Georgian. In March 1977 the union's executive board noted that they were "totally delighted that we no longer have the Nixon-Ford administration in Washington and would work just as hard to elect Carter and Mondale if elections were held next week." The new administration, they hoped, would be "more responsive" to the needs of working Americans. This optimism overlooked the fact that the Democratic Party as a whole was becoming less sensitive to the needs of a waning labor movement. In addition, no union had ever tried to conduct a boycott against a company as large and diverse as Stevens, and history suggested that the firm's officers were unlikely to capitulate quickly.[53]

SIX

Stirring the Nation's Conscience

Since the late 1960s the union had tried to gain as much publicity for the Stevens case as possible, hoping this would create outside pressure on the firm that would force it to moderate its antiunionism. By the mid-1970s this long-running media campaign against Stevens had already secured national press coverage and mobilized the support of some northern congressmen and the national AFL-CIO. In launching their boycott, union strategists stepped up these efforts to build public backing. Over the next few years, they effectively portrayed the Stevens boycott as a fight for social justice against a lawless employer that had no respect for workers' rights. "This struggle," proclaimed Jacob Sheinkman, "far transcends the boundaries of a traditional labor-management conflict. The struggle at J. P. Stevens is for justice." ACTWU's efforts to secure public backing and positive publicity were an important and effective part of its boycott campaign. As *Fortune* noted in June 1978, "the true purpose of the boycott is to drum up wide public support for the union cause, and there it is successful."[1]

Within a couple of years, the union had secured an impressive range of endorsements for its boycott. The effort was backed by major civil rights groups such as the NAACP and CORE, as well as the largest women's organization in the country and a variety of church and senior citizens' bodies. In addition, students at seventy-five universities and colleges set up boycott support groups. Political help was not lacking either, as the boycott was endorsed by several U.S. governors, fifty-six U.S. representatives, and a variety of senators. Other high-profile supporters included actress Jane Fonda, economist John Kenneth Galbraith, author Michael Harrington, and ABC sports commentator Myron Cope. The wide range of support buoyed the confidence of union leaders. As early as March 1977, Murray Finley asserted that the union had secured enough backing to "win" their long struggle against J. P. Stevens. By the end of the decade, Jacob Sheinkman claimed that the boycott, which had been launched to "stir the American conscience," had become "the economic and social force of the seventies."[2]

The strongest support for the boycott came from the North. In states where unions were strong, many were shocked to learn that some American workers were still unable to organize freely. At the same time, most northerners had witnessed how local firms had closed down plants and moved south in search of cheaper wages, just as Stevens had done. The company seemed to epitomize the "runaway shops" that had turned large parts of the Northeast and Midwest into a declining "rust belt." Northern liberals were also outraged by the company's record of racial and sexual discrimination, and by its poor safety record, all of which were publicized effectively by ACTWU. In 1979 the Oscar-winning movie *Norma Rae* gave a further boost to the union's efforts. Union leaders proved adept at capitalizing on the film's popularity, sending Crystal Lee Sutton, the "real life Norma Rae," on a successful national publicity tour. In the large northern cities, in particular, Sutton was well received, and she emerged as an articulate and able spokeswomen for the workers' cause.[3]

The union was especially effective at mobilizing public backing by concentrating on Stevens's record of lawlessness. "Since 1964," noted one appeal, "the NLRB has found J. P. Stevens guilty of illegal anti-union activities on 13 separate occasions and three additional cases are currently pending." The company had established "a persistent pattern of flagrant and massive law violations" that the NLRB had been unable to stop. As a result, workers' right to organize had become a "hollow promise." ACTWU's material also emphasized workers' desperate need for a union. Their low wages—"some 31% below the national manufacturing average"—were widely publicized, especially to a northern audience, as was their powerlessness to speak out to improve the situation.[4]

The union also accused Stevens of having a poor health and safety record, and of discriminating against both African American and female employees. ACTWU's case was effectively summarized in informative "fact sheets" that were widely distributed to sympathetic audiences. "The conditions under which J. P. Stevens employees work," declared one, "are fraught with serious health and safety hazards." Effectively combining the union's allegations of lawlessness and racism, another sheet asserted: "Black men and women suffer discrimination in employment practices at the hands of J. P. Stevens, America's second largest textile manufacturer and the nation's no. 1 Labor-Law-Breaker!"[5] At the same time, a catchy "Don't Sleep with Stevens" slogan caught the public's attention. Americans, insisted the union, should not let the renegade firm's sheets into their bedrooms. As Sol Stetin put it, the whole effort was designed "to bring the story of J. P. Stevens to as many people as possible." Over the next few years, these publicity efforts made the Stevens campaign into a cause célèbre for many Americans.[6]

The union was particularly successful at mobilizing support from students, especially on northern campuses. Many of the younger generation were outraged by the company's record of lawlessness. At Princeton University, members of the J. P. Stevens Boycott/Princeton Support Group waged an on-campus campaign in support of the Stevens workers. In October 1976 they demonstrated against the dual role of R. Manning Brown, the chairman of Princeton's board of trustees and a Stevens board member. The following spring, they succeeded in preventing a visit by company executive Whitney Stevens, who planned to defend the firm's position before a closed gathering at the Princeton Club. Members of the Support Group objected, insisting that Stevens should take part in an on-campus public discussion. If he refused, they promised to demonstrate against his visit to the campus. Facing this pressure, officials of the Princeton Club canceled, saying that "they didn't want their members subjected to that kind of thing."[7]

Similar activities took place at a wide range of universities. At New York University, concerned students distributed thousands of leaflets and initiated a letter-writing campaign to try to ensure that Stevens linen was not used in university dormitories. At the University of Illinois, volunteers also circulated literature and carried out surveys to determine the amount of Stevens products used on campus, while at Cornell University students organized an education week to raise awareness of the boycott. Teach-ins were held at a number of schools, including Columbia, NYU, Rutgers, and Princeton. Although they varied from place to place, most teach-ins featured talks by faculty members and former Stevens workers, along with films, songs, and general leafleting. At Stanford University, students organized a major campaign after they discovered that the university was an important owner of Stevens stock. After collecting what they called "an enormous number" of signatures, boycott supporters pushed the university to vote in favor of ACTWU-backed resolutions at the 1977 annual stockholders' meeting.[8]

Comparable efforts produced results elsewhere. At Harvard and Princeton, student activists secured pledges from official stores to drop Stevens products, while administrators at the University of Pittsburgh bowed to protesters' demands and stopped purchasing the company's goods. In general, however, it was the public image of the company that was most hurt by the students' activism. "The campus boycott may not have the power to hurt Stevens economically," admitted Marilyn M. Quinn, a student at American University, "but it has damaged the company's public image." As these activities highlight, most student support for the boycott was concentrated on northern campuses, although more than six hundred leaflets were also distributed by volunteers at the University of Texas.[9]

This activism challenged popular perceptions about the apathy and conservatism of students in the 1970s. "Everyone claims to understand the college student of the 1970's," noted the *New York Times* in December 1977. "Grade-conscious, career-oriented and politically moderate to conservative, today's undergraduate is supposedly intent on doing his or her own thing, rather than changing the world." In fact, the Stevens campaign encouraged other types of campus activism, especially at Princeton, where students formed one of the most active boycott chapters. "I see the boycott as a campus trend," noted Princeton senior David Salomon. "Vietnam is over, but activism hasn't died. It has simply changed its focus to holding corporations here and abroad accountable for their actions." In the fall of 1977, Princeton students also protested against President Carter's economic policies, organizing a demonstration when Secretary of Labor F. Ray Marshall spoke on campus. Other student groups protested against American trade with apartheid South Africa, spoke out against world hunger, and lobbied for more rights for Chicano workers within the United States. The student protesters, reported the *Chronicle of Higher Education*, had revived "a spirit reminiscent of the 60's."[10]

ACTWU's fight drew considerable support from church groups. Many religious leaders felt that the company was morally wrong to break the law. In June 1979 the American Jewish Congress endorsed the boycott "for as long as the Company refuses to recognize (by utilizing a pattern of delaying tactics, intimidation, or coercion) the legal right of its employees to organize." A wide range of other religious groups, including the National Council of the Churches of Christ and the Synagogue Council of America, gave similar reasons for their support.[11] Church support again followed regional lines. In May 1979, for example, the boycott was endorsed by the United Presbyterian Church (the northern group) while the Presbyterian Church in the United States (the southern group) reaffirmed its earlier decision not to support the effort.[12]

While most church support came from the North, some southern church leaders also spoke out against J. P. Stevens. In March 1978 six Catholic bishops from southern dioceses issued a statement that strongly criticized the giant textile producer. Stevens, they insisted, had a "sad record of continued opposition to the formation of unions" that was "irreconcilable with the clear demands of social justice in the Christian Gospel."[13] Boycott strategists were proud of the support they secured from church groups. In February 1979 boycott director Del Mileski boasted to union leaders that "the Stevens issue has gained more religious support than either the Farah or Farm Workers' campaigns." The former ACWA activist felt that the religious endorsements created moral pressure on Stevens, and company officials certainly tried hard to give their own side of the story to church groups.[14]

Many civil rights groups also supported ACTWU's boycott. Shocked that Stevens workers were so poorly paid, these activists felt that unionization would raise their wages. The company's black workers continued to earn even less than their white counterparts. In the late 1970s civil rights activists were becoming increasingly concerned about black economic inequality, especially in the South. By this time, African Americans had secured legal equality but black income still stubbornly lagged behind. Harnessing these concerns, in December 1976 the union set up Southerners for Economic Justice (SEJ). The lobbying group was headed by prominent figures from the African American community, including Georgia state senator Julian Bond, former SNCC chair John Lewis, Atlanta mayor Maynard Jackson, and NAACP southern director Ruby Hurley. Working with community and church groups, SEJ conducted a "vigorous education campaign" to build support for the boycott within the South. Reflecting the involvement of former civil rights activists, SEJ leaders consistently linked the Stevens struggle to the dominant protest campaign of the previous decade. "The goal of economic justice," they asserted, was the South's "next great challenge following the civil rights era." By linking the boycott to the fight for civil rights, however, SEJ was always much more effective at securing support from the African American community than it was from southern whites.[15]

Other prominent African American leaders endorsed ACTWU's fight. In the late 1970s, Coretta Scott King publicly backed ACTWU on several occasions. In doing so, she cited her late husband's support of unionization as one of the most effective ways of lifting blacks out of poverty. "The outcome of this struggle," she claimed, "will determine whether millions of Southern workers, black and white, win their right to union representation and to a fair and equitable share of the wealth that production creates." Mrs. King was on friendly terms with several ACTWU leaders, and she maintained that the union could provide "competent and committed representation for working people of all races."[16]

The union also joined with civil rights activists in a campaign to stop Woolworth's from stocking Stevens products. In the early 1960s, student civil rights demonstrators had protested against the retailer's whites-only lunch counters, trying to push the firm to take a moral stand against segregation. Two decades later, they returned to the company's stores and urged managers to condemn J. P. Stevens. In May 1980 Jibreel Khazan, one of four men to participate in the first sit-in, joined eighty other demonstrators in a protest at a Woolworth's store in Boston. Publicizing Woolworth's refusal to support the Stevens boycott, many protesters linked ACTWU's fight with the civil rights movement. "It's essentially the same struggle," commented Canon Ed Rodman, missioner to minorities for the Episcopal Diocese of Massachusetts. "Now it's black people and white people—they're not being allowed to organize. Of course, then it was civil rights. Now it's economic rights."[17]

The union went to considerable lengths to mobilize the civil rights community behind its boycott. Boycott publicity material made much of the discrimination faced by African Americans at the company, linking it with Stevens's broader record of lawlessness. As one flyer put it, "Hiring on the basis of race, discriminating against blacks in layoffs and recalls, paying black males substantially less than white males—that's only part of the appalling Stevens record. It's time to end racial discrimination at J. P. Stevens." Testimony from individual workers was used to graphically illustrate these points. "I asked why I couldn't get the same thing the white man was getting," explained black worker Robert Mallory in one flyer. "And I never got an answer whatsoever out of all of them."[18]

Stevens consistently answered these allegations of racial discrimination by arguing that it was hiring more and more blacks. In a 1977 pamphlet, the company asserted that minorities made up 23 percent of its workforce, an increase of "over 200 percent during the last ten years." Stevens steered clear of discussing these workers' job assignments, as officials knew that blacks were still more likely to be concentrated in lower-paying positions. By singling out percentage increases, the company was also able to make the pace of change appear as dramatic as possible, as African Americans had only recently gained access to production jobs.[19]

The union was particularly effective at attracting support from women's groups. The women's divisions of church groups responded enthusiastically. In April 1978 the Women's Division of the United Methodist Church endorsed the boycott, citing workers' right to organize into unions. Representing about fourteen million women nationwide, the executive committee of the National Council of Catholic Women soon added their backing. Both Methodist and Catholic women also organized local actions such as store visits, letter writing, and the collective destruction of credit cards in front of store officials. Other religious groups encouraged their members to challenge the company's conduct. "We believe," explained the National Coalition of American Nuns, "that those multinational corporations proven guilty, as J. P. Stevens has been on numerous occasions, of depriving American citizens of the benefit of labor law, must be challenged by Christians in the name of the Lord."[20]

The National Organization for Women was a particularly strong boycott supporter. Founded in 1966, NOW was an activist feminist group that aimed to integrate women "into full participation in the mainstream of society, exercising full privileges and responsibilities in a truly equal partnership with men." The group claimed to be "the oldest and largest feminist organization in the world," and in the late 1970s it had more than seven hundred chapters in the United States and abroad. In June 1977 NOW passed a resolution in support of the boycott and asked its members to solicit support from other feminist organizations. In October 1978 a second resolution supported the workers' right to organize, endorsed an international boycott of the company's products, and called on NOW members to participate in local activities to place pressure on the renegade textile firm.[21]

NOW activists supported the boycott for a number of reasons. The group noted that nearly half of the company's workers were women and claimed that they faced "massive discrimination" in the mills. NOW argued that unionization would raise workers' wages and provide women with better opportunities to bid on higher-paying jobs. Noting the prevalence of cotton dust in the company's mills, the group were also concerned with cleaning up

Stevens's plants. As women were the "primary consumers" of the firm's products, NOW leaders asserted that they could work with other feminist organizations in "this important battle for justice, equality and workers' rights."[22]

Many NOW members placed pressure on retailers to sever their relationship with J. P. Stevens. Posing as local shoppers, NOW members went into department stores, located Stevens products, and asked that they be removed from sale. Many of these actions were undertaken as much to generate publicity and awareness as they were to get the offending merchandise taken off the shelves. In a similar vein, in July 1977 NOW's New York chapter staged a street theater in front of Madison Square Garden that culminated in a burning of the firm's sheets. In large northern cities such as New York, Philadelphia, and Boston, branch members also tried to get meetings with store managers in order to persuade them to change their position. In the summer of 1977, for instance, a delegation of members from the Brooklyn NOW, together with women from a variety of church groups, met with managers of Abraham & Strauss stores to try to persuade them to support the boycott. Pointing out that A&S officials had been reluctant to meet with them, NOW member Jo Milnar started the meeting by insisting that the firm had "slighted" the group "as women." A&S chairman Alan Gilman defended his position, insisting that it was not his firm's responsibility to make "moral judgments" about labor disputes. Ultimately, A&S executives refused to back down, but the NOW representatives were satisfied that they had convinced the company of their concerns.[23]

In March 1978 a wide variety of women's groups met in Washington, D.C., to organize the National Women's Committee to Support J. P. Stevens Workers. In all, thirty women's groups attended the meeting; they included the National Women's Party, the Women's Equity Action League, the National Council of Catholic Women, the National Consumer League, and United Methodist Women. NOW president Eleanor C. Smeal told the meeting that "the Stevens boycott so ties in with everything that the women's movement is doing that it is part and parcel of it." In particular, the campaign gave feminists the opportunity to refute criticisms that they were middle-class reformers who did not tackle bread-and-butter issues. "The guts of the feminist movement," asserted Smeal, "is the economic issue. It is about the economic equality and economic survival of women." The NOW leader also linked the Stevens campaign with the fight to ratify the Equal Rights Amendment, claiming that both fights centered on the conservative South. Firms like

Stevens, she explained, opposed the ERA precisely because it would bolster the drive for equal pay for men and women who performed the same jobs.[24]

At the conference, participants mapped out an action plan. As women were the major purchasers of bedding and towels, the company's staple products, they reasoned that they had the ability to place real pressure on Stevens. Following the conference, a delegation of feminist leaders went to the White House to bring the company's "systematic exploitation of women and black workers" to President Carter's attention. Although the Georgia Democrat did not meet with the protesters personally, he deputized presidential assistant Midge Costanza to do so. In an animated meeting with Costanza, the women asked for a review of the Pentagon's contracts with Stevens. But the Carter administration, like its predecessors, was not willing to bar the company from government business.[25]

The committee also initiated a letter-writing campaign directed against retailers who stubbornly stocked Stevens products. In the spring of 1980 the committee wrote Woolworth's chairman Edward F. Gibbons. "Members of the National Women's Committee to support J. P. Stevens Workers have been active for over two years now supporting the struggle of the J. P. Stevens workers to achieve decent working conditions and wages which will allow their families to live in human decency," they noted. "As the major purchasers of domestic products we are using our consumer power to help bring justice to the workplace at J. P. Stevens." Despite this appeal, the large retailer continued to be a major stockist of Stevens products.[26]

At the same time, the committee mobilized many of its members to write letters. In April 1979, Mary C. Steele wrote to chairman Ralph Lazarus of Federated Department Stores, arguing that J. P. Stevens was a corporate renegade that flouted both labor and civil rights laws. Referring to Federated's Richway Stores division, she asked, "Why should I buy J. P. Stevens products sold at Richway?" New York resident Joy Chute also argued that Lazarus should not condone Stevens's lawlessness by stocking their products. "I am not 'a special interest group,'" she wrote. "I am a citizen who believes in fair labor practices, and I feel that the Stevens Company has consistently violated these." Many other women cited Stevens's willingness to break the law, together with its record of discrimination against both women and blacks, as compelling proof that the company needed to be isolated from the rest of the corporate community.[27]

In an effort to gain concentrated publicity for its campaign, on November 30, 1978, the union organized Justice for J. P. Stevens' Workers Day, a

Figures 5 and 6. Boycott activists in New York City, 1977. (Images Unlimited/Kheel Center for Labor-Management Documentation and Archives, Cornell University.)

series of coordinated protests that were held right across the country. These activities were well publicized in the press, with the largest demonstrations taking place in major cities—New York, Philadelphia, Detroit, Indianapolis. In New York City, more than three thousand demonstrators noisily marched past Stevens Tower in midtown. In southern cities such as Birmingham, where Ray Rogers addressed a rally at the Central Labor Council, and Knoxville and Atlanta, the protests were smaller.[28] The events were well backed by ACTWU's allies, including representatives from other unions, women's and civil rights groups, and religious organizations. At a rally in Allentown, Pennsylvania, local NOW leader Dixie White explained that she was determined to secure fair wages for Stevens's female workers. "Labor issues and feminist issues are the same issues," she asserted. In Cincinnati, Rev. Tecumseh X. Graham was one of many church leaders who took part in the nationwide protests. "We must do everything we can to ensure decent wages for J. P. Stevens's employees," he declared. "We must march on, march to dignity. The labor movement is the backbone of this country."[29]

Many political leaders also took part in the Justice Day protests. In Portland, Oregon, Governor Bob Straub was one of several state political leaders to endorse a local rally in support of the Stevens workers. In northeastern cities, many local political leaders enthusiastically backed the protests. "Our point," commented Connecticut state senator Joseph Lieberman at a rally in New Haven, "is to send consumers a message to avoid Stevens products, to support the workers and to get the company to recognize the workers' union."[30] In New York, Governor Hugh L. Carey personally backed Justice Day and called Stevens a "notorious corporate scofflaw," saying, "J. P. Stevens has violated the National Labor Relations Act, the cornerstone of labor law, more than any other company in American history."[31]

Despite securing extensive press coverage, Mileski felt that journalists focused too heavily on local actions, overlooking the fact that simultaneous protests had taken place in seventy-four cities. J. P. Stevens also hit back by releasing its own widely circulated press statement. In it the company mounted a vigorous defense of its record, claiming that its workers were better paid than most textile employees and that they should not be "forced into a union." Stevens insisted that its employees had repeatedly rejected outside representation, and it challenged the union to call elections at any of its plants.[32]

The Justice Day protests confirmed that the union's support was largely concentrated in the North. Here many felt that Stevens had contributed to their region's economic problems. In the summer of 1979 the American Jewish Congress asserted that Stevens's low wages had encouraged "the exodus of business from the urban areas of the Northeast to the Sun Belt." Many northern politicians also backed the boycott on these grounds. In August 1978 a letter signed by three New York state senators and four assemblymen claimed that Stevens was "a glaring symbol of runaway shop," and added, "Their actions have encouraged other companies to relocate their manufacturing operations to localities that neither recognize nor respect workers' legitimate right to advocate trade unionism without fear of reprisal."[33] In some northern areas, press coverage noted that local textile plants had been closed by Stevens. Union flyers capitalized on the runaway shop theme. The company's move south, declared one ACTWU leaflet, had caused "tens of thousands of jobs lost in the Northeast."[34]

Virtually all the political endorsements that the union received were from northern Democrats. By July 1978 the boycott had been backed by the governors of Connecticut, Massachusetts, Minnesota, Colorado, and Rhode Island. In addition, four lieutenant governors and three secretaries of state had expressed their support. The boycott was also endorsed by a range of

Figure 7. Boycott demonstration in New York City, late 1970s. (Ed Snider, Images Unlimited/Kheel Center for Labor-Management Documentation and Archives, Cornell University.)

northern senators and city government officials. The same pattern was repeated when it came to members of Congress: of the fifty-six whose backing the union had secured by July 1978, none represented the states of the former Confederacy. Representatives from Michigan, Massachusetts, and New York, all heavily unionized states, were the most numerous.[35]

Other unions joined in supporting the boycott because they were worried about the flight of union shops to the southern states. Asserting that the response of other unions had been "overwhelming," Mileski wrote in October 1977 that "the runaway shop issue, and its relation to J. P. Stevens, has been an important theme in mobilizing this support. The issue has been personalized for the members' understanding and involvement." In the fall of 1978 the Coalition of Labor Union Women typically endorsed the boycott because it felt that Stevens's lawlessness was "undermining our hard-earned wage and working standards by encouraging plants to move into non-union Southern strongholds."[36] Many union members who took part in the Justice Day protests felt that they were also fighting to uphold the labor standards of northern workers. In Allentown, Pennsylvania, local UAW leader Louis Yandrisevits told marchers that other unions should support the boycott because in time they would "have to face the same problems in the South" that ACTWU was facing. Yandrisevits's prediction proved to be accurate, especially for the automobile industry. In the 1980s and 1990s a number of non-union automobile plants were set up in the South, hurting union workers in the north.[37]

While many other unions supported ACTWU's fight, the UAW was particularly active. In the late 1970s the UAW's Community Action Program coordinated what Mileski termed an "extensive program of support" for the Stevens boycott. Right across the country, UAW members participated in boycott activities such as marches and store visits. The autoworkers, wrote Stetin, provided "terrific support" in ACTWU's "crucial struggle with J. P. Stevens."[38] In the Justice Day protests, officials from many central labor councils took part. ACTWU's campaign was even praised by UTW leaders. In the recent past, the two rival textile unions had frequently fought one another, but these differences were put aside when it came to the Stevens campaign. "I hope they're successful," reflected UTW president Francis Schaufenbil in 1978. "If anybody ought to have his ass tanned, it's J. P. Stevens." Viewing the company as a symbol of corporate opposition to unionization, the labor movement united behind ACTWU. "Where Stevens is concerned, all union disagreements disappear," claimed labor law professor Benjamin Aaron. "The Teamsters, Meany, and the U.A.W. can all come together on the Stevens issue, where there's great ideological harmony."[39]

While they were effective at mobilizing northern opinion, union leaders realized that they needed to recruit more support within the South as well. The setting up of SEJ was an effort to address this inbalance. But with SEJ support limited to the African American community and a small group of liberal whites, union strategists hoped that they could use the brown lung issue to build broader support within the South. These efforts were not wholly successful, as most concern about the prevalence of byssinosis again came from northerners. Within the South, community leaders continued to stress the economic benefits that the textile plants provided. Even those who recognized the dangers of cotton dust reasoned that it was a price worth paying for the thousands of jobs that the mills supplied.[40]

Until the early 1970s, the textile industry's economic and political clout successfully blocked efforts to clean up the mills. In 1972 the first federal cotton-dust standard was introduced, but activists complained that it was far too lax. The Nixon administration promised to introduce more stringent controls, yet pressure from southern textile industrialists helped to ensure

Figure 8. Utilizing the "runaway shop" theme in the north. (Kheel Center for Labor-Management Documentation and Archives, Cornell University.)

that they never delivered on this commitment. In 1978 OSHA did implement a new federal standard that set permissible exposure levels for different parts of the plant. The move came after considerable pressure from the newly formed Carolina Brown Lung Association. In the spring of 1977, for example, sixty CBLA members traveled to Washington to tell federal officials why a stricter dust standard was needed. Even with the new directive, it was still estimated that 13 percent of all textile workers would contract byssinosis at some point in their lives. Working with the CBLA, the union pressed for stricter cotton-dust regulations and more effective compensation for victims.[41]

In the North the union was effective at using the brown lung issue to strengthen its calls for the boycott. "Coughing . . . choking . . . gasping for breath" is how one union flyer claimed thousands of southern textile workers spent their days. "In some J. P. Stevens plants," it added, "state and federal inspectors have measured dust and lint in concentrations **up to 12 times** higher than recommended standards." ACTWU effectively publicized the case of Louis Harrell, a Stevens worker who died of byssinosis while the campaign was in full swing. In one widely circulated photograph, Harrell was captured just five days before his death. Lying on his hospital bed, he

Figure 9. Holding aloft a picture of "brown lung" victim Louis Harrell, ACTWU president Sol Stetin leading a boycott protest by union activists. (Kheel Center for Labor-Management Documentation and Archives, Cornell University.)

held up a plaque from Stevens that thanked him for "28 years of loyal and faithful service."[42] In another fact sheet, retired Stevens worker Thomas Malone similarly emphasized the company's ruthlessness. "After 37 years of loyal and faithful service," he reflected, "I have a plaque, $1,360, and brown lung."[43]

Many organizations cited occupational health and safety as the key motivator of their support for the boycott. In a letter to Federated boss Ralph Lazarus, the American Civil Liberties Union claimed that Stevens's "outrageous violations of civil rights" were illustrated by its poor health and safety record. "Permanent physical injury and disfigurement are common in the unsafe machine operations of Stevens," wrote ACLU executive director Ramona Ripston. "Brown Lung disease is an almost inescapable 'retirement benefit' after working for Stevens." In another letter, Emma I. Darnell of Church Women United claimed that "working conditions at many Stevens plants are hazardous and inhumane. Cotton dust levels exceed U.S. government standards; many workers (47% of whom are women) have been the victims of 'Brown Lung' disease."[44]

By the end of 1979, the boycott had also succeeded in gaining some high-profile endorsements from media figures. During the 1979–80 football season, ABC sports commentator Myron Cope personally went to Gimbel's management after ACTWU supporters reported that the retailer's Pittsburgh branch was selling towels made by Stevens. At Pittsburgh Steelers games the fans twirled "terrible towels" in the team colors, black and gold, to put a jinx on the opposition, a practice Cope had helped to popularize. After the union made it known that Stevens manufactured the black towels, the broadcaster intervened. Following considerable media publicity, the store withdrew the offending items from its shelves. Around the same time, actress Jane Fonda also visited Gimbel's in Pittsburgh to protest their continued sale of J. P. Stevens products. When managers refused to meet with her, the actress leafleted outside and spoke to gathering journalists, securing newspaper and television coverage. Stevens responded with a statement denying that they were antiunion and calling Fonda's involvement "ludicrous and misguided."[45]

In 1979 the release of *Norma Rae* gave further impetus to ACTWU's efforts. The film was loosely based on the story of Roanoke Rapids worker Crystal Lee Sutton, a union activist who was fired by the company during the 1973–74 campaign. In August 1973 freelance journalist Henry P. Leiferman first told Crystal Lee's story in a *New York Times Magazine* article on the Stevens campaign. He later wrote a book about Sutton's life and secured

Figure 10. Leafleting a Los Angeles Dodgers baseball game, August 1977. (Kheel Center for Labor-Management Documentation and Archives, Cornell University.)

movie rights, which he sold to *Norma Rae* producer-director Martin Ritt. Filmed at Opelika Manufacturing Company in Opelika, Alabama, *Norma Rae* depicts workers' struggle to organize at the fictional O. P. Henley Textile Company. Although it concentrates rather extensively on the personal relationship between Norma Rae (played by Sally Field) and northern organizer Reuben Warshovsky, the movie gives a generally sympathetic account of the workers' struggle. In its most powerful scene, derived from the incident that led to Norma Rae's discharge, she is ordered out of the plant for trying to copy down an antiunion notice from the company's bulletin board. In protest, she climbs onto a table. Technically obeying the company's orders not to talk about the union during working hours, she then scribbles the word "UNION" onto a piece of paper and holds it above her head. One by one, workers respond by shutting off their noisy machines. The determined employees subsequently succeed in organizing a union, but the film ends with the euphoria of the election victory and conveniently overlooks Stevens's subsequent refusal to sign a contract.[46]

Rather than focusing on abuses of union power, *Norma Rae* identified the viewer with the underdog, low-paid workers simply fighting for the right to improve their working conditions. Overall, the film was a clear boost to ACTWU, especially as Hollywood had traditionally dished up negative portrayals of organized labor. In April 1980 Jacob Sheinkman wrote Sally Field to thank her for her "moving portrayal," concluding, "we have found that a public whose consciousness and awareness has been awakened by the experience of seeing you as 'Norma Rae,' is a public most receptive to lending the active support that the Stevens workers need." As the *Washington Post* noted, the movie certainly helped the union's cause. "Unless the moviegoers happened to be charter members of the National Right to Work Committee," it noted in an editorial, "chances were better than good that he or she would emerge from the theater cheering for Norma Rae and the Union and against the Big, Powerful, Impersonal Company."[47]

Despite the publicity surrounding *Norma Rae*, on the eve of the film's release Sutton herself was still struggling to make ends meet. Although the NLRB eventually reinstated her, she failed to settle and soon quit the mill. In her efforts to find work, Sutton's notoriety as a union activist scared local employers. Sol Stetin also claimed that Stevens had compounded Sutton's problems by writing her a "vicious" reference that mentioned her union activism. She was able to secure only low-paid work in a local Hilton Inn. In August 1979 Sutton reported to Stetin that she had quit this job after a new

Figure 11. Crystal Lee Sutton with ACTWU president Sol Stetin (right), circa 1979. (Cliff Kalick/Kheel Center for Labor- Management Documentation and Archives, Cornell University.)

owner had taken over the hotel and abolished her insurance. "The job itself was bad enough," she noted wryly. "But that was 'the straw that broke the camel's back.'" Despite her problems, and her annoyance that *Norma Rae* had concentrated too much on her tangled personal life, Sutton's faith in trade unions was undiminished. "It makes me feel good," she noted, "to know that the Union is interested in seeing that justice be done to the workers that JP constantly continues to harass, even after the Supreme Court of the United States of America has said this will not be tolerated. Shit, if this happens again, someone will go to jail."[48]

Union leaders were genuinely concerned with Sutton's plight, and they also sensed that she was a "hot news item" that they could use to their advantage. The problem, as Mileski framed it, was "How to pay Crystal Lee without giving the appearance of having bought her." During October and November 1979, the union came up with a plan to pay Sutton $295 a week while she toured the country as "the real Norma Rae," giving speeches and interviews along the way. Her schedule was managed by Gail Jeffords, a professional public relations agent who skillfully concealed the salary that Sutton was receiving.[49]

In the first half of 1980, the union sent Sutton on a nationwide tour of nineteen cities, and they were pleased with the media coverage that she secured. The former Roanoke Rapids textile worker made an appearance on *Good Morning America* and was interviewed by a range of high-circulation newspapers, including the *Detroit Free Press* and the *New York Daily News*. Overall, the tour brought the Stevens story to a potential audience of some seventy-five million people and secured fifty-seven newspaper feature stories, sixty-three local television appearances, and thirty-nine radio appearances. "The most remarkable fact about this campaign," beamed Jeffords, "is that there has NOT BEEN ONE SINGLE NEGATIVE STORY at any time since Crystal's appearances began." Sutton certainly won over journalists with her honesty and modesty, and she effectively conveyed the message that all southern mill workers needed to fight for decent wages and better working conditions. "The election victory at Roanoke Rapids," she asserted, "wasn't just done by the organizer and me as it looks like in the movie. It took a lot of people pulling together to make it work. The workers realized that sticking together—being a union—was the only way."[50]

Sutton highlighted the prominent role that many women played in the Stevens campaign. Throughout the long battle, women were often enthusiastic union recruits and they proved especially skillful at articulating their grievances to a broader audience. In Statesboro, which the union used as a graphic example of Stevens's antiunionism, the workers' struggle for justice was eloquently told by activists such as Myrtle Cribbs and Addie Jackson. "At J. P. Stevens," declared Jackson, "before we started organizing, it wasn't much different than slavery. No lunch hour. Just eat your sandwich while running your machines. And then Stevens closes the plant. They shut us out. . . . that's what they said they'd do and that's what they did. Teach us a lesson."[51] Even after the plant had closed, Jackson claimed that she hoped to return one day "to let them know I'm still around and still kicking." Time and time again, women expressed the power of collective protest well. "Times have changed," maintained Stevens worker Evie Bass in 1978. "People aren't afraid anymore. You know, when just one person stands up or speaks out, it's easy to be afraid. But when a thousand stand up together, there's a lot they can do."[52]

On the whole, the union's campaign certainly succeeded in creating a great deal of positive national news coverage. The northern liberal press provided some of the most favorable. In the summer of 1979, journalist Gloria Emerson slammed Stevens in a lengthy article in the progressive New York publication *Village Voice*. After a visit to the firm's plant in Walterboro, South Carolina, she compared the mill to a "plantation" and accused the company of having a "disgraceful record" of lawlessness. "For years," she wrote, "Stevens has successfully managed to keep the union out, often

Figure 12. Crystal Lee Sutton with Sally Field, who won an Oscar for her depiction of Sutton's life in *Norma Rae*. (Cliff Kalick/Kheel Center for Labor-Management Documentation and Archives, Cornell University.)

through coercion and reprisals, to preserve its immense profits and its control over employees." Writing for the *Nation*, journalist Ed McConville took a similar line. Organizing attempts at the firm's plants had failed, he wrote, not because workers rejected the union but because of the vicious antiunion "war" waged by an intransigent employer.[53] In 1979 northern journalist Mimi Conway's *Rise Gonna Rise* also sympathized with the workers' plight and stressed Stevens's ruthlessness. A lively and accessible account of the Roanoke Rapids conflict, *Rise Gonna Rise* proved popular with readers. The *New York Times* remained an ally for the union, describing the company as "virulently anti-labor" and "a symbol of labor lawlessness." Television coverage was also generally sympathetic. In 1977 special features by CBS's *Sixty Minutes* and PBS's *MacNeill/Lehrer Report* were both favorable to ACTWU. Union strategists circulated the programs as widely as they could. "60 Minutes segment on Stevens campaign generated excellent response in boycott cities around nation," noted Mileski. "We recommend that a print of this segment be made available to all field staff for local use."[54]

ACTWU's leaders took great satisfaction in the broad backing that their campaign had secured. In March 1978, Murray Finley told the executive board "that our union has an image we can be proud of. You cannot pick up a newspaper without seeing something about our union and the campaign." In October 1977 a campaign report made similar claims. "The Stevens story," it stated, "has been told to the American people with such dramatic effectiveness that the name of J. P. Stevens has become a household word." The union had certainly succeeded in its efforts to make many Americans feel that they were part of a broad fight for justice. In March 1980, Hilda Howland M. Mason, cochair of the Citizens Committee for Justice for J. P. Stevens' workers, summed up how many felt: "Millions of Americans, from all walks of life, have come together to view the issues raised by the efforts to organize the J. P. Stevens Company labor force as a compelling cause of social justice—one which far transcends the usual dimensions of labor-management controversy. An impressive coalition of prestigious religious, minority, labor and community groups and leaders have joined to back the J. P. Stevens workers' cause, and have pledged to boycott J. P. Stevens products until the Company grants humane and fair treatment to its employees."[55]

With such backing, ACTWU's leaders were confident of victory. By effectively isolating Stevens, they insisted, their campaign was influencing consumer behavior. "This campaign," claimed Sheinkman, "has established an awareness factor in the American public's mind and even in those who buy for the department stores—a much greater awareness than was manifested in the Farah campaign." It remained to be seen whether these claims were accurate, especially as union strategists were well aware of the difficulties of conducting an effective economic boycott against a company as large and diverse as J. P. Stevens.[56]

SEVEN

Corporate Campaigns and Boycotts

In the late 1970s, ACTWU's leaders concentrated a great
deal of effort on undermining Stevens's public image
partly because they recognized the difficulty of hurting
such a large firm financially. They realized, however, that
their efforts needed to have some economic impact on the
textile giant in order to force a change in its behavior. As
Paul Swaity put it, "The philosophy behind it was that, unless you can hurt their pocketbook, you aren't going to
bring this company down."[1]

An economic boycott against Stevens certainly faced
formidable obstacles. The textile firm sold only around
one-third of its products direct to the consumer, and even
these goods were packaged under a confusing variety of
brand names. Company executives repeatedly claimed
that the boycott failed to hurt their operations, and they
cited record sales figures to bolster their case.[2] In money
terms, union leaders could not claim that their efforts
were a complete success, as many retailers argued that
they could not get involved in an outside labor dispute.
Several of Stevens's biggest customers, including F. W.
Woolworth and J. C. Penney, also insisted that it was their
duty to offer the best range of merchandise possible, and
that it was up to consumers to decide whether they wished
to boycott Stevens products on moral grounds.[3]

Despite these difficulties, a great deal of evidence suggests that the boycott did have a mild impact on the
company's operations. While some retail stores refused to
yield to pressure, others clearly were affected by the cam-

paign. In particular, the boycott undermined Stevens's profits: as several mainline retail stores stopped stocking the company's products, Stevens was forced to sell its goods through discount stores instead. The behavior of Stevens's workers also suggests that the boycott was affecting the firm's operations. Across the South, antiunion workers mobilized into Employee Education Committees (EEC) largely because they felt that the boycott was threatening their job security. The union's corporate campaign, which aimed to create pressure on Stevens by forcing its directors to resign, also undoubtedly secured some positive results. In the late 1970s a series of high-profile resignations rocked the company, and even the business press expressed concern about Ray Rogers's tactics. ACTWU also forged some pioneering bonds with unions in other countries, conducting what it claimed was the first successful international boycott. The union collaborated especially well with Zensen Domei, the Japanese textile union, although it struggled to replicate this success in other countries.[4]

ACTWU leaders hoped to model the Stevens boycott on the Farah campaign, which had hurt the apparel maker and forced it to recognize the ACWA. The comparison was misleading, however, because virtually all of Farah's products were sold on the retail market and offered under the company name. In sharp contrast, Stevens made a wide variety of goods, and many of them were not identifiable brands. In December 1976 only 34 percent of the company's revenue was derived from the sale of its products directly to the retail market, with most income coming from the sale of fabric to other apparel producers. If the union had tried to hurt these sales, it would have been conducting an illegal secondary boycott. Even when Stevens sold direct to the consumer, it was difficult to identify the company's products. Its sheets and pillowcases alone retailed as Beauti-Blend, Beauticale, Fine Arts, Peanuts, Tastemaker, Utica, and Utica and Mohawk, as well as being produced for designer labels such as Yves St. Laurent and Dinah Shore. In 1976 the company also had some 20,900 customers, none of which accounted for more than 5 percent of total sales.[5]

Aware of the problems that confronted the union, company officials repeatedly boasted that the boycott had failed to hurt their operations. In March 1978, Stevens's annual report asserted that sales and profits had "not been affected" by the boycott. Sales figures seem to support this position: in 1978 they were a record $1,651,451,000, a 7 percent increase compared to 1977.[6] Overall, Stevens's sales rose 16.2 percent in the two years after the boycott began, compared to 12.5 percent in the two years before it. In 1979 and

1980 the company continued to enjoy sales growth, reporting gains of 11 percent and 4.5 percent. Earnings per share did fall in the two years after the boycott was launched, but this drop was in line with broader industry patterns.[7]

It is very difficult to assess the boycott's exact economic impact upon Stevens, especially as the company did not break down its earnings to reflect the profitability of those products that it sold to the retail market. In general, however, the records of the campaign suggest that it did have a mild impact on sales. Written in February 1980, one confidential report found "weakness in the recent performance of Stevens' home furnishings segment," which the boycott was concentrating on. In this segment, income fell from 34 percent of total sales in 1978 to 29 percent in 1979. The report also documented that the number of customer accounts fell from more than 20,000 in 1978 to around 16,000 in 1979, confirming that the union's efforts to persuade private consumers to withdraw their patronage were having some effect.[8]

Concentrating on Stevens's profitability, rather than its sales, presents a different picture. In 1979 a research paper by Rutgers University student George A. Kelly looked at Stevens's profit margins, derived by dividing net profits for a twelve-month period by net sales. Kelly concluded that Stevens was underpricing its product line in order to sustain high levels of both sales and earnings. His data showed that the company's profitability was well below the industry average. Executives seemed to be trying to mask the impact of the boycott by offloading their products cheaply, a dangerous tactic because it reduced the company's ability to reinvest in its operations. In December 1978, James Finley admitted that his company had sold many products "substantially below cost" over the previous two years. Around the same time, even the promanagement *Business Week* acknowledged that the boycott was at least partially effective. "The boycott," it noted, "as well as union attacks on Stevens' management, are having an increasing impact on the big textile producer." A survey by the journal found "some evidence" that Stevens products were not being displayed in major department stores as much as they had been previously.[9]

The company's workers also claimed that the boycott was having an impact, and many set up antiunion committees to express their concerns. Although ACTWU charged that these groups were controlled by the company, their members did not ape Stevens's efforts to downplay the boycott's effectiveness. In March 1977 several antiunion workers were interviewed by CBS reporter Mike Wallace. "With the boycott, my job has been shut down," claimed one Roanoke Rapids worker. "Hundreds of looms standing in there. It doesn't look good at all. I think the union should help us sell our products instead of boycotting our products." Gene Patterson, a leading figure in the Roanoke Rapids EEC, similarly claimed in December 1976 that, "This union come in . . . they put a boycott against our company, and that's forcing us out of our jobs, and I don't think that the people in Roanoke Rapids really need that." Although workers may have blamed the boycott for curtailments that would have occurred anyway, their concerns were deep-rooted and were based on firsthand experience in the plants.[10]

Some retail outlets did clearly prove receptive to the boycott campaign. At Richway stores in the Atlanta area, union pressure undoubtedly made a difference. Boycott activists initially met with the president of Rich's, the parent company of Richway, but he refused to make specific commitments. Following pressure from protesters, the company's line changed. "Since Christmas 1977," reported local coordinator Joel Gay, "the amount of JPS products carried by Rich's has been small. Usually one or two designs. Before the stores had many designs." By the summer of 1979, Gay noted triumphantly that "Richway, the discount division of Rich's, has almost cleared its shelves of JPS products." Working with women's, church, and civil rights groups, the union mounted a widespread letter-writing campaign against Rich's, with many customers promising never to shop at the store until it stopped ordering from Stevens. "I have been a shopper at Rich's for many years," wrote Decatur resident W. J. Ford in one typical letter. "I support the consumer boycott against J. P. Stevens and will not buy J. P. products. . . . I will inform my friends and neighbors about the consumer boycott, and that Rich's is selling Stevens products."[11]

Union pressure on Jordan Marsh, a major outlet for Stevens products in New England, also produced results. In a September 1979 meeting with the Women's Committee for Justice for J. P. Stevens' Workers, Jordan Marsh chairman William Tilburg insisted that he could not cut back on Stevens products while his competitors were continuing to stock them. Repeated petitioning and letter writing, including approaches to Thomas Macioce, president of Jordan Marsh's parent company, Allied Stores, eventually led to a change. In a series of meetings with Macioce, the Allied boss made private pledges to reduce his firm's reliance on Stevens, following through on these commitments by reporting sales figures to the boycott strategists. He also told these staffers that thanks to the union's campaign Stevens had "lost a lot of main-line department stores" and was trying to sell its products through discount stores instead.[12]

It was in the large northern cities that the boycott was able to attract the strongest support. Philadelphia, for example, was described by Mileski as a "model for all boycott cities." By March 1977, strong citizens' and labor committees were engaged in a campaign of store visits in the Pennsylvania metropolis. With careful planning, their efforts were producing results. Aware that Wanamaker's leading executives were Presbyterians, boycott staff selected several Presbyterian ministers to meet with them. "Wanamaker's subsequently announced cancellation of entire line of Stevens products," noted Mileski, "with exception of one line of towels." In New Haven, Connecticut, an active boycott chapter also reported positive results. In February 1978 area director Mike Szpak related that a range of retail stores and hotels, including both the Sheraton Park Plaza Hotel and Macy's stores, had voluntarily canceled Stevens lines.[13]

The union's success should certainly not be exaggerated, as many companies proved resistant to outside pressure. Despite repeated efforts, boycott supporters were unable to make any progress with the management of Woolworth's stores. A boycott delegation told Woolworth representatives in June 1980: "There has been no change despite all the groups that have met with you." Strategists were also dissatisfied with the position taken by Zayre's, a major retailer with more than 250 stores. In March 1979 the firm's top executives met with campaigners but made few commitments. "Zayre's met reluctantly as a result of national pressure and the VP.'s were insulting to the committee throughout the meeting," reported Mileski. "The voluntary cutbacks which the Zayre's management proposed were totally inadequate."[14] Both Sears and J. C. Penney also sold a great deal of Stevens products under their own brand names and proved reluctant to change suppliers. Between them, the two retailers had more than two thousand stores and remained crucial customers for the southern textile firm. Sears was especially valuable because it also sold the firm's products through its 1,470 retail telephone sales offices. Montgomery Ward similarly provided Stevens with a great deal of telephone-generated business and proved equally unwilling to find an alternative supplier.[15]

Retail executives gave a variety of reasons for refusing to honor the boycott. Most commonly, they insisted that they had to remain neutral during labor disputes. Montgomery Ward vice president Richard C. Scheidt re-

Figure 13. Protesters targeting Gimbel's store in Philadelphia. (Press Associates/Kheel Center for Labor-Management Documentation and Archives, Cornell University.)

sponded to pressure to boycott Stevens by citing "our Company's long standing policy of not becoming involved in labor disputes between Wards suppliers and their unions." Executives argued that, if they abandoned this principle, they could be subjected to pressure from other "special interest" groups. They also asserted that it would be wrong to try to influence the behavior of another firm. "Our position with respect to this dispute is one of strict neutrality and 'hands off,'" wrote Sears vice president C. F. Bacon.[16]

Many firms also asserted that it was up to customers to choose which products they would buy, and that stores should not influence their decision. At Woolworth's, "our policy is to offer our customers quality merchandise at competitive prices, and we believe we do that better than any other retailer in the nation," explained vice president J. F. Carroll. "As is their prerogative, those customers may freely choose to buy or not buy any of the products or services available to them. We do not believe that we should impinge on that prerogative nor take any action inconsistent with our position with respect to this controversy." Executives were reluctant to take a moral stand. In September 1980 a J. C. Penney official typically argued that his company was "solely a merchandising organization and must judge our suppliers on the value of the goods or services they produce for us."[17]

Some executives chided the union for attempting a boycott of Stevens products. Richard C. Scheidt argued that the effort would hurt "the very employees" that the union was seeking to assist. He also asserted that there were only "limited available sources in the United States" for the type of products that Stevens made. "Turning to non-U.S. employers for such products would not assist the United States economy," he declared. Scheidt added that it was up to the NLRB and the courts to resolve the Stevens case, an argument repeated by other executives. Randall E. Copeland, president of Strawbridge and Clothier, fended off boycott pressure by arguing that it was important not to take a position in the dispute until "the final judgments have been rendered by the proper regulatory and legal bodies." Some executives were also keen to refute suggestions that they lacked a social conscience. In meetings with boycott leaders, Woolworth's managers pointed out that their company made sizeable donations to many nonprofit organizations, including some civil rights groups.[18]

As part of its campaign, ACTWU also tried to place international pressure on J. P. Stevens by working with unions in countries where the company operated facilities. At the time of the boycott, Stevens jointly owned textile plants in Mexico, Australia, New Zealand, Canada, France, and Japan. In its campaign, the union forged important bonds with unions in these countries. In particular, Japanese trade unionists campaigned fervently against the textile maker, donated funding to the cause, and helped to stop Stevens goods from entering their country. Del Mileski also made trips to Europe, where he enlisted the support of union leaders in England, Holland, West Germany, and Belgium. ACTWU leaders took pride in the endorsements they received from labor colleagues around the globe. In December 1977, Jacob Sheinkman told his executive board colleagues that they were coordinating "the first international boycott that is being undertaken successfully." Such claims were overstated, as efforts to boycott Stevens goods in international markets were often ineffective. Still, ACTWU did pioneer the strategy of working with overseas unions to create pressure against a multinational corporation.[19]

During the boycott, ACTWU cooperated most effectively with Zensen Domie, the Japanese textile union. The Asian union became involved in the campaign after its president attended a meeting of international labor leaders in Washington, D.C., in September 1977, a gathering that brought together union heads from several countries where Stevens ran plants. Presided over by George Meany, it sought to develop strategies for exerting pressure on the textile giant in these overseas markets. Upon their president's return, Zensen Domei's executive council voted to try to extend the boycott to Japan. Mobilizing support from their members, leaders also showed a dubbed account of the Stevens struggle at their annual convention. Following this, delegates passed a unanimous resolution in favor of a boycott. "We can never tolerate," it declared, "the use of products made by J. P. Stevens, which goes against democracy, oppresses its workers, dares committing 1,500 violations of laws, and repeats many offenses trampling down social justice." According to Takashi Izumi, who headed the Stevens boycott in Japan, this resolution led to the union setting aside a "substantial operating budget" to fund its efforts. Izumi noted that the Japanese unionists were keen to help their American counterparts because they had a strong belief in international solidarity. Many Zensen Domei members were especially grateful that the TWUA had sent them money and moral support in the mid-1950s when they had been engaged in a major dispute with Ohmikenshi Cotton Shipping Factory.[20]

The Zensen Domei committee organized a number of protest actions, including demonstrations in Tokyo, Nagoya, and Osaka where union members wore "devil-style" black cloaks and skullcaps. "These masks represent demons," explained Izumi, "and for us unionists Stevens is the demon." The union also distributed handbills outside major department stores, placed posters in commuter trains, took out newspaper advertisements, and issued press releases. Most important, it was able to stop the importation of Stevens goods into Japan. The union's efforts were helped by the fact that all textile imports into the Asian country were funneled through trading agencies that had sole rights of marketing and distribution. The boycott in Japan was clearly effective, as the sole Japanese importing agent quickly confirmed that it was not importing from the American firm "for some time until the situation clears up."[21]

Mileski and his staff were able to secure expressions of support from several other overseas unions. The Brussels-based International Textile, Garment, and Leather Workers' Federation (ITGLWF) endorsed the boycott and encouraged its affiliates to get involved in the campaign. Some responded by pressuring local stockists of the firm's merchandise. In May 1980 the Belgian union SETCA, which represented clerical and technical employees, wrote to managers of the Innovation and Bon Marché stores, both of which sold Stevens goods. The American firm, they noted, "defies the fundamental rights of workers and disregards the law with impunity. . . . In this company discriminatory hiring practices and the firing of trade unionists is a regular practice. . . . We request you to examine the possibility of ordering such products from other firms."[22]

The International Confederation of Free Trade Unions, a worldwide body with over five million members, also supported ACTWU's efforts. In May 1977 the ICFTU's executive board met in Rome and heard a report on the Stevens situation from the ITGLWF. They then pledged their support for a "worldwide boycott campaign of J. P. Stevens and Co. products . . . with a view to pressuring this multinational company to respect trade union rights of its employees in the U.S.A." ACTWU leaders were pleased to receive these endorsements. Such solidarity, claimed Murray Finley, "clearly announces to labor-exploiting companies worldwide that there is no refuge for them in foreign markets."[23]

ACTWU staffers also used their contacts with British trade unionists to try to improve the boycott's effectiveness. In September 1979 representatives from the British Tobacco Workers' Union had a "formal discussion" with the board of directors of British American Tobacco, Gimbel's parent company. The union leaders wanted BAT to influence its American subsidiary to stop trading with Stevens. Although they were sympathetic, BAT's directors declined to interfere in the controversy, insisting that Gimbel's operated in a different labor relations climate. As Trades Union Congress general secretary Lionel Murray reported, BAT's directors "said that they understood that British trade unions would not expect to fight for recognition for thirty years but that US legislation made the situation in America wholly different."[24]

Despite the support of international unions, it proved very difficult to implement an effective boycott in European markets. A major obstacle was the familiar problem of accurately identifying Stevens products, which were sold under a wide variety of brand names. In European countries, the company's merchandise was even harder to identify. Many stores in Great Britain, for example, sold American-made towels and sheets under their own label, making it impossible to know whether they were supplied by Stevens or other American firms. Hired to spread the boycott to stores in London, Norwegian unionist Helge Christophersen reported on the problems to ACTWU leaders. "The very nature of my task in fact turned out to be very complicated," she explained. "I checked thousands of towels, sheets, carpets, etc. in London and looked more and more desperately after the Stevens label as known in the U.S. These labels I did not see; however, a remarkably big part of the towels, sheets, etc. had the mark *Made in the U.S.A.* . . . . A basic problem I was faced with was the fact that all the chain stores and supermarkets on nearly all products *had their own label.* . . . So looking for Stevens labels was no easy thing."[25]

A variety of other problems held back an international boycott. In France a boycott was illegal, and American staff also complained that French unions were not sufficiently cooperative. British unions were more sympathetic, but as Stevens had no plants in the U.K., the British campaign lacked focus.[26] In Europe, getting the boycott off the ground proved problematic, as both sides complained that they were not receiving sufficient information from the other. Attempting to kick-start their efforts, American staff hastily encouraged the Europeans to boycott Fruit of the Loom products. The brand name was commonly seen in Europe, and staffers initially believed that all Fruit of the Loom merchandise was produced by Stevens. They later discovered, however, that the U.S. textile firm was licensed to use the brand name only for women's hosiery. This resulted in considerable confusion, as Europeans had already received literature telling them to boycott all Fruit of the Loom products. Fred Dyson, general secretary of the British National Union of Dyers, Bleachers, and Textile Workers, was angry about the mix-up. "This Union has gone to a great deal of expense to assist our American colleagues," he wrote, "but, in future, we shall be very reluctant to take part in any similar campaign if we are not issued with correct and detailed information."[27]

Several of Stevens's foreign plants were organized. The Stevens-Bremner factory in Foxton, New Zealand, was under contract with the New Zealand textile workers' union, and the labor agreement provided for a union shop and automatic checkoff. A plant in New South Wales, Australia, also had a contract providing for the union shop, dues checkoff, and arbitration. National labor laws ensured that Stevens was pushed to agree to terms that it steadfastly refused to grant in its American plants. In addition, the managers of overseas operations, many of which Stevens did not own outright, were given considerable autonomy in labor relations. Overseas union leaders were concerned about the vigor with which company officials resisted unionization in the United States. In September 1977 a group of foreign union leaders from Stevens's plants in Australia, New Zealand, Japan, Mexico, and France publicly pledged to help ACTWU's fight. The labor leaders also noted that Stevens workers in their countries were much better off than their American counterparts. "The workers in the Stevens plants in our countries enjoy relatively higher wages, more extensive benefits and far better working conditions than those in the company's U.S. plants," they asserted.[28]

Despite the public assurances of support, in some cases the good relations that unions had established with Stevens affiliates made it difficult to build support for an international boycott. In Australia, where the joint venture Stevens-Bremner operated a carpet manufacturing plant, textile union leader Bill Hughes reported to American unionists that the plant was "a 100% Union organised establishment." Stevens-Bremner paid above-average wages, abided by the conditions of a national bargaining award, and had a good health and safety record. As a result, Hughes flatly refused to support the boycott and wrote that "the Australian Textile Workers' Union would not be party to any ban being applied to any of the commodities of the above Company which are produced by Australian labour in Australia as the rapport that exists between the Company and the Union is of the highest order."[29]

In any event, working with international union leaders was unlikely to bring Stevens to the bargaining table in the United States, since only a small portion of the company's products were sold overseas. Stevens's reports to the Securities and Exchange Commission indicate that exports amounted to less than 5 percent of total net sales, while the firm's holdings in foreign ventures were modest investments.[30] While the company's overseas interests were limited, however, they should not be dismissed as unimportant. Profitability was higher in the foreign plants, and Stevens recognized that it was unlikely to increase its market share in the fiercely competitive U.S. market. As *Fortune* noted in April 1963, Stevens was interested in overseas expansion and had made "a deliberate but growing commitment to the markets of Western Europe."[31]

The union's efforts were more successful in producing negative publicity against the company in foreign markets. In France, activists concentrated their campaign upon the mass media, holding press conferences in Lille and Paris, arranging for screenings of *Norma Rae*, and issuing media kits to more than five hundred journalists. In Great Britain, similar efforts resulted in press coverage in two leading newspapers, as well as in union publications. The international edition of *Newsweek* also carried a story detailing the Zensen Domei campaign. "Japanese textile workers," it noted, "have answered a call from American textile unions to organize a boycott of J. P. Stevens Co. products in Japan because the big U.S. firm has resisted union efforts to organize employees at its plants in the United States."[32]

While ACTWU did mobilize a considerable degree of support from other unions, both at home and abroad, U.S. staffers complained that their own local unions were not sufficiently supportive. One December 1978 analysis grumbled about a "lack of activity" by ACTWU members. "The most important problems in sustaining and expanding boycott activity," explained strategist Tom Thompson, "continue to be the lack of involvement of ACTWU affiliates, and the lack of labor council activity."[33] Primarily concerned with their own grievances, many ACTWU members were too removed from the Stevens struggle. In the summer of 1978, the union tried to remedy this by instituting a Worker-to-Worker program. Under this initiative, the union paid its own members to be temporary organizers on the Stevens campaign. Designed to raise members' awareness of the struggle, the program also gave unorganized workers the chance to talk to rank-and-file unionists. The number of workers hired through the program was relatively small, however, and strategists continued to complain that their members were not sufficiently involved in the fight against Stevens.[34]

In an effort to exert economic pressure against Stevens, the union launched a corporate campaign that ran alongside the boycott. This effort was headed up by Raymond Franklin Rogers, a maverick campaigner whose controversial and innovative tactics gained a considerable amount of media attention. Described by the *Charlotte Observer* as a "vegetarian, weight lifter, and social activist," Rogers was in many respects an unconventional union staffer. He had, however, been raised in a labor household in Massachusetts, where his father worked at the General Electric plant in Lynn. A heavily built man, Rogers was an offensive lineman for the high-school football team, and he later set a New England weight-lifting record for the Olympic press. After graduating from the University of Massachusetts with a sociology degree, he first became active in the labor movement in the early 1970s. During the Farah campaign of 1973–74, Rogers played a key role in pressuring merchants in Birmingham, Alabama, to stop selling the firm's slacks. In mid-1976 he returned to work for the ACWA, who were in the process of merging with the TWUA. Impressed by his work on the Farah campaign, TWUA leaders were eager to involve Rogers in the Stevens struggle. Confident of success, Rogers quickly used the opportunity to launch the very first "corporate campaign."[35]

When applied to the Stevens campaign, Rogers's strategy involved extending the union's battle with the company to the financial and insurance industries that provided its financial footing. By harassing and annoying these companies, Rogers aimed to pressure Stevens to capitulate. "The focus of the corporate campaign," he explained, "is Stevens' corporate headquarters and those institutions that are heavily tied in with Stevens interests through interlocking directorates, large stockholdings, and multimillion-dollar loans. The goal of the corporate campaign is to cause those institutions to exert their considerable influence on Stevens and persuade them to recognize the rights and dignity of the workers, and to sit down and bargain in good faith. We understand, however, that they will exert their influence only when they realize that it is in their own primary self-interest to do so."[36]

Rogers's first target was New York–based Manufacturers Hanover Trust Company, selected because two Stevens officers, James Finley and David W. Mitchell, sat on its board. The bank, which held more than $1 million in union trust and pension funds, was also selected by Rogers because of its "indebtedness to the labor movement." Although all of their resolutions were soundly defeated, the union contingent effectively disrupted the Manufacturers Hanover shareholders' meeting, as protesters accused Stev-

Figure 14. Ray Rogers, pictured at the height of the corporate campaign. (Images Unlimited/Kheel Center for Labor-Management Documentation and Archives, Cornell University.)

ens of maintaining dangerous and unhealthy working conditions. Timothy Smith, director of the Interfaith Center on Corporate Responsibility, typically charged that executives had employed "obstructive and illegal tactics" in order to thwart unionization. In addition, Rogers helped to organize a popular letter-writing campaign that allowed union supporters to keep up the pressure on the two embattled executives.[37]

In the spring of 1978, the campaign secured real results when Finley announced that he was being forced to leave the Manufacturers Hanover board. Mitchell also confirmed that he would not seek reelection, although he cited the pressure of work as his major consideration. Union leaders were having none of it; the move, they asserted, was the reflection of their threats to withdraw union funds. "This is the culmination of a campaign," noted ACTWU spokesman Burt Beck. "The hot seat was put under Manufacturers Hanover," added Rogers, "and they had to get rid of those two directors." Unlike Mitchell, Finley made it clear that he had not wanted to leave the board. He would not run for reelection, he explained in a terse statement, because "You don't go where you are not wanted."[38]

Rogers now shifted his focus to other targets. In particular, he publicized that Stevens board member Mitchell was the chairman of Avon Products, the high-profile cosmetics manufacturer. A wide-ranging campaign effectively connected Mitchell with Stevens's aggressive opposition to the unionization of its women workers, and the pressure eventually told. As *Newsweek* explained, "Avon Products chairman David W. Mitchell resigned from the Stevens board after receiving a rush of mail and telephone calls questioning his affiliation with a company that has long been organized labor's number one pariah."[39] Women's groups played an important role in securing Mitchell's resignation. At the 1977 International Women's Year Convention in Houston, delegates sent thousands of postcards to Avon, while many more wrote letters after the convention. "This deluge of mail," claimed boycott staffer Carol Somplatsky-Jarman, "made it clear to Avon that the company's glamorous image was being tarnished among broad sectors of the women's movement by its association with the notorious labor law violator J. P. Stevens."[40]

Mitchell cited pressure from the union as the cause of his resignation. "I cannot permit Avon," he explained in his statement, "to be drawn into the conflict and to be subjected to the pressures which the union is exerting as a result of my Stevens board membership." Saying that his position had become untenable, Mitchell added that even Avon's door-to-door representatives were being questioned by customers about their company's relationship with Stevens. As he later reflected, "when it became apparent to me that my membership on the Stevens board was becoming detrimental to Avon, I had to get off; that was the only factor."[41]

Other victories soon followed for the corporate campaign. In September 1978, Ralph Manning Brown Jr., chairman and CEO of New York Life Insurance, resigned from the Stevens board because of union pressure. At the same time, James Finley gave up his directorship on the board of New York Life. Both men resigned after the union had announced plans to contest their reelections to the New York Life board. This would have required ballots being sent to millions of policyholders, a costly and time-consuming undertaking. Probusiness publications repeatedly complained about the union's tactics, demonstrating that they were effective. In one typical editorial, *Barron's* claimed that ACTWU was using unfair blackmail tactics. "The ACTWU dispute vs. J. P. Stevens," it warned, "is no labor dispute: it is class warfare in disguise." Stevens replaced Brown and Mitchell with an attorney and a college president, and Rogers insisted that powerful business figures were no longer willing to sit on its board. The appointment of North Carolina attorney Winifred T. Wells was also a partial victory for the campaign, as union staffers had complained that the Stevens board was composed entirely of white men.[42]

As part of his "campaign of exposure," Rogers tried to secure the resignation of E. Virgil Conway, a Stevens director and chairman of the Seamen's Bank for Savings. In October 1979 protesters in New York City targeted Conway. Along Park Avenue, pickets formed a human billboard that was more than twelve blocks long. In the downtown financial district, a similar demonstration took place, grabbing press attention. In both cases, protesters stood on sidewalks and waved signs reading "Break the J. P. Stevens–Seamen's Bank Connection." Rogers claimed that more than two thousand people took part in the demonstration, although Conway himself asserted that the number was more like four hundred. Although the embattled executive was reluctant to resign, union pressure eventually forced him to do so.[43]

Union strategists took heart from the negative publicity and embarrassment that they had caused Stevens. "This campaign," boasted strategist Alan Derickson, "continues to succeed in generating embarrassment for JPS in the business 'community.'" Rogers agreed, asserting that Stevens's "stature on Wall St." was "diminishing." Derickson boasted that while firms did not openly condemn Stevens, most were standing back and allowing them to

Figure 15. Members of the International Ladies Garment Workers Union taking part in the Seamen's Bank protests. (Images Unlimited/Kheel Center for Labor-Management Documentation and Archives, Cornell University.)

"get blasted publicly." Rogers's tactics evidently worried many business leaders and helped to pave the way for the eventual settlement in the fall of 1980.[44]

The union's successes should not be exaggerated, as not all those targeted by ACTWU succumbed to the pressure. Goldman Sachs had several executives who served as Stevens directors, and they stood by the company. "To us," explained one, "the company is making substantial efforts to conduct itself as a responsible corporate citizen." In the South, in particular, much of the business community remained broadly supportive of Stevens. In addition, the boycott and corporate campaign encouraged the company to launch a counterattack against the union. From the start of the boycott, it was clear that Stevens was in no mood to compromise, and it would take more than four years of campaigning before the two sides could finally reach a settlement.[45]

EIGHT

The Backlash

Just as the boycott led to the mobilization of liberal groups, it also acted as a rallying cry for conservatives. In the late 1970s much of the business community mobilized behind J. P. Stevens, feeling that the firm was being unfairly victimized by the union and its allies. In the South, many executives backed the embattled textile company because they did not want unions to increase their presence in the region. Conservative groups took up Stevens's traditional argument that the vast majority of its workers did not want to be represented by a "third party." The voices of these workers, they argued, were not being heard; as a result, they funded a range of antiunion employee committees to speak out against the boycott. Between 1976 and 1980 these groups emerged as a formidable opponent for the union.[1]

At the same time, the boycott led Stevens executives to become much more vocal in defending their position. Swiftly abandoning their previous policy of not responding directly to the union's allegations, Stevens now produced a full range of polished position papers and letters. These efforts did help the company to undercut the union's campaign. In the South, Stevens continued to receive a lot of community support, helped by the fact that most of ACTWU's allies came from outside the region.[2]

Stevens's officials were determined to fight back against any boycott. As early as June 1976, before the official launch of the boycott, the company issued its first public warning shot: "It has been the policy of Stevens for many years not to engage in public debate with the Textile Workers Union.

The boycott now makes it necessary that the public at large hear our side of the controversy and be informed of the circumstances which have led to a deliberate endeavor by the merged union to paralyze Stevens." Over the next few years, Stevens became increasingly adept at fighting its own public relations battle, laying out systematic and well-argued responses to ACTWU's allegations.[3]

CEO James D. Finley led the way, penning several well-written letters that were mailed to all of the company's workers. Finley consistently viewed the boycott as a destructive tactic that highlighted the irresponsibility of an overly powerful labor movement. "The union and the leaders of Big Labor," he claimed, "are openly trying to destroy our Company and with it the jobs of 45,000 people. Their actions indicate that they have no concern for Stevens employees." Finley admitted that his company was not "perfect," but he denied that executives had deliberately tried to violate the law. He encouraged workers to speak out and lobby against the boycott, and to publicize the union's own "violations of the law, including criminal convictions for violence and destruction of property." The indignant executive was in no mood to compromise. "We believe J. P. Stevens is a fine place to work," he noted. "You can be sure of one thing—it is the full intention of your management to keep it that way."[4]

The company also tried to undercut the support that the union was receiving from outside organizations. Between 1977 and 1980, company executives gave many addresses to church leaders, students, and other interested citizens. During an April 1978 visit to Cornell University, director of administration E. Marshall Palmer emphasized the company's "positive aspects," including its provision of jobs to 45,000 people and its "good reputation" within the South. Cornell students had expressed considerable support for the boycott, and the executives did not get an easy ride. Referring to Stevens's health and safety record, one student even accused the firm of "literally murdering people," and fumed, "I want to know how you sleep at night." Company executive Stewart Apragginis responded angrily; the student, he claimed, simply had the "wrong facts." In a more conciliatory follow-up, Palmer admitted that some of the union's charges did have "some basis in fact," but added that "many have been distorted out of proportion."[5]

Company executives spent a considerable amount of time in meetings with church leaders, including representatives from the United Methodist Church and the Churches of Christ. In November 1976, Palmer also gave a lengthy speech to a gathering of Presbyterian church leaders, complaining that Stevens's workers did not want to be unionized and that a reputable company was being unfairly targeted. "To put all this in some perspective," he commented, "it must be recognized that the union campaign has been waged with unrelenting pressure against Stevens over a thirteen-year period. Its length, its intensity, and its marked lack of success are probably without parallel in the history of union organizing campaigns."[6] Some of these efforts clearly secured results; the Presbyterians, for instance, failed to offer a national endorsement of the union's campaign. In addition, the company's position was strongly backed by individual Presbyterian, Methodist, and Baptist ministers, particularly in the South. Keen to show that not all religious leaders supported ACTWU's campaign, Stevens gathered these endorsements into its own well-disseminated dossier.[7]

Many of the ministers who supported the company lived in communities where Stevens was the dominant employer. For them, the textile firm was a vital economic provider. As one cleric from Halifax, Virginia, put it, "In our community the local J. P. Stevens plant is a good employer and a responsible part of our community life." Ministers cited the boycott as proof that the union would only jeopardize local workers' well-being. "I am mystified," claimed a Presbyterian pastor from Greenville, South Carolina, "by an organization that claims to have the worker's welfare at heart, and conducts a boycott that may cost many jobs." Some religious leaders pointed out that ACTWU's supporters were mainly outsiders. "Boycott support," claimed a Baptist minister from Anderson, South Carolina, "comes largely from people far removed from my community. They are separated by distance— and misinformation—from those of us most affected by their actions."[8]

The company's position was similarly supported by much of the southern press, particularly in communities where it operated its plants. Concerned about ACTWU's proposed boycott, in mid-1976 both the *Greenville News-Piedmont* and the *Greenville Piedmont* ran antiunion editorials. Such an effort, they argued, indicated that the union really cared little for the welfare of Stevens's southern workers.[9] In 1977 the local paper in Hendersonville, North Carolina, also came out strongly against the textile union. Hendersonville was located in a western part of the state that was heavily dependent on the textile industry, and its local paper pictured the Stevens campaign as an effort by northern union leaders to recapture an industry that they had lost to the "unorganized South." Like other southern papers, the *Hendersonville Times-News* argued that union wage demands were themselves to blame for these shutdowns. "Nobody in the South is starving," it boasted, "but unemployment in Detroit, Buffalo, Utica, New York is high because of taxes and union wage scales." The *Times-News* insisted that local people were better off with stable jobs, even if they did receive less pay than their northern counterparts. "The J. P. Stevens drive," it concluded, "is an example where external forces are at work to decide a state and regional question."[10]

Stevens itself played on the regional divide by trying to picture the union and its supporters as outsiders who were "badmouthing" the South. "Reduced to its essence," claimed Palmer, "the Union's position seems to be that there's something inherently better if a plant is opened in the North (where unionization tends to be higher) than if expansion takes place in the South." In fact, the company argued that southern economic growth had not hurt the North. Instead, it was union wage demands that were responsible for the deindustrialization of the northern states. Stevens managers also asserted that wages were lower in the South simply because the cost of living was lower. The entire South, concluded Stevens, was a "pawn" for union leaders who were really trying to protect the high wages of their northern members.[11]

In a range of forums, Stevens also mounted a vigorous response to the union's health and safety campaign. Executives now acknowledged that byssinosis could be caused by breathing cotton dust, yet they insisted that it was "very difficult" to separate the condition from "other lung diseases which can be caused by smoking cigarettes or the general environment in which a person may live." In January 1978 they also claimed the company had recently spent around $6 million on efforts to reduce cotton dust levels. As a result, they insisted, their mills were clean places to work.[12] Overall, the company was making "every reasonable attempt to lick the problem of brown lung disease." It was not possible to comply fully with federal health and safety regulations, they added, in view of the "staggering cost."[13]

In the fall of 1977 the company's willingness to publicly respond to the union's campaign was demonstrated well. A decade earlier, Stevens had refused to participate in a congressional hearing on labor law reform, insisting that its side of the story would not be listened to properly by the House's labor subcommittee. Now, however, executives mounted a spirited defense of their case in the nation's capital. Accusing the union of making "false and fraudulent" allegations, they argued that Stevens had always complied with the NLRB's timetables. What the union disliked, they insisted, was that the company had defended itself to the fullest extent of the law. They also argued that it was the union that had initiated "the contest and controversy which now centers around this Company," repeating their claims that the workers themselves did not desire outside representation. Rather than wanting to help these workers, managers insisted, ACTWU leaders were simply using the company's employees in a drive to ensure their institutional survival. "For the Union leaders," they claimed, "the stakes are high. They are not interested merely in unionizing Stevens. They view Stevens as the gateway to broader horizons. Their further target is the Southern Textile Industry generally—which in turn, in their long-range projections, will open the way to the unionization of all areas and industries not now unionized in this Country. This is the true motivation for the systematic and continuous denunciation of our Company—no matter, as we have shown, that it is unjustified and false in truth and fact."[14]

Many other executives viewed the Stevens case as a test of union power. In particular, textile industrialists saw the case as vital in determining the fate of union efforts to organize the South. Writing in the *New York Times,* respected labor columnist A. H. Raskin noted that southern textile manufacturers regarded Stevens as "their prime bulwark against engulfment in a union tide that would undermine their freedom to manage their business and wreck profitability." Robert E. Coleman, president of the South Carolina Textile Manufacturers' Association, even admitted to Raskin that the union's efforts had industrialists "running scared." Textile executives rallied around Stevens. In March 1977, just a few months after the launching of the boycott, the southern-dominated American Textile Manufacturers' Institute chose James Finley as their new president. In a public display of support for the Stevens official, the ATMI also held up Finley as their Textile Man of the Year. "The textile industry," noted the *MacNeill/Lehrer Report*, "considers J. P. Stevens its standard-bearer in the ongoing fight to prevent unionization of some 700,000 southern textile workers."[15]

It was not just textile companies that viewed the Stevens dispute as a line in the sand. In 1979 ACTWU obtained a copy of an interview with George Hood, an antiunion consultant who had helped to organize several of the employee committees. The confidential interview was conducted by staff at *Southern Exposure,* a liberal journal based at the University of North Carolina. In it Hood emphasized that he was helping Stevens because he felt that broader issues were at stake. "The longer I've been at it," he reflected, "the more I feel that it isn't the Stevens fight, it's everybody's fight, and it's either help Stevens or we all sink together." The fate of the campaign was also closely monitored by Patrick B. Comer Associates, a promanagement consultancy based in Greensboro, North Carolina. *Labor Analysis and Forecast,* Comer's newsletter, devoted special issues to the Stevens struggle that were widely circulated to southern firms. "J. P. Stevens, with 46,000+ workers, is considered by all unions as the key to organizing the industrial South," it explained. "So all industry should be interested."[16]

In one 1977 issue, *Labor Analysis and Forecast* noted with concern that the union had been successful in recruiting a wide variety of supporters. The management journal claimed that these allies had been duped by the union's calls for "social justice." In reality, it explained, the real goal of ACTWU's leaders was to gain more dues-paying members. "Obviously, civil rightists, church groups and others aren't being swayed by the expectation of fattening union treasuries," it noted. "They're interested in social justice. And, unfortunately, unions have convinced such people that the worker cannot achieve social justice without a union's help." The consultants urged executives to hit back. In particular, they should create the "opportunity" to tell their own employees that the boycott threatened the jobs of Stevens workers. In a separate issue, the publication expressed concern about ACTWU's efforts to reform labor law. The so-called Stevens Bill, it argued, was the "most important" piece of labor legislation in "many a year." Executives were encouraged to get involved in the campaign to defeat the proposal. "So stay on your guard, and let your own people in Washington know how you feel," it urged. "Do it *now* for H.R. 77."[17]

These appeals were widely heeded. During the hearings on the labor reform bill, a few employers sought to distance themselves from persistent labor law violators such as Stevens. Many others, however, did not react in this way. "Few representatives of the business community," claimed Frederic Feinstein, general counsel to the House Subcommittee on Labor-Management Relations, "have come forward in any type of official capacity and said, 'We deplore what J. P. Stevens is doing, we deplore violations of the labor laws.'" Even when the corporate campaign forced leading executives to resign, they did not publicly criticize Stevens's labor policies. An angry George Meany felt that the business community was two-faced. "When these business leaders who proclaim their respect for the rights of their employees to bargain collectively act in concert to defend such immoral lawbreakers as J. P. Stevens by seeking to gut labor law reform, we are left no alternative but to question their good word," he noted. The labor reform bill was defeated by a well-funded industry campaign, showing that few executives accepted that workers' right to organize needed to be strengthened.[18]

Many executives expressed their support for Stevens by helping to fund the Roanoke Rapids Employee Education Committee. In the fall of 1976 the group was formed after loom fixer Wilson Lambert went to see a local attorney about how Stevens employees could protest against the boycott. The lawyer referred Lambert to Robert Valois, a Raleigh-based labor consultant with considerable experience of representing companies during organizing campaigns. Determined to help the group, Valois in turn hired Robert Click, another experienced labor consultant. According to the Institute for Southern Studies, which researched the two men's backgrounds, they were both seasoned antiunion campaigners with *"a history of working for management in decertification campaigns* and using workers' groups for their purposes."[19] The EEC's efforts were clearly financed by southern textile industrialists who were determined to keep unions out of their region. Although most kept their donations private, its public supporters included Martin Processing, a textile dyeing firm based in Martinsville, Virginia. In August 1978 the firm's vice president noted in a letter to conservative North Carolina senator Jesse Helms that Martin supported the EEC "voluntarily and *openly"* because it felt that ACTWU's efforts were hurting innocent workers.[20]

The Roanoke Rapids EEC received much of its support from the North Carolina Fund for Individual Rights, a nonprofit organization that aimed to defend private citizens from "bureaucratic excess and illegal government actions." In addition to passing on funding to the EEC, the NCFIR also represented the group in its legal efforts to decertify the local union. NCFIR leaders were prominent conservative activists in the Tar Heel State. Hugh Joseph Beard, the group's attorney, was a University of North Carolina graduate who was engaged in a longstanding fight with the *Daily Tar Heel,* the campus newspaper, on the grounds that it endorsed political candidates while accepting a university subsidy. Both Beard and group president Wilson Bryan were active in the Republican Party and in the North Carolina Conservative Union. The group's founding president, Richard J. Bryan, was also an administrative assistant to Jesse Helms. The NCFIR received major donations from several southern textile firms, including the Deering Milliken Corporation and Chatham Manufacturing Company, two companies that vigorously resisted unionization. In a 1979 interview, Wilson Bryan admitted that the Roanoke Rapids EEC was a NCFIR client. The chemical industry executive added that he had been able to secure a good base of funding for the Stevens group: "That's brought in a lot of money, the Stevens case has, from a lot of individuals and some companies. . . . We have developed over our short time of existence a pretty darn good mailing list from people that contributed to other things."[21]

Although it clearly received funding from other companies, the Roanoke Rapids EEC vigorously denied that it was directly supported by Stevens. ACTWU representatives repeatedly charged that the group was controlled by the company, but the allegation could not be substantiated because the EEC successfully fought off efforts to open its papers. In early 1980, Secretary of Labor F. Ray Marshall petitioned the U.S. District Court for the group's records to be subpoenaed on the grounds that company support for the committee would have been a violation of the 1959 Labor Management Reporting and Disclosure Act. The EEC vigorously resisted Marshall's request, arguing that it would subject EEC members to retaliation from union members. According to Wilson Lambert, EEC members were aware of "the reputation of all unions, and this union in particular, for violence and other coercion against those who do not agree with them. Consequently, many workers who support us have told me that they do not want the union to know their identity." Taking note of these fears, North Carolina District Court Judge Franklin T. Dupree ruled that there was a "reasonable probability" that opening the files would lead to "economic and physical reprisals" against committee members.[22]

From its inception, the EEC's main goal was to decertify the ACTWU local union. They argued that the union had won the 1974 election by only a slim majority and that its boycott had now turned a majority of workers against it. Following an extensive campaign, in November 1977 the EEC submitted a petition to the NLRB that called for a new election. Although the federal body refused to consider the demand because of other charges that it was still investigating against the company, the EEC continued to fight the union, producing a great deal of publicity material in the process. It asserted that Stevens's workers were being used as "guinea pigs" by a union that wanted to organize the entire southern textile industry. The committee also argued that many of the union's new allies actually understood little about southern textile workers. "Students should stick to their books," claimed one flyer, "ministers to their flocks, and do-gooders to other chores."[23]

Committee members put forward a number of other arguments to support their contention that a union was unnecessary. They repeatedly associated the labor movement with strikes and violence and asserted that ACTWU's presence was divisive and negative. "This was a nice quiet little town," claimed one member, "and everybody was happy, like one big family, and all at once the union came in and a bunch of young people, they went to join the union and get something for nothing. It split the town in two, you've got troubles." Many also reasoned that supporting the union was pointless because Stevens would never agree to a union contract. Well aware of the Statesboro case, they argued that the firm would shut its mills rather than sign a deal with ACTWU. "I don't think J. P. Stevens will sign a contract," claimed EEC activist Janie Hawkins. "They have said that they would not sign a contract, and they will not and they will close these plants down. It has been done before, and they are shutting them down little by little now. . . . they'll do it before they sign a contract. I believe that."[24]

Many antiunion workers also insisted that they enjoyed working for J. P. Stevens and that the company had "been good" to them. "My job is the reason I got a chance to send my daughter to college," commented one EEC member, "and that is the reason that she has got an education, because of J. P. Stevens giving me a job. And I am proud to work for J. P. Stevens." Some were acutely aware of their own lack of formal education, arguing that Stevens provided stable work for those who had not finished high school. They contrasted the mills with Albemarle Paper Company, where workers needed more formal qualifications in order to secure a job. "One thing," noted EEC member Eula McGee, "J. P. Stevens has a lot of people that's not educated, like myself; and to work at the paper mill where they're unionized, here in this town you have to have a high-school education. There's quite a few people that work for J. P. Stevens that doesn't even have grammar school."[25]

The Roanoke Rapids EEC was certainly a formidable opponent for ACTWU. The group channeled workers' fears that the boycott was threatening their job security, undermining ACTWU's strength in Roanoke Rapids. At the group's first meeting in October 1976, the *Roanoke Rapids Daily Herald* estimated that between 600 and 700 people attended, although the union claimed that the real figure was between 300 and 400.[26] From this start, the EEC clearly picked up strength. In November 1978, Paul Swaity himself admitted that the union had been unable to overcome the fears of the "large majority" of workers in the North Carolina town. By the fall of 1978, the EEC claimed to have received backing from more than 1,400 of the 2,700 employees.[27]

Although the Roanoke Rapids EEC was the most vocal, similar committees sprang up in Slater, South Carolina, Tifton, Georgia, and Wagram,

North Carolina. All of these groups were well supported by what ACTWU general counsel Arthur Goldberg termed "the organized extreme right." Like other New Right groups, the employee committees were able to spread their message through the use of sophisticated direct-mail techniques. A new technology at the time, conservative groups were among the first to exploit the potential of direct mail, as it allowed them to quickly send their emotive material to thousands of recipients. Overall, the various employee committees were very effective at thwarting ACTWU's organizing efforts. As Goldberg commented in 1980, "These employee committees are one of the most effective means to defeat an organizing campaign. . . . I don't think any union has the resources to lick them on its own."[28]

Across the South, the committees hit back at the union's organizing campaigns. In Tifton and Wagram, they kept workers fully informed of union defeats in NLRB elections. The committees also pointed out that ACTWU was losing members, arguing that the union was a waning force that had little to offer. "You can see," concluded one communication, "that voting this union in would be like jumping on a sinking ship." The union responded by arguing that it could offer workers a better deal. "Why do textile workers make so much less than auto workers, steel workers, tire workers, beer workers, and paper workers," it asked. "The answer is simple—MOST OF THE WORKERS IN THOSE INDUSTRIES BELONG TO UNIONS."[29]

In the battle to determine whether unions really could offer economic improvements to their members, the committees repeatedly used material from Roanoke Rapids. Here, they argued, more than five years of union representation had not benefited the workers. Rather than receiving better wages, Roanoke Rapids workers were actually being denied the increases that Stevens was giving to its nonunion employees. "The nearly 3000 hourly employees at the seven Roanoke Rapids plants of J. P. Stevens," noted one Wagram letter, "have received several pay checks with NO raises in them!" Unions, insisted the committees, simply did not deliver on their promises.[30] In another communication, antiunion workers in Roanoke Rapids told their counterparts in Wagram of how they were "losing over $250,000.00 every month that we don't receive a general increase in wages like you got at your plants." As a result, they claimed that it was only a matter of time before ACTWU was ejected from their plants. "The union hasn't done a thing here in *five years*," claimed EEC leader Gene Patterson, "except to make life miserable and *turn friends and relatives against each other.*"[31]

The committees claimed that ACTWU was promising workers unattainable economic benefits. Union organizers were consistently portrayed as untrustworthy, even being compared to unscrupulous used-car salesmen. "Buyer Beware," screamed one flyer that included a picture of a decrepit car. "If someone tried to sell you this old 'heap,' what would they talk about—the tires, of course, they are the only items of value on the entire car. This is the oldest sales trick in the world—only talk about the good points; ignore the bad ones. . . . Don't be fooled by the union's 'selective' sales pitch—remember that the organizers may only be telling you about the good parts."[32]

Antiunion flyers also played on workers' fears of losing their jobs. "The world knows the results of the ACTWU BOYCOTT at Farah Textile Co., El Paso, Texas 3,000 Jobs Lost," claimed one. Workers were reminded that unions invariably caused economic insecurity. "Union Demands," claimed another communication bluntly, "destroy companies."[33] Workers were even threatened with blacklists, a traditional weapon of southern textile employers. "If <u>YOUR</u> JOB IS CUT BACK OR CUT OUT, <u>WHAT WILL YOU DO</u>?" asked the Wagram committee. "Those J. P. STEVENS EMPLOYEES who are blindly jumping into the union may not realize the magnitude of their mistake UNTIL THEY APPLY FOR A JOB SOMEWHERE ELSE." Unions, according to the committees, failed to appreciate that textile firms operated in a highly competitive industry. ACTWU's unrealistic demands, they argued, could be the final straw for hard-pressed U.S. textile companies that had to compete with cheap imports. One antiunion flyer asked whether workers had noticed the increasing amount of foreign-made clothing stocked by local stores. Referring to ACTWU's wage program, it asked: "How many 15% raises do you think STEVENS and the rest of the textile industry in the good old U.S.A. could stand before EVERYTHING in the stores would be 'Made in _____'??"[34]

Committee members also argued that workers' individuality would be lost if they belonged to a union. Unions were pictured as dictatorial organizations that rode roughshod over the interests of the individual. Workers would be powerless to stop them raising their dues and calling damaging strikes. "With enough power," claimed one flyer, "there would be nothing to stop the union from <u>RAISING dues, fees, fines and assessments</u> to any amount. Also, sit-downs, slow-downs, walk-outs, and strike losses cost <u>YOU MONEY</u>." The committees asserted that workers were better off having a direct relationship with the company. The committee in Tifton urged, "Every human being that GOD created is an important individual. . . . HANG—ON To Your Independence. IT IS PRICELESS!!!" Wagram workers, meanwhile, were urged to "join the growing number of southern workers who are standing up for their freedom of choice and independence."[35]

In the late 1970s, antiunion workers also created Stevens People and Friends for Freedom. Based in Greenville, SPFF was led by Mildred Ramsey, a fifty-two-year-old grandmother who worked at the Dunean plant. A tireless activist who claimed to have started the group on her own initiative, Ramsey argued that SPFF grew to represent "thousands of satisfied Stevens employees who are opposed to unionism." Ramsey portrayed her supporters as independent citizens who were struggling to get their side of the story across. "Big labor," she asserted, was a dominant force and it was difficult for nonunion employees to be heard. "This is not a fair fight," insisted Ramsey. "The union right, the organizer right, the NLRB's rights, are always in the news. The rights of our company, and the *great majority* of us who do *not* favor the union, are being denied."[36]

Claiming to be carrying out God's work, Ramsey worked diligently to encourage workers to sign cards that pledged to "Stop the Union . . . Stop the Boycott." With enough cards under her belt, the SPFF leader intended to use them to disrupt union attempts to secure bargaining rights on the basis of their own authorization cards.[37] Ramsey also lobbied on behalf of broader efforts to restrict union rights, insisting that she wanted to "keep our beloved Southland free of all the crime, violence, corruption, strikes, destruction of property, and general chaos that always comes with unions just like sticky comes with molasses." An effective organizer, she collected many signatures from workers who supported right-to-work laws. "We know," she warned, "that what the union Bosses really want is to repeal the right to work (without a union) Law."[38]

In sharp contrast to the union, which drew a disproportionate amount of support from African Americans, the procompany workers were overwhelmingly white. Scott Hoyman recalled that "the anti-union group in Roanoke Rapids . . . They were all white." In 1977, television reports graphically captured these racial divisions. At union meetings the majority of those attending were African American, while at the EEC gatherings there were no black faces. Many EEC members voiced fears that the union was too supportive of black civil rights. Wilson Lambert told CBS's Mike Wallace that the union supported "nigger rights," adding, "Most of the ones you get at the union hall are colored." EEC member Kermit Smith claimed that the union's membership was 85 percent black, and that "they have been promised a lot of things that the union cannot possibly deliver." Black workers also felt that race was

Figure 16. Procompany workers demonstrating in Greenville, South Carolina, 1980. Mildred Ramsey is on the far right. (Kheel Center for Labor-Management Documentation and Archives, Cornell University.)

crucial in determining union support in Roanoke Rapids. "The whites resented the union," recalled Jettie Purnell, "because they was told that union would elevate black above them, and they believed that. . . . So that's why they didn't want it to happen."[39]

The antiunion groups also tended to attract more support from older workers than the union did. These senior employees were often close to retirement and were reluctant to fight for a change in working conditions. Many also felt that their pay and conditions had steadily improved without a union. Both men and women were well represented in the antiunion groups, although most of the leaders of the EEC in Roanoke Rapids were male loom fixers. Since the beginning of the campaign, many loom fixers had spearheaded opposition to the union; as the highest-paid production workers, they felt that they had the most to lose if their mill closed down, and many also harbored hopes of progressing into supervisory positions.[40]

The mobilization of procompany groups highlighted that the boycott did not simply have positive consequences for the union. As successful as ACTWU was in building support for its case and embarrassing Stevens, these efforts also emboldened its opponents to become more vocal. This opposition disrupted the union's efforts to sign up the firm's workers, contributing to the plethora of problems that organizers faced on the ground.

NINE

The New Stevens Strategy

In the latter stages of the J. P. Stevens campaign, the union made another major effort to organize the company's workers. As the Roanoke Rapids group represented less than 7 percent of Stevens's employees, ACTWU leaders were acutely aware that they needed to make further organizing gains. But while the boycott and corporate campaign secured results, the organizing efforts were the least successful part of the union's strategy. Publicly, the union trumpeted the success of the organizing campaign, which it claimed was "gaining momentum on a broad front." Arguing that it had secured majority support in several plants, the union boasted that it had established "emerging locals." In reality, these claims were overblown. By the time of the 1980 settlement, ACTWU had again failed to organize any of the company's major facilities.[1]

In a sharp contrast to its campaign in the 1960s, these organizing efforts did not fail primarily because of illegal opposition from Stevens. Rather than openly threatening its workers, the company increasingly relied on antiunion workers to fight ACTWU for them. Using the boycott to bolster their case, the antiunion committees effectively linked the union with economic devastation. Scaling back their reliance on breaking the law, managers also increasingly used economic incentives to deter unionization. This change was generated by court decisions and the widespread publicity surrounding the case, both of which reduced the firm's ability to violate the law. This shift in tactics caused difficulties for ACTWU strategists who still demonized Stevens as "the nation's Number one labor law violator." The union's organizing strategy relied on the company continuing to behave as ruthlessly as it had in the past, and planners struggled to adjust to the shift in their opponent's tactics.

Following the launching of the boycott, ACTWU's leaders decided that they would no longer seek elections at Stevens plants. Instead they supported the AFL-CIO's efforts to have unions granted bargaining rights if a majority of the workforce signed authorization cards. Organizers encouraged as many workers as possible to sign cards and waited on the outcome of the AFL-CIO's labor law reform bill. In the meantime, they reasoned, the bill would be bolstered by continuing violations by Stevens. When this bill was defeated in the summer of 1978, the union's organizing strategy was derailed. Although the union contested (and won) three small elections in 1979–80, union leaders remained reluctant to authorize a complete change of strategy, partly because they knew that election campaigns would give the company a golden opportunity to use the boycott against them.[2]

From late 1976 on ACTWU leaders gradually escalated their organizing efforts. Within a year of the merger, thirty-three full-time organizers were working on the campaign. Although Stevens's plants were clustered to some extent, the staff still faced a daunting task. At the start of 1977, for example, the company operated seventy-five mills in the region, in forty separate communities. Campaign planners divided the region up into ten sub-areas, establishing an office in each one. As the boycott gained momentum, union leaders expanded their organizing efforts even further. By February 1979 the number of full-time organizers had risen to forty, while an additional thirty staff were employed on a part-time basis through the Worker-to-Worker program, which took workers out of the plants and paid them a small stipend while they assisted the drive.[3]

The key to the union's organizing strategy was its policy of not petitioning for NLRB elections. At some sites, elections could not be held because of pending unfair labor practice charges, while at others the union argued that it would not seek a vote unless it could be "free and fair." "That means," explained Murray Finley, "the atmosphere has to be cleansed, not only in the plants but also in the communities." In February 1977 a key organizing document outlined the reasons for the strategy in full. In particular, the union insisted that Stevens had always refused to recognize it through conventional channels. Rather than winning isolated elections, the union also hoped to use its card majorities to secure bargaining rights at a number of facilities at once. "The campaign to organize J. P. Stevens is being planned with objectives that are far more ambitious and far reaching than the normal traditional organizing campaigns we generally pursue," noted the document. "Mindful of the southern anti-union conspiracy and that our goal is to get bargaining rights for the entire J. P. Stevens chain; confronted by a situation where we've been trying to convince the NLRB that in light of all the past intimidation and violation by the company, a free and uncoerced election in any Stevens plant is no longer possible, and that even if it were possible to win an election in one or two plants, it would not contribute that much to our total objective, but would undermine our case before the NLRB; recognizing a condition where after years of bargaining we have not been able to get contracts in Statesboro or Roanoke Rapids and a similar roadblock would confront us in other plants—we are not gearing up for any elections at this time."[4]

On the ground, this policy was not always popular with either workers or organizers, especially when they felt that they could win an election. Workers frequently questioned their organizers about when a vote would take place, and these queries were passed on to union leaders. Some workers grew disillusioned with the slow pace of organizing, feeling that they had signed cards for nothing. By November 1977 the union had obtained authorization card majorities in eleven plants, including two in Tifton, Georgia, and two in Wallace, North Carolina. Maintaining members' enthusiasm without being able to promise them an election was not easy. "Having gained majorities or near majorities in a number of plants a good deal of staff time must be spent in maintaining the interest, loyalty and involvement of the workers," noted an overview report. Despite this, field staff were warned by organizing director Harold McIver to "play down the N.L.R.B. election as only one of the many ways to achieve collective bargaining."[5]

Stevens's executives also capitalized on the union's reluctance to call elections by repeatedly arguing that "union bosses" were trying to take away workers' democratic right to choose whether they wanted to be represented by an outside organization. The company thus used the move to bolster their long-standing claims that unions were undemocratic organizations that really cared little about what their members wanted. The company also disputed ACTWU's claims that any election could not be "free and fair." "Although it has been asserted by the union that fair elections are not possible in Stevens' plants, this assertion cannot withstand examination," they noted. "The election at Roanoke Rapids which the union won is regarded by the union as a 'fair' election. The allegations of unfairness have only come in instances where the union has lost elections." Throughout the late 1970s the company repeatedly challenged the union to call elections, placing ACTWU's strategists on the defensive.[6]

The union's reluctance to hold elections was also related to its fear that the company would use the boycott against it on the eve of any vote. Aware that the boycott made organizing "more difficult," they felt that a change of strategy was justified. "Now that we are undertaking a boycott against J. P. Stevens," noted an AFL-CIO meeting in June 1976, "the type of organizing activities we conducted in the past directed at winning NLRB elections will have to be carefully reviewed and modified. The probability is we will not hold any elections but will try to build up strong support among the workers to prevent the company turning those workers against the union and preparing for a time when we can seek representation rights in the unorganized plants."[7]

In order for ACTWU's strategy to work, it was vital for the labor reform bill to become law. ACTWU was a major sponsor of H.R. 77, introduced in January of 1977 by New Jersey Democrat Frank Thompson. Thompson's bill sought to require the NLRB to automatically certify the union as the bargaining agent in any plant where 55 percent of the workers had signed authorization cards. If this proposal was secured, ACTWU would then automatically win bargaining rights in several plants without calling elections. The bill also sought to require that an NLRB election be held within forty-five days of the board receiving a petition, thus undermining an employer's ability to destroy a union's preelection majority. Dubbed the Stevens Bill, H.R. 77 also sought to prohibit companies that had committed "flagrant or repeated violations of NLRB orders" from doing business with the federal government for three years.[8]

ACTWU leaders argued that these provisions would allow them to make real progress in the South. As executive council member William Gordon declared, the bill was a "vital necessity" if the union was to overcome the "southern conspiracy." This feeling was shared by others in the labor movement. In the summer of 1977, ACTWU's executive board minutes reported that labor law reform was "high on the AFL-CIO agenda." In urging support of the bill, George Meany claimed that Stevens was the "classic case" of an employer who had kept the union out by breaking the law. ACTWU leaders themselves used the Stevens case in an effort to secure the speedy passage of H.R. 77. As Sheinkman reported to the executive board in June 1977, "the labor law legislation is now known as the Stevens bill—the Stevens record is a good basis for trying to get legislation through."[9]

The bill was strongly opposed by the business community. Managers argued that it gave excessive power to unions, which were trying to use the law to erode workers' freedom to choose. Stevens mounted a particularly vigorous defense of the status quo. Company officials spoke out against the proposal for elections to be held within forty-five days of the union's petition, arguing that this undermined management's ability to give its side of the story. Unions, they pointed out, already controlled when elections were called. They likewise rejected provisions that called for an employer to allow a union representative to enter the plant and address the workforce on the eve of elections; managers, they argued, did not have the right to go into union halls and speak to workers there. They also opposed the proposals to bar repeated labor law violators from receiving government contracts. Federal agencies, they asserted, should not step into "the dubious sphere of blacklisting and boycotting, merely upon 'opinions' of the Labor Board." Overall, Stevens executives forcefully enunciated the business community's position that H.R. 77 was little more than a power grab by greedy union leaders. "Again, and always," they insisted, "the single aim and thrust of the proposed new law is the accomplishment and spread of unionization and Union contracts. . . . Instead of being titled the 'Labor Reform Act of 1977,' a true description of this Bill would be the 'National Unionization Act of 1977.'"[10]

Corporate opposition to H.R. 77 ultimately won the day. In all, the labor movement spent more than $1.4 million trying to ensure the bill's passage, yet this was considerably less than the amount expended by its opponents. Using direct-mail techniques, lobbyists for industry groups such as the National Association of Manufacturers secured the support that they needed to uphold the status quo. Although the labor reform bill passed the House by a big margin, 257–163, a successful filibuster by Senate conservatives meant that the bill was sent back to committee to die. In June of 1978, reform supporters tried in six cloture moves to get the sixty votes they needed, but narrowly failed. It was a major blow to the Stevens campaign.[11]

Union leaders were especially disappointed with the performance of new president Jimmy Carter. When Carter was elected, many labor leaders had been cautiously optimistic. A Democratic president, they reasoned, would bolster their efforts to level the playing field. After a year in office, however, George Meany gave Carter a C-minus rating, expressing particular disappointment with the administration's failure to do more to achieve full employment. Union leaders then had to tone down the labor law reform bill in order to win the president's support, but the measure was still fiercely attacked by conservatives. Labor leaders also charged that Carter should have tried harder to break the Senate filibuster. The relationship between organized labor and the Democratic president further deteriorated over the remaining years of Carter's term. Like his predecessors, Carter refused to take a strong stance against J. P. Stevens, and the firm continued to receive lucrative government contracts despite union protests.[12]

The failure of the labor law reform bill added to the difficulties faced by ACTWU's organizers. In an effort to increase their effectiveness, ACTWU now required all organizers working on the drive to fill in a detailed weekly report. Staff had to outline the "major problems" they were facing, and to suggest how these could be "overcome." While some staff failed to fill in the forms conscientiously, many did record the wide variety of problems that beset them.[13]

Again and again, organizers claimed that workers were too afraid to support the union. Acutely aware of how previous union activists had been fired or intimidated, most workers were unwilling to stick their necks out. The company's history of labor law violations meant that its workers remained reluctant to join the union even when few new NLRB charges were being generated. In August 1979, Evan S. Hamilton reported from High Point, North Carolina, that the major problem he faced was "fear as usual." Similarly, Ernestine Spencer wrote from a plant in Laurens, South Carolina, that "overcoming fear is the major problem." From Rock Hill, South Carolina, organizer Eddie Nichols related that workers worried that the company would "fire them or put them on a less desired job" if they signed an ACTWU card. Like most organizers, Nichols stuck to his task, hoping that he could slowly gain workers' confidence. He "worked like hell" on house calls, but his campaign still petered out.[14] Many workers also continued to fear that the company would close their plant if they supported the union. From Allendale, South Carolina, Henry Mann complained that workers sensed that their isolated mill would close if they signed union cards. "Big issue is plant closing," he noted succinctly. The Statesboro and Darlington shutdowns lent weight to these fears, as both cases were still before the courts in the late 1970s.[15]

In those years many of Stevens's workers were particularly aware of the unhappy fate of their coworkers in Statesboro, the small Georgia town where the TWUA had secured bargaining rights a decade earlier. In September 1976 the Court of Appeals for the Fifth Circuit found Stevens in contempt of court for violating its bargaining obligations under two earlier court decrees. Sixteen months later the court issued its remedial order, imposing strong affirmative relief if the plant reopened and ordering Stevens to cease and desist from making unilateral changes in any plant within the court's jurisdiction where the union was certified. If the company refused to comply, it would be fined $10,000 for each violation and its officials could be jailed. In legal terms, the decision was a victory for the union, but by this time the company had already used the Statesboro case to undermine several organizing campaigns.[16]

The decision also failed to help those who had lost their jobs. In July 1977 a journalist who visited the small Georgia town found that many former mill workers had struggled to find work. Some were living on food stamps, while others were driving long distances to perform low-paid jobs. Former union activists claimed that local employers were particularly reluctant to hire them. As Addie Jackson put it, "They won't give me a job and they won't give me anything to live on either." Despite this, former activists had few regrets and still hoped to return to the mill one day. The plant itself stood idle until October 1978. When it was reopened by a New Jersey–based scissors manufacturer, the workers' hopes seemed to have been realized. But union supporters soon found that the new owners were also unwilling to hire them.[17]

To some degree, the union had unwittingly helped to make workers wary of becoming active in its campaign. Throughout the late 1960s and 1970s, in its highly successful publicity push, the union made extensive use of George Meany's characterization of Stevens as "the No. 1 labor law violator in the country," together with the U.S. Court of Appeals's 1977 declaration that Stevens was "the most notorious recidivist in the field of labor law." Stressing such ruthlessness could be two-edged when the union was simultaneously trying to encourage Stevens workers to take on the company. In 1979 strategist Richard Rothstein privately acknowledged "the past difficulties we have had in reconciling a focus on Stevens repression and lawlessness with the need to inspire confidence and hope in unorganized workers."[18]

Ultimately, however, it was the company that was largely responsible for increasing workers' fear. Organizers found that Stevens had a multitude of ways of making its employees afraid. On some occasions workers found antiunion literature placed in their pay envelopes, while on others supervisors spread rumors of impending layoffs. When such curtailments did occur, they were well publicized.[19] By the late 1970s, rising imports were causing layoffs across the textile and apparel industry, and many workers worried about their job security. As organizer Mark Pitt reported in September 1979, fear of plant closing was "very difficult" to overcome because the industry was in "bad shape." Across the Stevens chain, more than seven hundred employees were laid off between December 1977 and December 1978.[20]

Acutely aware of the risks of joining the union, many of Stevens's employees assessed their situation and decided to steer clear of controversy. Even in the late 1970s they often reasoned that textile jobs were the best around. In Aberdeen, North Carolina, union supporters complained that ACTWU's message was not getting through to many of their coworkers. "Most of them never had anything," noted worker Debbie Tedder. "They think they're doing good now, getting $3.90 an hour." Eddie Nichols confronted similar problems at a plant in Laurinburg, North Carolina. "Employees at this plant hav ben very poor," he wrote, "a textil wage seems good to them." These problems had been faced by textile organizers before, especially as most mills were located in small towns where the mill was the main employer. Traditionally, textile companies had also sought to discourage higher-wage firms from moving in and raising their employees' expectations. Although new industry was moving into the Piedmont in the 1960s and 1970s, Sun Belt growth was patchy and there were still many towns where textile mills remained economically dominant.[21]

Stevens encouraged these feelings by steadily improving the wages and benefits of its workers. Company officials were especially careful to ensure that their wages matched those paid by unionized southern mills. They also informed their workers that joining the union would not lead to higher wages. In Tifton, Verney L. Cumbee related that "the company tell people that they don't need a union because they have the same as the union plant have now." Company propaganda made much of the fact that workers' wages were increasing. One 1977 flyer reminded employees that the company had been able to improve their wages and benefits for fifteen consecutive years. Stevens noted that such increases were possible only because of the company's profitability, which the boycott was threatening. In a similar vein, workers in Wagram were informed that the union did not guarantee better wages. Belligerently titled "ACTWU Facts," a flyer cited the case of the organized Pacific Mills in Columbia, South Carolina. "Can the union guarantee better wages?" it asked. "Of course not! If they could, why are Pacific Mills' employees paid less than you after years of paying union dues."[22]

The company used wage and benefit data as a key part of its public relations battle with the union. In a June 1979 "Position Paper," Stevens argued that its workers already received "good wages and benefits." The company claimed that its employees earned $4.69 an hour, thirty-one cents more than the industry average. According to Stevens, weekly take-home pay was also above the industry norm, and all workers earned more than the federal minimum wage. Highlighting how it had steadily improved its fringe benefits, Stevens now funded medical insurance, a pension plan, and vacations based on service. Most of these benefits had been introduced since the early 1960s, when the union had begun its organizing efforts. In 1978 Stevens also made Christmas Eve a paid holiday in several of its nonunion plants, as well as increasing the vacation benefits of long-serving employees. Both moves worried the union.[23] The steady improvements certainly hurt ACTWU's efforts, as many workers reasoned that conditions were getting better without a union. Roanoke Rapids worker Opal Nethery commented in 1976: "Now, we have had increases in our salaries from time to time throughout the fifteen years that I've been working, and I consider them reasonable increases. And I've been perfectly satisfied with mine, and I'd much rather see our country come back to a normal living than to see it just keep going like it's going, and there's bound to be a stopping point somewhere."[24]

By the late 1970s, even the union's opponents admitted that its presence had pushed the company to improve both pay and benefits. In a revealing interview, antiunion consultant George Hood credited the union with forcing the textile firm to treat its employees better. "Stevens pays better than any other large textile employer in the South, and its benefits are better," he asserted in 1979. "People don't understand that. Of course it wasn't always that way. The union has done a lot of good, there's no question about it, at Stevens. Things are much better today because of the union presence. . . . This union presence has made them get into the employee relations game—kind of late, but they're doing it." So the union's campaign did secure positive results for the company's workers, but this was little consolation for a declining organization that desperately needed new members.[25]

On the ground, Stevens managers also made renewed efforts to encourage workers to identify with the company. In Laurens, South Carolina, Susan Sachen reported that managers responded to the organizing drive by involving workers in a variety of activities, including company-sponsored sporting events. As she concluded, these tactics were effective: "all the Co. handouts (baseball etc.) have slowed down activity." The company often blended reprisals and incentives. "Each time our campaign builds," Sachen noted with frustration, "the Co. hits us with something; Besides layoffs they are starting basketball and volleyball."[26] In some campaigns, Stevens's response was a world away from its famously harsh tactics. In Walterboro, South Carolina, the union spent five years trying to organize a plant that employed around six hundred workers. ACTWU leaders asserted, however, that the company was using a more conciliatory approach to effectively deter unionization.

In February 1979 the union sent respected staffer Nick Builder to work out what had gone wrong in Walterboro. "The Company's nicey-nicey policies have always been and continue to be a problem," he concluded. "Walterboro management seems always to have played it soft—even in the election no one was fired apparently—and the new Stevens strategy seems to have been carried to extremes here. . . . Currently lax, sometimes very lax, enforcement of rules, easy going management styles and a careful avoidance of direct conflict with the stronger committee-members mean that good, positive issues are hard to find." The company's reasoned approach had left the union with few grievances to exploit. As Builder noted, "Recent incidents that Bob investigated evaporated quickly—a worker was 'persuaded' that an unfair shift transfer was his own voluntary choice; investigation of cases of favoritism turned up union supporters who had been allowed to get away with as much, or more, etc." There seemed little prospect of the union ever making a breakthrough in the South Carolina town, and the campaign was later abandoned.[27]

By the late 1970s there were other signs of a broader change in Stevens's approach. As *Fortune* journalist Walter Guzzardi Jr. noted, the company's losses in the courts and the union's ability to secure public support had "compelled a change in Stevens policy." In 1978 this shift was spotlighted as the company brought in a new legal team that included J. Frank Ogletree, a lawyer with a reputation for compromise, together with former NLRB trial attorney Jerold Lehlman. Shortly after taking over, this new team settled with the NLRB when it demanded an unprecedented nationwide injunction that would have expanded the harsh terms of circuit court rulings to several Stevens plants. With new general counsel James Grady at the helm, the company worked out a settlement and the injunction was never issued. The exact details of the agreement remained private, but what was clear was that Stevens had convinced board officials of its willingness to comply with their rulings.[28]

Around the same time, there were other signs of a shift in the company's posture. In March 1978 top company officials initiated secret talks with

ACTWU's leaders, and the two sides began to make real progress. On the ground in Roanoke Rapids, ACTWU leaders argued that the union's presence had also pushed Stevens to become more moderate. "We have had a major influence on tempering the company's activities, normal activities," claimed Paul Swaity in 1978. Over time, the company began to address workers' grievances, although managers refused to give the union credit for this change. By dealing with the union on a daily basis, company officials had overcome their own fears and established a working relationship that paved the way for the eventual settlement.[29]

By the late 1970s the company had also given much clearer guidelines to all of its plant managers in order to reduce the number of NLRB charges. In the fall of 1978, human resources staff issued all plants with a written set of rules and regulations. The new rules for the first time established clear procedures for disciplining and discharging workers. Hal Addis, Stevens's vice president for industrial relations, claimed that this manual helped to prevent management from committing unfair labor practices and thus undermined the union's strategy of building up labor board cases against the firm. In the late 1970s the number of workers fired by Stevens for union activity certainly fell; even by the union's figures, only twenty-nine employees were unfairly discharged in 1976–77, compared with more than seventy in the first year of the campaign. Between 1978 and 1980 few workers were discharged by Stevens, and the NLRB upheld many of these dismissals.[30] NLRB officials themselves felt that the company's blatant violations of the law were now a thing of the past. "With all these contempt decrees and orders, we've got them covered like the dew covers Dixie," claimed an NLRB lawyer in North Carolina. "If they do anything serious, all we've got to do is whip out the papers." In the last two years of the Stevens campaign, NLRB officials decided against taking the company back to the appeals court and seeking harsh fines. As a spokesman admitted, the complaints that they issued against Stevens between 1978 and 1980 were technical rather than deliberate, and did not contain the "clear and convincing" evidence of guilt that was required to secure a contempt hearing.[31]

In the summer of 1979, for instance, the board dismissed several charges that the union had brought against Stevens. The violations that did occur were not as flagrant or widespread as they had been a decade earlier. "This record," concluded the board in August 1979, "contains limited violations of a less than serious nature and does not appear to have the scope of past conduct of this Respondent." In a case covering the company's plants in Tifton, the board also dismissed many of the charges brought by the union. Administrative law judge David L. Evans ruled that "in this case the three violations of Section 8(a)(1) of the Act were not so egregious as to preclude the holding of a fair election. . . . the unfair labor practices established herein are minimal in nature."[32]

Union leaders certainly noticed a change in the company's strategy. Still vigorously opposed to unionism, Stevens was relying less on violating the law, instead fighting ACTWU through the employee groups and a sophisticated public relations campaign. In May 1977 organizing coordinator Harold McIver noted privately that Whiteford Blakeney, the architect of Stevens's earlier strategy, was no longer representing the firm. In a letter to organizing staff, he directly contradicted the union's public claims that Stevens's tactics had not changed at all since the early 1960s. "Obviously," he noted, "the opposition that we are running into now from J. P. Stevens is different from what we have encountered in the past." In 1978 a report prepared by union strategists summed up the company's change of tack. It explained that, while Stevens was still fighting the union, the type of opposition had changed. "Stevens has switched to more subtle tactics," it noted, "and is making a major effort to involve more directly the employees and the community in its anti union activities. The boycott is being whipped up into a major issue."[33]

Court decisions were particularly influential in forcing a change in the company's behavior. On August 31, 1977, the Court of Appeals for the Second Circuit had found J. P. Stevens in contempt for violating a previous order. The court ordered broad remedies that covered all of Stevens's plants in the Carolinas. In particular, the company had to allow union representatives into the plant and give them access to bulletin boards. These representatives were also permitted to make preelection speeches on company property. If it failed to agree to these provisions, Stevens would be fined $5,000 a day. In December 1977, NLRB trial examiner Bernard Ries also found that Stevens had bargained in bad faith in Roanoke Rapids and had exploited its bargaining-table recalcitrance to "chill" the union's organizing efforts. Ries extended a cease-and-desist order to cover any company facilities where the union could establish bargaining rights, and ordered Stevens to pay the legal expenses of both the union and the NLRB.[34]

In a biting decision, Ries slammed Stevens's past conduct. Executives had, he asserted, approached the Roanoke Rapids negotiations with "all the tractability and open-mindedness of Sherman at the outskirts of Atlanta." The decision was hailed by ACTWU leaders as "monumental," and they noted that the strident criticism had forced Stevens to undertake remedial action. In June 1978, Jack Sheinkman reported privately that there had been "a change in Stevens' tactics. The number of Stevens' unfair labor practices are declining as they are being more careful because of the strict restrictions of the court order."[35] In the winter of 1979–80 the union contested elections at two Stevens plants, in High Point, North Carolina, and Allendale, South Carolina. In both cases, organizers were able to use their access to the plants to counteract the effect of captive-audience speeches and achieve narrow election victories. As neither mill employed more than a hundred workers, these victories had limited significance. In the larger plants, ACTWU still lacked the support that it needed to call elections with confidence, especially as Stevens was likely to offer greater resistance when more was at stake.[36]

While the courts' criticism of Stevens pleased union leaders, it described the company's past behavior much more accurately than its current conduct. By the summer of 1978 the company's change of approach was causing major problems for the union's organizing campaign, which had been predicated on the assumption that the firm would continue to behave as it had in the past. "For the past year or two," noted Paul Swaity in August 1978, "our organizing approach to gain bargaining rights in as many J. P. Stevens plants as possible was largely based on a strategy of combining authorization card majorities with unfair labor practices on a plant by plant basis and seeking NLRB recognition on grounds that the company's record of unfair labor practices made no fair election possible." The union found that Stevens was no longer violating the law on a wholesale basis, leading Swaity to conclude that their progress "has not been very encouraging." In early 1978, he explained, "it became apparent that achieving bargaining rights in additional plants by means of this strategy was very unlikely. Under pressures of Court Contempt, the type of violations we were experiencing in the past stopped. Although some borderline violations continued to take place these were very limited and scattered." Swaity argued that the union should petition for elections in the plants where it was strong, but the card authorization strategy was never completely overturned.[37]

In short, in the late 1970s the failure of union efforts to organize J. P. Stevens could no longer simply be associated with the company's illegal tactics. Instead, many of ACTWU's problems were caused by a shift in its opponent's tactics. The failure of the labor reform bill also hurt the campaign, as it derailed the strategy of trying to secure bargaining rights based on card majorities. The organizing campaign was held back by a wide variety of other problems, including fallout from the boycott and conflict within the union's own ranks. Right across the South, organizers also found that many white workers were reluctant to join with blacks, confounding their expectations that the influx of African American employees would boost the campaign.

TEN

"We Need More White Involvement"

By the late 1970s it was clear that, in the fifteen years since the union had started the Stevens campaign, the organizing climate had changed considerably. As well as confronting an opponent whose tactics had become more sophisticated, organizers were now trying to mobilize a workforce that contained far greater numbers of African Americans. Between 1967 and 1977, the number of blacks working for J. P. Stevens more than tripled.[1] Union strategists had reasoned that the influx of these new recruits would help their campaign, but the presence of black workers created unforeseen problems. Across the South, the organizing campaign was also held back by a variety of other problems: many unorganized workers disagreed with ACTWU's boycott, there was conflict within the union's own ranks, and southern community leaders remained largely supportive of Stevens.

African Americans now made up around a quarter of Stevens's workers.[2] As union leaders had anticipated, many of these workers had been radicalized by the civil rights movement and responded enthusiastically to the campaign. Disproportionately assigned to lower-paying jobs, black workers also had more reason to join the union. Organizers all across the South found that blacks quickly signed membership cards and were willing to assume leadership roles. Scott Hoyman recalled, "We would have an experience of a greater percentage of support by black workers than whites, on the average." The problem was that black activism tended to scare off whites. Viewing the union as "black," many whites adamantly refused to join, despite repeated efforts by organizers to bridge the racial divide.[3]

Organizers vividly recalled the strong support that African American workers gave to the union. In the late 1970s Vonnie Hines worked for several years on the Stevens campaign in both the Carolinas and Georgia. "The black workers," she recalled, "seemed to understand more that sticking together meant something, that they could accomplish something by doing that. . . . If you went into a campaign where it was predominantly black workers . . . you had more support than you would with a white ratio." A former Stevens worker, Hines felt that blacks saw the union as a way of fighting the discrimination that they continued to face in the mills: "They knew how they had been discriminated against and how hard it was for them to get in the plants. I remember when I worked for Stevens, I was a mender. . . . Well, the menders were supposed to be sort of the upper echelon, and I quit Stevens in—I worked for them probably until '60—and there was not a single mender that was a black mender. . . . They had the menial jobs, you know, cleaning the bathrooms, sweeping the floors."[4]

The civil rights movement had helped to prepare many black workers for the union's campaign. As Hines recalled, the movement had driven home the importance of collective action, especially as mass protest had played a decisive role in securing the abolition of segregated public facilities.[5] "The blacks had an entirely different set of social attitudes to the white textile workers," added Hoyman. "The blacks were influenced by the civil rights activist doctrine, and their churches became the organizing center." After playing a key role in the civil rights protests, black church leaders also proved more responsive to the union than their white counterparts. During the Stevens campaign, several organizers ended up using African American churches as meeting places, partly because few white ministers were willing to support ACTWU.[6]

Organizers complained repeatedly about how difficult it was to secure white support. At the company's plant in Shelby, North Carolina, Louis Agre faced real problems in recruiting whites. In September 1978 he reported: "We still have a completely Black committee on 2nd [shift]." Agre's first-shift committee was also predominantly black. "There is still a need to build a stronger 1st shift committee and to get more White," he related. Agre's efforts to address the problem yielded few results. White workers took the lead in the antiunion movement, and managers allowed them to pass out damaging propaganda in the mill. Although ACTWU staffers tried hard to tackle these problems, the union never succeeded in breaking through in Shelby.[7]

Lack of white support was a problem in several other campaigns. In Milledgeville, Georgia, organizers arrived in town in the summer of 1976 and quickly signed up many blacks. While this was initially viewed as an encouraging sign, drive leader Mel Tate was soon expressing his concern that the drive needed "more white involvement." In Laurens, South Carolina, several ACTWU organizers faced the same situation. In September 1979, Jimmy E. Smith related that his main task was "getting white people active." Blacks had signed up to the union in large numbers, causing whites to reason that the union was not "for everybody."[8] Similar difficulties were reported by Susan Sachen, who also worked on the Laurens campaign. In May 1979 she identified one of her key problems as "developing militancy and leadership among white workers."[9]

In Pamplico, another small town in the Palmetto State, organizer Phillip Pope complained about a "lack of white support" in the plants, which were about 40 percent black. A summary of the campaign produced by Richard Rothstein confirmed that white inactivity was a serious problem. "Pamplico-Cypress," it noted. "It has not been possible to correct the serious racial inbalance of this campaign by recruiting a significant number of white committee-persons. . . . if whites can become involved, this should be a good campaign."[10] In December 1978 organizers arranged a Christmas party for their supporters, but only one white worker attended.[11] Staff in other locations were equally frustrated. In Wagram, Donna Krenik complained in October 1979 that she was "having [an] awful time with whites." In Walterboro, Rothstein reported that blacks had taken up most leadership positions. "The plant is nearly half black, the committee much more so," he wrote.[12]

Across Stevens's plants, black workers continued to face widespread discrimination. Over the course of the 1970s, workers at several mills banded together to bring class-action racial discrimination lawsuits under Title VII of the 1964 Civil Rights Act. Alleging that they were still denied equal opportunity for promotion, more than three thousand black employees in Roanoke Rapids participated in *Sledge et al. v. J. P. Stevens* (1970), a major class-action case that stayed before the courts for twenty years. In the smaller case of *Sherrill et al. v. J. P. Stevens* (1973), the company was ordered to improve black workers' promotion opportunities at its plant in Shelby. The original suit was brought by A. C. Sherrill, a black employee who claimed that white workers had threatened him with "bodily harm" when he had tried to secure an entry-level supervisory position. The case vividly highlighted the resistance that blacks often faced when they tried to obtain nontraditional jobs.[13]

By the late 1970s, blacks had made progress into many production jobs, but they were still more likely to be confined to lower-paying positions than their white coworkers. As late as December 1980, data from the Roanoke Rapids complex showed that a white male worker with a sixth-grade education made $4.64 an hour, while a black male employee with the same level of education made $3.97.[14] The pattern was repeated at other plants. Whites were also much more likely to be working on the preferred first shift than blacks. Organizers related that whites consequently felt they had more to lose by joining ACTWU. Robert Tim Brown reported from Milledgeville: "Most of the support for the campaign comes from the black employees; the whites well recognize their superior position in the plant and are extremely difficult to organize."[15]

Older whites were especially difficult to sign up. Many were near retirement and did not want to take risks, especially as they had often worked their way into higher-paying positions. Several organizers described these problems. "There is still a real shortage of older white committee folks on 1st shift," reported Louis Agre.[16] Organizers also alleged that the company hired more whites when it wanted to undermine the union's efforts. In Laurens, staff suspected that the company was deliberately taking on as many whites as it could. "They aren't hiring many Blacks," wrote Harold Bagwell. "We are watching this action for possible charges." Bruce Raynor claimed that this type of racial hiring was commonplace. "It's always been a problem," he reflected in 1995. "Racial hiring went on all through the seventies and eighties, and even today when a company is fighting us, their hiring pattern will be to hire whites."[17]

Across the South, leaders of EECs tried to use the race issue to undermine the union. As EEC members were overwhelmingly white, the committees attempted to undercut black support for the union by defending Stevens's record on race. One Wagram flyer claimed that Stevens had given "over a MILLION dollars to the NEGRO COLLEGE FUND." Reminding workers of the company's economic contribution to local communities, it also noted that Stevens provided more than 40,000 jobs for both black and white southerners. Other material attacked the union more directly. In one appeal specifically prepared for black workers in Tifton, the local EEC gleefully publicized organized labor's own history of racial discrimination. Timmons Boyce, a nonunion black employee, claimed that the union had done little to help black people in the past: "IF THE UNION EVER RE-ALLY WANTED TO HELP THE BLACK MAN . . . WHERE WERE THEY WHEN WE WERE PICKING COTTON FOR A LIVING???" Back in the 1940s, Boyce claimed, he would have "been GLAD to join the union . . . because My family and I really needed a 'better life.' BUT A BLACK MAN COULDN'T EVEN GET 'IN' THE UNION UNDER ANY CIRCUMSTANCES. DID YOU KNOW THAT???" By the late 1970s, Boyce claimed, opportunities had improved and he was keen to hold on to his higher-paying job. Such polemical material was not always histori-cally accurate. The TWUA had always accepted black members, although it had generally failed to challenge segregated job assignments. There were, however, many craft unions that had refused to accept blacks even as late as the 1940s.[18]

Official company material was not as emotive, yet the essential message was the same: J. P. Stevens provided steady work to thousands of blacks and whites and was much better placed than the union to look after its workers' economic interests. In *The Issue—The Right to Choose*, a company film pro-duced in the late 1970s, Stevens carefully included material from both black and white workers. White workers asserted that Stevens jobs had allowed them to buy new cars and own their own homes. Black employees added that textile jobs had also allowed the black community to make major economic strides. One unidentified black man from Wagram commented that his job had already allowed him to send three children through college, while two more were still completing their studies. An African American woman added that her employment at Stevens had enabled her to obtain bank loans, over-coming the traditional problems that African Americans had faced in gaining credit. The film also stressed the company's role in giving jobs to blacks who did not have a formal education.[19]

The company argued that the boycott threatened black workers' eco-nomic security. In the film, one unidentified speaker claimed that "the pro-posed boycott of J. P. Stevens Company can very well hurt rather than help black people, remembering that twenty-three percent of the employees of J. P. Stevens are black." Another speaker insisted that unions could not help the black community because they were undemocratic and corrupt: "Are you working in the interest of the black people when you take away their rights to join or not join a union? Are you working in the interest of black people when there is a tremendous amount of graft involved in pension funds, retirement funds, and you name it? Are you working in the interest of black people in the power-grabbing situation?"[20]

Such propaganda failed to undermine black support for the union, especially as many African Americans were acutely aware of the discrimination that still existed in the company's mills. When African Americans comprised a majority of the workforce, organizers did particularly well. Black support was central to the union's victory at the company's mill in Montgomery, Alabama. In August 1976 organizers traveled to the city and succeeded in signing up a majority of the workforce in less than two weeks. Out of 425 workers, 275 were black, yet they were more likely to be concentrated in lower-level jobs and to work on the night shift. Organizer Robert Tim Brown noted that the campaign had been received enthusiastically by the African American employees, who clearly wanted better opportunities in the plant. At the same time, many of these workers had participated in civil rights protests, including the famous 1955–56 bus boycott that had helped to launch the civil rights movement. "It does appear," wrote Brown, "both because of the success of the campaign thus far, and because of the location of this plant and the history of the black movement in Montgomery, that this plant might be an excellent opportunity for winning a Stevens election." His analysis proved accurate. In early 1980 ACTWU won an election by drawing heavily on the support of African American activists.[21]

As most plants had white majorities, the union could not secure bargaining rights simply by mobilizing blacks. While organizers frequently struggled to unite blacks and whites, they faced an even greater challenge at the company's complex of plants in Wagram. These mills were located in a part of southeastern North Carolina that had a significant Native American population. Around 30 percent of workers at the plant were Native American, while a slightly smaller proportion were black. In August 1979, Verney Cumbee reported that one of the main problems in Wagram was "getting the Blacks and Indians to be strong together." John Barry, Cumbee's colleague, claimed that blacks responded more enthusiastically to the union than the Native Americans, who had adopted a wait-and-see attitude. Barry warned workers "not to be dragged into racial set-to," yet he was never able to recruit sufficient support from the Native Americans.[22] In a detailed analysis of ACTWU's problems in Wagram, he argued that the union was partly to blame for its difficulties because it did not have any Native American organizers. "Indian workers repeatedly resent the absence of Indian organizers," he wrote. "There are black and white organizers, as there are black and white workers; but there are no Indian organizers for Indian workers. This is perceived as though the Indians don't count. Unfortunately, they have often voted accordingly in Scotland and Robeson County union elections." With whites also reluctant to join the union, organizers struggled to make effective progress in Wagram.[23]

By the late 1970s, the union had made some progress in integrating its staff, yet its organizers were still predominantly white and male. In May 1977 thirty organizers were working on the campaign, of whom six were black and only four were women. Leaders acknowledged the need for further progress. "There is a need for at least five more black staff to insure at least one black staff representative in each sub-area," noted one report. "Hopefully, some of the additional black staff might be women." There was no recognition of the need to recruit Native American organizers, however, despite the fact that Stevens's plants in Rock Hill, South Carolina also employed a significant number of Native Americans.[24]

The organizer's job was a difficult and frequently unrewarding one. It was certainly not well paid. In the late 1970s, organizers earned around $5 an hour, little more than a textile worker. In return they worked long hours and drove long distances. As most mills ran twenty-four hours a day, organizers had to work at night and on weekends in order to contact workers effectively. Campaigns could last for several years, requiring staff to live out of motel rooms. They were permitted to go home only every other weekend, a rule that some flouted. By the summer of 1978, campaign directors Richard Rothstein and Harold McIver both expressed concern that staff were spending too long at home. "The situation is completely out of control," they noted. "It is getting to the point where staff who would like to be conscientious are feeling that they are being taken advantage of and it is creating a morale problem."[25]

Other internal problems hurt the campaign. Many organizers disliked having to pay their expenses up front, especially as it was many weeks before they were reimbursed. In May 1979, Charles Marsh threatened to "raise the roof" after a holdup in receiving his expenses. "It is ridiculous," fumed another indignant organizer, "that we must pay out our own money and then wait so long to get it back. It's time ACTWU financed the organizing campaigns instead of expecting their staff to do it for them." Some organizers challenged the orders of their directors. Jonathan Heller resigned in the summer of 1979 after having "policy differences" with his superiors, whom he accused of overriding the recommendations of field staff and not being sufficiently militant.[26] Turnover among organizers was damagingly high. In the Greenville area, workers complained that the unexpected departure of several organizers had prevented them "from building a strong campaign." Staff also frequently complained that they were overworked. In a typical report, Georgia-based organizer Fred Nye wrote: "We need someone else added to the Georgia Staff so that we can cover the Plants better." Mel Tate, who coordinated the union's activities in Georgia, similarly lamented that "there is just not enough time to get to all the locations."[27]

There were also disagreements between campaign strategists. The relationship between Richard Rothstein, who coordinated organizing from international headquarters, and Harold McIver, who ran the campaign on the ground, was particularly poor. A veteran of the civil rights movement, Rothstein was appointed full-time director of the Stevens organizing campaign in the spring of 1979. He replaced Paul Swaity, who was now free to concentrate on other drives. The new director soon resented McIver's influence over staff in the field. McIver, complained Rothstein, "intervenes in random ways in our direction of the campaign, making a consistent approach impossible and leaving the staff in doubt as to whom to follow."[28] These disagreements were partly a reflection of the fact that the campaign had two directors, who inevitably competed for control; amalgamating the positions or establishing a clearer chain of command seemed the obvious solution. Rothstein also complained about the ineffectiveness of some organizers. "Rudolph Downing," he wrote in a typically biting memo to McIver, "is a very good house caller, but is incapable of building a committee or planning a campaign in Anderson. He should be reassigned to Shelby."[29]

As union strategists had feared, the boycott also hurt the organizing drive. In June 1976 a letter that Stevens mailed to all of its workers claimed that the proposed boycott threatened "the jobs and the livelihood of thousands of Stevens workers." It provided, added Stevens, "additional and conclusive evidence that the union organizing campaign has not been to benefit our employees but to benefit the union." Both Scott Hoyman and Harold McIver reported that this letter had a "general chilling effect" upon organizing.[30] While not as damaging, the corporate campaign also complicated ACTWU's efforts to sign up new members. Like the boycott, the campaign attempted to disrupt Stevens's business operations and could therefore be used against the union. Rothstein urged that Ray Rogers's efforts not be publicized in the field. "While the corporate campaign cannot be portrayed as so direct a threat to our members' jobs as the boycott," he noted in August 1978, "it is still not very far removed."[31]

Throughout the late 1970s, company officials referred often to the boycott in their fight against ACTWU's organizing campaign. In a June 1978 letter to workers at Stevens plants in Wagram, local manager Ellis S. Reynolds asserted: *"The Union does not want customers to buy our products. The Union wants to 'Wipe Out' our Company. The Union is engaging in the world-wide boycott of the products you make. The Union wants to take away your jobs and your job security."* Within a month Rothstein commented to colleagues that "the company is increasingly using the boycott against us to some effect."[32]

The boycott also encouraged southern community leaders to rally behind Stevens. The local press in Greenville were particularly supportive. The *Greenville News-Piedmont* claimed that the boycott was "inherently tyrannical," adding that "innocent people inevitably get hurt in boycotts." The *Greenville Piedmont* went further, falsely accusing the union of launching an illegal secondary boycott. Bogged down in efforts to organize workers at two of Stevens's mills in the area, organizers were furious. "The effect of these editorials on the organizing campaign," reported Michael Krivosh, "seems to be extremely detrimental according to community contacts." It was difficult to know how to respond. As Krivosh put it, the union's opponents were far more "vocal" than its supporters, and it was unlikely that either paper would even print a rebuttal from ACTWU.[33]

In the towns where it operated its plants, the company continued to receive a great deal of backing from community leaders. Organizers claimed that Stevens was supported by other local employers, with the partial exception of some unionized construction firms. They also complained that some merchants refused to give credit to their supporters. The views of store owners in Roanoke Rapids were typical. "If Stevens hadn't taken over those mills, there'd be nothing here and everyone would be on welfare," noted one in 1977.[34] Many merchants were reluctant to rent office space to the union. In several cases, union meetings were held in black churches simply because there were no alternative venues. In the Georgia towns of Dublin, Tifton, and Milledgeville, staff spent a great deal of time searching for office premises, where they could hold their meetings. In Statesboro, where ACTWU maintained a skeletal organizing staff, the union was only able to rent a run-down building and was eventually pushed to vacate the premises after the owner refused to maintain it.[35]

The lengths to which some local officials would go to keep unions out of their communities were revealed well in Milledgeville, where mayor Robert Rice and police chief Charles Osborne hatched a plan to spy on organizers Mel Tate and Louis Washington. Unable to rent a meeting space in the small city in the summer of 1976, Tate and Washington instead conducted regular union meetings in their rooms at the local Holiday Inn. A "personal friend" of Rice, motel owner J. C. Green told the mayor that the two organizers were operating out of his premises. Claiming that he felt an obligation to take a "leadership role" in community affairs, Rice called a meeting with Osborne and local plant managers where they agreed to conduct surveillance of the organizers' activities. The meeting was attended by representatives from a range of local companies—J. P. Stevens, Concord Fabrics, Grumman Aerospace Company, Griffin Pipe Products, Meadow Industries, Holytex Corporation—who agreed that they had worked hard to attract industry to their community and were determined, as Rice put it, "to try to keep the union activities out of Milledgeville, Georgia."[36]

To this end, Rice promised to "monitor the meetings of the union organizers to obtain tag numbers." These details could then be run through the computer at the Milledgeville Police Department and their owners identified. Following the meeting, Osborne selected detectives James D. Josey and William Donald Miller to carry out the surveillance. The two officers would pick up a key from Green, who assigned them a room above those used by the two organizers. Although the city of Milledgeville offered to pay for the room, Green refused to accept any funds. The detectives were told to dress in plain clothes and to watch Tate and Washington, recording the name of anyone else they could identify who was seen with them. In addition, they were instructed to compile a list of license plate numbers and pass it on to Osborne. The chief warned his men not to use Milledgeville Police Department stationery when collecting the numbers, and to keep the surveillance confidential. "Mr. Osborne instructed Mr. Josey and myself not to discuss this surveillance with any other persons," recalled Miller, "including members of the Milledgeville Police Department or our wives." Altogether, the two detectives passed on more than a hundred license plate numbers to Osborne.[37]

Another key figure in the scheme was Rev. Dr. C. Wayman Alston, an African American minister who agreed to undermine black support for the union. Claiming that unions discriminated against black workers, Alston asserted that "blacks should not exchange one master for another, at the very moment that we appeared to be 'overcoming.'" Alston, however, later fell out with the mayor over his failure to promote more women and blacks into city government. In addition, he charged that Rice had harassed two respected African American leaders who had helped the union. According to Alston, Rice possessed a "union phobia, akin to the late Senator Joe McCarthy's fear of communists in government." Shocked at how far the mayor was willing to go to keep Milledgeville union-free, Alston broke details of the secret scheme to the press, resulting in a rash of articles in both local and national newspapers.[38]

In many ways, the events in Milledgeville were a reminder of Stevens's continuing willingness to violate the law in order to deter unionization. At the same time, there were again clear signs that the company was being more cautious than it had been in the past. Grumman Aerospace supplied its own security agents to help with the surveillance, but Stevens's legal department told its plant manager to avoid active involvement. The willingness of other firms to participate in the spying also suggested that Stevens's vigorous antiunionism was hardly unusual.

In the plant, union supporters did complain that they were refused overtime or treated more harshly, but there was no program of mass firings.[39] Of course, if the union had called an election, the company was armed with information that would have allowed it to pinpoint union supporters. As it was, the scheme became public in July 1978, effectively killing off the union's faltering efforts, when Alston, feeling used, told the mayor that he should find himself "another nigger" and contacted the press. Once news of the surveillance broke, attendance at union meetings plummeted. "Workers have told me since the news stories that they are afraid to meet or be seen with me or the other organizers," asserted Tate in July 1979. "[They] fear that they may lose their jobs, as well. Consequently, worker attendance at our meetings has dropped substantially." The union sued, and those involved in the scheme ended up paying damages. Concord Fabrics, for example, paid ACTWU $18,000 and pledged to refrain from further surveillance. It was another moral victory for the union, but they never succeeded in organizing the Milledgeville plant.[40]

Taken as a whole, the union had little to show for its extensive organizing efforts. Between 1977 and 1982, ACTWU strategists aimed to organize 20,000 new members a year, but they never achieved it. In 1978 and 1979, organizers succeeded in signing up around 9,500 workers, but this dropped to 6,400 in 1980 and just 4,400 in 1981. Across the country, employers were increasingly able to defeat union organizing drives, and the South proved particularly hard to crack. In 1978, a peak year of organizing activity, the union won 55 percent of all the votes it contested, but in the South it was victorious in only three elections and lost seven. In Dixie organizers' productivity, as measured by election wins, was the lowest in the country. In the late 1970s, ACTWU's leaders found that even an extensive commitment of resources did not lead to widespread organizing gains in the textile South.[41]

ELEVEN

Settlement

In October 1980, representatives from J. P. Stevens and ACTWU announced an historic settlement. Under it, the company finally signed a contract covering the sites where the union had won bargaining rights, while in return ACTWU agreed to call off its corporate campaign and boycott. The union and its supporters were euphoric; they took great satisfaction in the fact that Stevens, a company that had fought so hard to keep its plants union-free, had now agreed to deal with organized labor. "Finally," declared Jack Sheinkman, "after declaiming for years that the Union represented some sort of evil, and that the Company had an obligation to its workers to preserve their 'right' to be free of a union, in this Settlement Agreement Stevens acknowledges that it can live 'civilly' with the union."[1]

Although the union had won an important point of principle, Stevens only agreed to deal with ACTWU at the sites where it had won bargaining rights. At all of its other plants, managers vowed to resist subsequent organizing efforts. For another three years the union continued to try to sign up the firm's workers. In the fall of 1983 the two sides finally settled all remaining NLRB cases and brought their twenty-year battle to a complete halt.

The union could certainly take credit for helping to achieve the historic breakthrough in 1980. ACTWU had conducted an innovative campaign that had secured a great deal of positive publicity and had created real pressure on the company to settle. In particular, the corporate campaign had clearly unnerved Stevens. A key part of the settlement was the so-called Ray Rogers clause, which Stevens insisted on in order to stop ACTWU from ever using its corporate campaign tactics again.[2]

Rogers's ability to put pressure on the Metropolitan Life Insurance Company was especially significant. The union had decided to target the firm after learning from Securities and Exchange Commission records that much of Stevens's long-term debt, around $111 million in all, was owed to Met Life. In the past, the insurance company had been able to select its board members without opposition, but in 1980 the union announced that it would offer two alternative candidates. This would have required Met Life to spend more than $9 million on conducting the election, a burden that it was understandably anxious to avoid.[3]

In early October 1980, Met Life chairman Richard Shinn met with Whitney Stevens to express his concern about the union's tactics. Shinn later denied pressuring the new Stevens CEO in the meeting, but the textile executive soon decided that settlement was in his firm's best interests. He had been thinking along these lines for some time, and the meeting with Shinn helped Stevens to make up his mind. In particular, Stevens's executives worried about the company's continuing exposure to the corporate campaign. In the summer of 1979, company director James R. Franklin had referred in a trade publication to the union's attempt to "isolate Stevens from the rest of the corporate and financial world by driving experienced and valued leaders from the Stevens Board of Directors," and admitted, "Surprisingly and regrettably, the union has achieved a modicum of success using this destructive tactic." In September 1981, vice president for industrial relations Hal Addis told an industry gathering that the corporate campaign had been the "most effective" part of the union's efforts. Addis confirmed that Stevens became keen to reach a settlement because it feared "an even stronger impact from the campaign before it was over."[4]

Press observers credited the corporate campaign with a key role in securing the settlement. As *Time* concluded, "ACTWU's corporate harassment campaign . . . turned out to be very potent." Business sources agreed. *Business Week* called the corporate campaign "the union's ultimate weapon." Stevens settled, added the *Economist*, "partly because the campaign by the union to turn Stevens into a corporate pariah was taking its toll." Many business observers viewed Rogers's tactics as "something new and disturbing," and they were eager to ensure that Stevens settled before the maverick activist inflicted more damage on both the company and the broader corporate community.[5]

Ultimately, what secured a settlement was not simply the corporate campaign but the broader willingness of the union to keep fighting. In particular, the boycott and the ongoing organizing drive confirmed that the union would not give up easily. Company officials began to see that a limited settlement might be better than fighting on with no end in sight, especially if they could persuade ACTWU to abandon the boycott and the corporate campaign. Scott Hoyman was convinced that Stevens realized the union was not going to give in. "The most important reason for the Stevens company to settle was the fact that the union had been there for seventeen years," he recalled. "We became the lesser of two evils, an ongoing campaign or some kind of settlement." According to *New York Times* journalist Philip Shabecoff, the company's executives felt a "general weariness" and decided that an agreement was preferable to continuing an unending struggle.[6]

As early as March 1978, Stevens's top executives had begun private meetings with ACTWU's leaders, and while these talks did not produce any immediate change, they helped to convince the company of the union's unwillingness to abandon the campaign without significant concessions. Held in New York City, the negotiations were initiated by the company and certainly buoyed the union's morale. Murray Finley privately termed them "a key factor" and told the executive board in February 1979, "While there was no settlement, it indicates that they would like to settle." The meetings encouraged ACTWU's leaders to keep up the pressure on the firm, and they became particularly upbeat in the final two years of the struggle.[7]

Behind the scenes, influential management and labor figures pushed for a settlement. On the union side, Harry Van Arsdale, longtime president of the New York City Central Labor Council, used his extensive contacts with labor and business leaders to urge the two sides to reach agreement. At the same time, Virgil Conway was instrumental in keeping talks going on the management side. "Everybody on both sides would like to see a negotiated settlement," he claimed in June 1980.[8]

These efforts were greatly helped when James D. Finley was replaced by Whitney Stevens. In explaining his motives for stepping down, Finley made no mention of the union but emphasized that the time was right for a change. He was entering his sixty-fourth year and had served as CEO for ten years. "By modern standards in major corporations," he noted, "10 years as Chief Executive Officer is a long period of time." Finley clearly disagreed with making a settlement, and he was reputed to be unhappy with the general softening in the company's position toward the union. The long-serving official stayed on as a member of the Stevens board, but he passed the key positions of CEO and chairman to Whitney Stevens, who took over on January 1, 1980. The union saw the move as very important because they had been told by industry sources that Stevens was "a push-over compared to Finley."[9]

Almost immediately, a change in the company's approach to the conflict was apparent. Whitney Stevens had much less invested in the struggle than Finley, who had been a potent symbol of the firm's antiunionism for more than a decade. On March 4, 1980, the new CEO told the annual stockholders' meeting that he wanted to settle the dispute, a clear shift from his predecessor's stance. "We believe it is clearly in the company's interest to seek a fair contract," he declared.[10]

In the summer of 1980, Whitney Stevens initiated a new round of talks with ACTWU's leaders. The two sides met secretly in the Statler Hilton's Empire meeting rooms, leaving their offices before each session without even telling their staffs where they were going. As they became more familiar with each other, attitudes gradually softened. In particular, Whitney Stevens established a much closer personal relationship with Murray Finley than his stern predecessor had been able to do. The ACTWU leader later reported, "This has been an intensive negotiation and the relationship with the company has grown more cordial and civil." By the fall, the two sides were able to reach agreement with what Finley termed "a very cordial shaking of hands."[11]

The progress made in New York City filtered down to Roanoke Rapids, where the details of the contract were being hammered out by local managers and union officials. In the small community, negotiations took place in the more humble surroundings of the Potato House, a storage shed that Stevens had converted into a conference room. Here the company also softened its position. "Talks began picking up on October 8," recalled union representative Clyde Bush. "That's when we began to see the light, when you could really see the company had a change of heart." In the closing two weeks, company officials agreed to the final and binding arbitration of grievances, which had been a major stumbling block. In addition, they offered Roanoke Rapids workers a $1,300 payment to compensate them for missed wage increases.[12]

Union officials were delighted to have secured a settlement. "In the judgment of the officers," reported Murray Finley to the executive board, "our union has made a major breakthrough in the South." Finley felt that the union could "take pride in the way it carried the brunt of this campaign," arguing that the settlement was proof that all of their efforts had been worth it. "We carried the fight," agreed Jack Sheinkman, "and the labor movement has gained as a result of this fight." Sol Stetin, the one executive board member who had been involved with the Stevens campaign from the start, proclaimed the settlement "a great one" and saw it as a validation of his decision to merge with the ACWA.[13] Other leaders felt that the agreement served as a reminder to textile employers that the union was still capable of launching a determined fight. As Scott Hoyman commented, "because of the Stevens campaign, ACTWU is more respected by all employers."[14]

In Roanoke Rapids the rank and file were also very pleased, and gave an "overwhelming acceptance vote" to the agreement. "It feels real good," commented Gene Love, who had worked at the plants for three decades. "It's hard not to feel good, not so much for myself but for all those people who spent forty years giving their life to the company and then ended up with no security." He added, "I know that Stevens has to make a profit, but not in blood, not out of the bodies of its workers." Others were optimistic about the future. "This is just wonderful. It's a whole new life," said Syretha Medlin. "I think things are going to get better now," said another.[15] The settlement clearly strengthened the local union. In the few days after the contract vote, dozens of workers joined for the first time. According to union secretary Joyce Bush, many of these new recruits told her, "If we're going to reap the benefits, we're going to pay our way."[16]

Rather than sharing this euphoria, most residents of Roanoke Rapids were simply relieved that the long dispute had finally been settled. Many worried that the conflict had given their town a negative image, and now they hoped that life could return to "normal." Merchants admitted that their businesses had been hurt when Stevens had stubbornly refused to give wage increases to the Roanoke Rapids workers, so they were also pleased with the wage agreement. "Things have been rough since the workers were denied the last two pay raises, and business has suffered," admitted one.[17]

Across the country, the settlement was widely celebrated by many of the union's supporters. Senator Daniel Patrick Moynihan, who had helped to arrange a showing of *Norma Rae* on Capitol Hill, termed the agreement "a victory for all American workers." Liberal writer Michael Harrington similarly praised the union for achieving a "terrific victory." Congratulations poured into the union's offices from many other individuals and groups. Catholic bishop Sidney Metzgar praised the workers for achieving their "wonderful victory," adding that the agreement was "an answer to prayer." Civil rights leaders such as Clarence Mitchell also celebrated. Like many others, Mitchell hoped that the settlement would lead to the spread of unionization "throughout the South."[18]

The Stevens struggle had mobilized many other unions, and they were understandably delighted that a breakthrough had finally been achieved. The National Football League Players Association congratulated the textile union on its "imaginative and determined battle against J. P. Stevens." The NFL players' leaders hoped that the settlement would be "the beginning of a decade of growth of unionism throughout the country, and in particular, the South." The Stevens campaign had been well supported by the AFL-CIO, and new president Lane Kirkland was also delighted. In a public statement, Kirkland called the settlement "a major victory for all of the working people of America."[19] "I firmly believe," he told ACTWU's convention, "that because the union members at Stevens would not quit, and because their fellow workers and trade unionists would not abandon them, that better days are ahead for workers throughout the American textile industry and throughout all other industries."[20]

In many ways, the union and its supporters did have much to celebrate. For nearly two decades Stevens had adamantly refused to recognize the union. As the *New York Times* commented, during the long battle the company had become "the chief symbol of industry's determination to resist unionization in the South." By signing a contract, the company had made "a dramatic shift in its position toward labor-management relations." Writing in the *Los Angeles Times*, labor writer Harry Bernstein also emphasized the symbolic importance of the breakthrough. In a piece entitled "The Fall of J. P. Stevens," Bernstein insisted that "victory was the very existence of a union contract" with a company that had spent millions of dollars to avoid recognizing organized labor.[21]

In the agreement, Stevens made a number of important concessions. One of the most significant was the "portability" provision. Under this, the company agreed to offer the terms of the agreement at any of its plants that the union could organize over the next eighteen months. As unions had struggled to secure strong contracts in the South, this provision was potentially very significant: it ensured that if ACTWU won other elections, it could automatically offer workers a contract that contained the key items of the checkoff and the independent arbitration of grievances. Health and safety had also emerged as important issues in the campaign, especially in its latter stages. Traditionally, Stevens workers had very little say over these issues, but here too they made some important gains. The company agreed to maintain joint worker-management health and safety committees in each plant to give employees the opportunity to bring up their concerns. The agreement also provided for some regulation of workloads, with incentive rates now calculated to include adequate "personal and fatigue" allowances.[22]

The establishment of a grievance procedure was very important to many rank-and-file workers. Aware that they were no better paid than their non-union counterparts, they primarily looked to the union to give them a voice inside the mills. Many welcomed the chance to talk back to overbearing supervisors. "Now," claimed Mary Robinson from Montgomery, "we have the right to go up to a supervisor and say, 'This is wrong. No, it's not like that.' We never had that before. Now we can say, 'You can't do that. You've got to go by the contract.'" Stevens had been forced to modify its unilateral management style. According to Scott Hoyman, this shift represented "a revolutionary change in the relationship between workers and Stevens management." The company had strongly opposed any union business being conducted inside its plants, but now ACTWU representatives were permitted to enter the mills to investigate complaints. Elected stewards were allowed to process these grievances during their paid working time. And, significantly, Stevens had finally agreed to a checkoff of union dues, ensuring that ACTWU's local unions would have the financial stability that they needed to operate effectively.[23]

The union too made compromises in order to secure the agreement. Although the company granted a 19.3 percent wage increase to its Roanoke Rapids employees, this hike merely gave them the same pay as the firm's nonunion workers. They now received $5.10 an hour, eleven cents more than the average textile wage. For the next eighteen months, the union also agreed to give up some of the organizing tools that it had secured through NLRB and court rulings, including the right to address workers inside the plants. ACTWU leaders argued that such compromises were inevitable. "The pudding didn't have as many plums as the union would have liked," concluded one analysis. "But the important thing, the miracle is, that we have a pudding at all."[24]

At the time, many union supporters overlooked these limitations. The understandable euphoria of victory led labor leaders to underestimate the barriers that still faced unions in the South. Instead, they claimed that organizers would now sweep through the region signing up willing recruits. Israel Kugler of the Workmen's Circle in New York was typically ebullient. "Words cannot convey our elation at the ACTWU's victory over J. P. Stevens," he gushed. "At long last labor's Operation Dixie is well on its way to fruition." Continuing to view Stevens as the key to organizing the entire South, other labor leaders hailed the agreement as highly significant. "The J. P. Stevens settlement," wrote International Ladies Garment Workers Union president Sol C. Chaikin, "is a great victory—a victory for the textile workers, for ACTWU, and for the entire labor movement. . . . Your unrelenting persistence and your innovative creativity in the J. P. Stevens campaign have opened up new vistas for labor in the South and in the nation."[25] ACTWU leaders themselves envisaged that the settlement would pave the way for further organizing gains. Murray Finley told his executive board that "organizing in the textile plants will continue in order to take advantage of the settlement in J. P. Stevens."[26]

The key weakness of the agreement was that Stevens adamantly refused to pay its unionized workers more than its unorganized employees. As a result, executives were confident that they could fend off subsequent organizing efforts. As the *Daily News Record* reported, "Stevens never could agree to give the workers at the organized plants anything more in wage and benefits than it has offered to its non-union workers. To do otherwise would mean total corporate surrender to future organizing efforts at other Stevens plants."[27] Executives from other companies agreed that ACTWU would continue to struggle. "If you compare wages to be paid those workers in the recently unionized Stevens plants with what non-union mill workers are receiving in South Carolina, you will see that there is no incentive there," commented one executive from the Palmetto State. "The wages are right in line with other non-union plants."[28]

As organizers continued their efforts, they found that the settlement was actually a hindrance. Working on the union's ongoing campaign in Wagram, John Barry described the problem. "Unfortunately," he wrote, "the record speaks for itself: the settlement has had little effect on unorganized Stevens workers at Wagram and elsewhere." The union had now lost its promise of delivering something better. "The settlement," he concluded, "makes clear that wages and benefits are the same in unorganized as in organized plants. Whether we like it or not, money talks."[29] The union faced similar problems when it tried to capitalize on the settlement by organizing other southern companies. Like Stevens, these employers studiously matched union wages and benefits, undercutting ACTWU's appeal. In September 1981 an internal analysis of the union's organizing program identified a central problem: "Many unorganized workers feel their wages and benefits are as good or better than those in union plants, and that they have little to gain by union organization."[30]

Despite making the settlement, Stevens remained strongly opposed to ACTWU's ongoing organizing efforts. The company's top executives drew a clear distinction between the situation in Roanoke Rapids, where they now accepted that the union represented the majority will, and their unorganized plants, where they continued to vigorously fight organized labor. Shortly after agreeing to the settlement, the company ran newspaper advertisements across the textile belt that laid out this position. "We sincerely believe the great majority of Stevens people also oppose unions," they reiterated, "and we intend to support them in their right not to be organized."[31]

Ultimately, neither side could claim a total victory from the settlement, especially as both had been damaged by such a lengthy and costly battle. As the *Raleigh News and Observer* noted, "Both sides came out with scars: for Stevens, a denting of the corporate image; for the union, a drain on the labor coffers." Despite settling with the union, the company never completely shook off its reputation as a lawless renegade, and this undoubtedly hurt its business. Officials refused to admit how much they had spent on the protracted fight with the union, but they later acknowledged that the battle had distracted them from making important investments in keeping their plants efficient. In this way, the lengthy war may have contributed to the firm's longterm economic decline.[32]

In all, the labor movement spent at least $30 million on its battle with Stevens. This included $11 million dished out by the TWUA between 1963 and 1976, up to $15 million expended by ACTWU on the boycott and corporate campaign, and $4 million contributed by the AFL-CIO. The amount was believed to be the most that a union had ever spent on a campaign against a single company. "Certainly, I can't think of anything that rivals it," admitted AFL-CIO research director Rudolph Oswald. The heavy expenditure took its toll. Between 1976 and 1983, ACTWU operated in the red, a predicament caused largely by the expense of funding the Stevens campaign.[33]

In the wake of the settlement, Stevens announced an overhaul of its operations, closing some plants and trimming the workforce at others. Now that it had resolved its battle with the union, the company insisted that it had to carry out these cuts to stay competitive. In 1981 alone, Stevens closed six of its southern plants, laying off more than two thousand workers. At the end of 1982 it also shut its unionized plant in Montgomery, Alabama, although the company agreed not to use the closure to hold back ACTWU's organizing efforts.[34]

This commitment notwithstanding, the cuts made many workers fearful of signing union cards. In August 1981 ACTWU lost a vote at a Stevens plant in Rock Hill, South Carolina, and at other sites the union failed to gain enough support to even contest elections. In February 1981 Stetin admitted to the executive board that "we are not making the progress we had hoped for in other J. P. Stevens plants." Finley added that the contract settlement had not led to the anticipated breakthrough, and he complained that the cost of organizing was "extremely burdensome."[35]

The major cause of the layoffs was the steady rise in cheap imports into the United States. Struggling to compete, many firms shed staff or folded up altogether. As its members lost their jobs, the union's ability to fund future organizing drives steadily dropped. Between 1976 and 1984, ACTWU lost around 90,000 members. "Reduced membership," noted the union's executive board in July 1982, "is a serious problem both financially and organizationally."[36] The majority of ACTWU's members worked in the apparel industry, and it was clothing plants that were the hardest hit by imports. In 1977 Murray Finley told the union's executive board how imports had gradually become a major threat. "From a little issue of importing of apparel in the sixties," he noted, "this has become today the single greatest threat to the livelihood of over two million American textile and apparel workers and to the continuation of a viable domestic industry. The penetration is becoming horrendous."[37]

Already in debt, the union was now forced to make cuts. Shortly after reaching a settlement with Stevens, ACTWU's leaders laid off many of those who had been working on the campaign. As the union had agreed to call off its corporate campaign and boycott, some of these layoffs would have occurred anyway, yet there was no hiding the fact ACTWU could no longer afford to finance such an extensive battle. "Two million dollars still has to be cut, and it will be done with fairness," reported Finley in January 1981. "We must sacrifice because there is no alternative." Shortly afterwards, Stetin reported that seven staff from the textile division had been laid off, including several organizers on the Stevens campaign. But still Sheinkman pushed him for more cuts. "Sol, I believe you said there were 9," he wrote. "I would like to get 10 by the time the GEB meets in April."[38]

In the early 1980s the union also confronted a conservative political climate. Incoming Republican president Ronald Reagan began his new term by firing 13,000 striking members of the Professional Air Traffic Controllers Organization (PATCO), a move that led to a wave of concessionary bargaining across the country. In the face of renewed corporate resistance, ACTWU's efforts faltered. In May 1982, Scott Hoyman reported that the union was receiving "many requests from textile employers for concessions." It was becoming difficult to resist these demands, especially as workers now feared that they would be permanently replaced if they went out on strike. As Stetin later reflected, the Stevens settlement had been a "step in the right direction," but the union had been unable to capitalize on it fully because "we got Reagan."[39]

With the political and economic climate hostile, the union struggled. In the early 1980s ACTWU lost an important election at the Linn-Corriher Corporation in North Carolina and abandoned a campaign at Cannon Mills without a vote. In 1980 the union was able to win only 37 percent of the elections it contested, and most of these victories were at small plants. The repeated lack of success took its toll on staff. In September 1981 an internal analysis concluded that organizers were "frustrated, having not been able to bring about an election victory in years. They are failing to excite workers to organize because they themselves are no longer inspired, self-motivated and self-confident."[40] In private, the union's leaders recorded their disappointment. As ACTWU president, Murray Finley had invested heavily in organizing, but he accepted that the union's efforts had still fallen short. "We have been ineffective," he acknowledged, "even though we spend about 50 percent of our income on organizing."[41]

Once it had called off its boycott and corporate campaign, the union found that it lost momentum. Lacking the focus that the Stevens campaign had provided, it no longer could transform the struggle to organize the southern textile industry into an issue of national concern. "The intensity is gone," declared the *Southern Textile News,* an industry publication. ". . . Now, the union's campaign is diffused and defused." Even the antiunion *News* acknowledged, however, that the union had achieved more by "focusing on one textile company" than it had through its previous "shotgun approach to textile organizing." A "forceful and comprehensive campaign" had brought one of the largest southern textile companies "to terms."[42]

Despite its difficulties in capitalizing on the settlement, the union could clearly take many positives out of the Stevens campaign. The fact that ACTWU had secured an agreement at all was very significant. Although the union had organized only a portion of the firm's workers, it still represented one of the biggest gains in the textile industry's history. "Although the agreement covers only ten of Stevens' 80 plants and just 3,500 of its 32,000 production workers," noted *Time,* "it is a union victory." With other major textile companies—Burlington Industries, Cannon Mills, Deering Milliken—remaining 100 percent nonunion, the establishing of even a limited union presence at a large textile chain was significant. As historian Clete Daniel has observed, "Stevens had bowed to the union only slightly, but even a partial capitulation caused leading employers in the southern textile industry to question their long-held assumption that unionism would, at some point, collapse under the crushing weight of the disappointments heaped on it."[43]

The significance of this breakthrough was reflected in the displeasure of some industry executives. Duke Kimbrell, president of the North Carolina Textile Manufacturers' Association, asserted at the time that he was "disappointed that J. P. Stevens would settle." The union, he added, represented a small minority of the company's employees, and executives could have continued to resist. Industry leaders in South Carolina had a similar reaction. Like their counterparts in the Tar Heel State, these officials worried that the agreement would deter industrialists from setting up new factories in the South.[44]

In Roanoke Rapids, building on the progress they had made during the settlement negotiations, the two sides were able to establish a constructive working relationship. In February 1981 a journalist from the *Raleigh News and Observer* visited the textile community and found that the two sides were now "getting along" well. "I guess, on the whole, everything is going pretty smooth," admitted union official Clyde Bush. Managers were growing used to the union's presence. "We respect them, and we think they respect us," commented a company official in October 1981.[45]

In the years immediately after the settlement, the two sides resolved their differences amicably. In May 1985 workers in Roanoke Rapids ratified a three-year agreement, their third since the historic 1980 breakthrough. The contract contained a number of improvements, including better severance pay and a stronger seniority clause. The union had become an established presence in the North Carolina community, with workers meeting at a smart new union hall named after Scott Hoyman. Hoyman himself remained active in servicing the local, and he was proud of the stable relationship he was able to establish with company officials. Above all, he felt it showed that unions did not stop companies from operating competitive plants. As he reflected in 1995, "The fact that a union was willing to spend seventeen years and a lot of money and a lot of staff time and win something in the end, and to have the company still continue to operate those plants successfully, that's a big change."[46]

In the fall of 1983 the two sides were also able to conclude a final truce. Ironically, this agreement came shortly after the death of the man whom many viewed as the architect of the firm's antiunionism. Robert Stevens passed away in January 1983 at the age of eighty-three after a brief illness. Since his retirement the former CEO had stayed on as an emeritus director, and many observers believed that he had continued to influence the firm's labor relations policies. Within a year of his death, the company agreed to pay the union $1 million to settle all outstanding charges of unfair labor practices. In addition, it pledged around $200,000 in back pay to eighteen discharged workers. ACTWU leaders welcomed the settlement, especially as it helped to push the union into the black for the first time in many years.[47]

In announcing the settlement, company attorney Robert T. Thompson indicated that Stevens had softened its stance considerably. The company, he noted, had made the agreement because it had "an ongoing relationship with the union where they do represent the employees." Executives had clearly reconciled themselves to a union presence in their plants. Confirming this, ACTWU counsel Arthur M. Goldberg noted that Stevens had made "a commitment to live with us on a civilized basis in the organized situation."[48] This change was more obvious in a private part of the settlement, as Whitney Stevens wrote NLRB general counsel William Lubbers to assure him that he would not "tolerate conduct by any of our personnel which would infringe upon employee rights." Satisfied with the company's commitment, Lubbers himself commented that Stevens's employees were now "in a position to exercise their statutory rights, free of coercive opposition."[49]

The truce was not as widely publicized as the original contract settlement, but it was important because it finally ended the twenty-year battle between the union and J. P. Stevens. ACTWU leaders stopped targeting the firm's plants. Both sides had been scarred by their lengthy fight, and now they realized that they had to address other challenges. Even in the early 1980s, it was clear that a massive joint effort would be needed to try to secure the industry's long-term economic future. Yet few could have predicted just how rapid the pace of the industry's decline would be over the next two decades.

EPILOGUE

In the years after the truce, both the textile and apparel industries fared badly. Like most U.S. textile firms, Stevens tried to stay competitive by laying off some employees and increasing the workloads of those who remained. In 1977, at the height of ACTWU's campaign, the firm employed 44,100 Americans, but this fell dramatically to 23,400 in 1987. By the late 1980s these efforts could not save the historic textile company from being bought out by a competitor. Throughout the 1980s and early 1990s, plant closings also hurt ACTWU. As their organization lost members, ACTWU's leaders began to look for a merger partner, and in 1995 they joined with the International Ladies Garment Workers Union to create the new Union of Needletrades, Industrial, and Textile Employees (UNITE).[1]

Rising levels of imports were the main cause of the decline. Between 1973 and 1985, imports into the U.S. textile market doubled, and they continued to increase in subsequent years. By the end of the 1980s, imports claimed a third of the U.S textile market and 48 percent of its apparel market. In both the textile and apparel industries, employment levels tumbled. In the major textile state of North Carolina, some 100,000 textile jobs were lost between 1989 and 1999.[2] In the apparel industry, the number of workers in U.S. plants fell from around 1.2 million in 1986 to 846,000 nine years later.[3]

Both union leaders and textile industrialists had complained about imports since the 1950s, but in the 1980s the problem became much more acute. "Imports have threatened the jobs in one or more of the ACTWU industries for nearly two decades," noted the union in 1987. "The last three years were somehow different. The U.S. markets were flooded with goods from all parts of the world."[4] Within the apparel industry, many imports came into the United States under Section 807 of the U.S. Tariff Schedule. Set up in 1964, the schedule stipulated that garments could be sewn or assembled elsewhere out of cloth cut in the States, incurring substantially less duty when they entered the country than garments both cut and sewn abroad. In 1985 the International Trade Commission reported that there were 825 plants in Mexico carrying out Section 807 work under the "twin plant program." In all, these facilities employed 250,000 workers. The central advantage of foreign production was lower wage costs, a key factor in the labor-intensive apparel industry. In 1984 the average wage in the U.S. apparel industry was $7 an hour, but it was only $1 in Mexico and just twenty-one cents in China.[5]

Despite their history of conflict, labor and industry leaders worked together to try to secure tariff protection. With their high-profile "Crafted with Pride in the USA" program, the two sides also encouraged the public to buy American-made textiles. These efforts yielded few results. Influenced by consumer groups who supported free trade, most politicians refused to support more stringent import restrictions. As ACTWU's executive board noted glumly in March 1984, "Congress believes in the gospel of free trade."[6]

Lacking effective protection against cheap imports, former giants such as Stevens were soon in danger of extinction. In 1987 the company issued what was to be its final annual report. In it executives noted that imports now posed "the industry's continuing and most tenacious problem." Nevertheless, as Stevens headed into its 175th anniversary year, executives remained publicly hopeful that they could meet the challenges ahead. These hopes were not realized. In 1988 one of the nation's oldest textile firms disappeared as a corporate entity when it was divided up into three separate companies.[7]

The split was initiated in February, when top executives led by Whitney Stevens made a $696 million leveraged buyout proposal. As one analyst put it, the move showed that "Stevens has got a 'for sale' sign on it and . . . there's going to be either another offer or a higher price from management." Soon afterwards West Point Pepperell, a Georgia-based competitor, paid $1.2 billion for Stevens and promptly split it up.[8]

Plant closures had a particularly harsh impact on small southern textile communities. Over the course of the 1980s, J. P. Stevens closed all three of its plants in Great Falls, South Carolina, eliminating 1,600 jobs in a settlement of just 2,600 people. Although not all of these workers had lived in

Great Falls, their wages had helped to sustain downtown businesses. In 1991 a journalist from the *New York Times* who journeyed to the small town found that the downtown area was full of abandoned stores. "You always thought," commented Randy Campbell, who had worked in all three mills, "that something that was here for so long could never close down, but it did, and there's not much left here to close anymore." He added, "I don't think in my lifetime this town will ever recover to what it was."[9]

The decline of the textile and apparel industries accelerated in the wake of the 1994 North American Free Trade Agreement, which encouraged low-wage industries to relocate to Mexico. NAFTA was strongly opposed by the AFL-CIO, which worried about the potential loss of jobs and the fact that the treaty contained no guarantee of enforceable labor rights. Their opposition was largely ignored by new Democratic president Bill Clinton, who had moved his party to the center in order to ensure electoral success. Across the country, the treaty led to a wave of job losses and undermined unions' bargaining power, especially as employers could now threaten to move to Mexico unless they secured significant economic concessions from their U.S. workers. Once NAFTA became effective, both the textile and apparel industries hemorrhaged jobs. In fact, of all the job losses in the U.S. textile industry between 1941 and 2002, 36 percent occurred after NAFTA. In 2001, the industry's worst year since the Great Depression, sixty-two mills in the Carolinas alone shut their doors for good.[10]

From the perspective of the twenty-first century, the textile industry's decline overshadows the Stevens campaign. In seeing Stevens as the key to organizing the entire South, union leaders reasoned that the textile industry would continue to dominate the southern economy. By the time of the 1980 settlement, some observers already sensed that the industry's days were numbered. In a thought-provoking editorial, the *New York Times* warned that U.S. unions needed to adjust to the fact that the markets for most goods were "increasingly international." It noted that "1980 is not 1935, nor even 1963, when this battle began. . . . even if the victory allows labor to show employers once again that they cannot run away from unions, that's not much of a lesson when the main suitors of labor-intensive industries are not in the Carolinas but in Asia." In recent years, the few breakthroughs that textile unions have been able to make have usually been eclipsed by the industry's chronic instability. In 1999 this was forcefully demonstrated when UNITE finally managed to organize the large complex of mills in Kannapolis, North Carolina, that had formerly been owned by Cannon Mills. In the wake of the vote, economic insecurity hung over the plants, and within four years the mill's new owners had liquidated the entire site. In the biggest layoff in North Carolina's history, more than 3,400 people lost their jobs, leaving former employees economically and emotionally devastated.[11]

Despite the decline of the industry, the Stevens struggle remains important. The campaign reminds us that some significant activism took place in the 1970s, an understudied decade that has often been dismissed as "generally quiescent." At the height of the battle, the union successfully recruited support from civil rights groups, demonstrating that these organizations continued to be active in the 1970s. In addition, they mobilized women's groups and encouraged activism from a generation of students who supposedly lacked the social conscience of their 1960s predecessors. The campaign also stimulated grassroots activism from conservative groups, mirroring the broader mobilization of the New Right in the 1970s.[12]

Above all, the Stevens campaign remains important because of the influence it had on labor relations. In the 1970s Stevens epitomized corporate resistance to unions. Even before Reagan's election, often viewed as the starting point for a corporate onslaught on unions, business opposition to organized labor was on the increase, and it was clear that the labor movement was going to face tough times regardless of who was elected.[13] In 1978 George Meany complained that employers were becoming increasingly antiunion. "Employer challenges to collective bargaining have never been greater since the late 1930s," he charged. Throughout the 1970s the percentage of NLRB elections won by unions steadily fell. In 1969 they were successful in 57 percent of the elections held, but this dropped to 45 percent in 1979. Between 1976 and 1979, deauthorizations and decertifications rose from 3 percent of all elections to 11 percent. As ACTWU's Paul Swaity reflected in 1979, "law-breaking J. P. Stevens style" was becoming increasingly common.[14]

In the 1980s and 1990s, many companies copied the tactics that Stevens had pioneered. These decades were characterized by the dramatic decline of the labor movement. Between 1983 and 1999, for instance, union membership tumbled from around 20 percent of the nonagricultural labor force to just 13.5 percent. While the decline of the manufacturing sector hurt many unions, rising corporate opposition was another major cause of organized labor's decline. As Stephen H. Norwood's recent *Strikebreaking and Intimidation* has demonstrated, in the 1980s and 1990s many executives fired union activists in order to defeat organizing campaigns. As the Stevens campaign had graphically highlighted to a national audience, it typically took several years for fired workers to be reinstated by the understaffed NLRB, and by this time disillusioned organizers had invariably left town.[15]

In the last twenty years, Stevens's tactics of openly violating labor laws have become increasingly common, partly because they make economic sense. As the case emphasized, employers could even deduct NLRB back pay awards from their taxes as a legitimate business expense. On a broader level, it was cheaper for large employers to fight the union than to accede to its economic demands. By 1977 Stevens had paid out $1.3 million in back pay and fines, yet it would have cost the company more than $8 million to give their 40,000 workers a modest wage increase of ten cents an hour. As Stevens noted, even the legal costs of fighting the union were "not material in the Company's overall operation."[16]

As striking has become increasingly ineffective, many unions have instead launched corporate campaigns against intransigent employers.[17] During the Stevens campaign, Ray Rogers launched the very first corporate campaign, and in the 1980s he tried to use similar tactics in struggles against Hormel Foods and International Paper. By this time Rogers's tactics were well known and he was unable to repeat his success. In the 1980s Rogers also influenced other unions to launch campaigns of their own. By June 1987, more than fifty corporate campaigns had taken place across the United States.[18]

During corporate campaigns, unions have been most effective when they have forged effective bonds with nontraditional allies. As the Stevens case highlighted, unions could hit back at multinational companies by uniting with labor leaders from other countries. In the 1980s, locked-out members of the Oil, Chemical & Atomic Workers Union worked with foreign unions and environmentalists in a successful struggle against German chemical firm BASF. In the early 1990s, international cooperation was likewise a central feature of the United Steelworkers' successful battle against RAC Corporation, which demanded major concessions from locked-out workers in Ravenswood, West Virginia. The workers resisted the company's demands by forging close links with unions in Europe, creating pressure on Marc Rich, the elusive international financier who controlled RAC. Tracking Rich across Europe, the union had, in the words of one of its leaders, "put up a picket line around the world."[19]

Despite these occasional successes, union leaders continued to complain that only labor law reform could create the level playing field that they needed to compete effectively against hostile employers. In 1994, AFL-CIO efforts to secure labor law reform were thwarted by a Senate filibuster, just as they had been in 1978. On both occasions, union leaders complained that Democratic presidents had not done enough to support their efforts.[20]

Without a change in the law, union leaders face an uphill struggle to organize new members and protect those that they have, yet at the start of the twenty-first century there are also grounds for optimism. In recent years, unions have recruited new members in service industries and the public sector, becoming increasingly responsive to minorities and women in the process. UNITE itself has made organizing breakthroughs in a wide variety of industries, increasingly reaching out to African American and Latino workers. In many ways, the Stevens case showed that labor can secure recognition from even the most powerful and intransigent employers. Modern-day union leaders look back on the Stevens campaign with pride, taking satisfaction in the way they forced such an antiunion company to moderate its behavior. As current UNITE president Bruce Raynor puts it, "No way should we win, but we did."[21]

NOTES

Introduction

1. For coverage of the Justice Day protests, see Del Mileski to General Officers and Leadership, January 8, 1979, pp. 6, 13, "Status Reports II" folder, box 401, ACTWU Papers, held at the Kheel Center for Labor-Management Documentation and Archives, School of Industrial and Labor Relations, Cornell University (hereafter cited as "ACTWU-Cornell"). Mileski's report includes a full range of clippings on the Justice Day protests from December 1, 1978, including "3000 March in Midtown to Attack J. P. Stevens' Anti-Union Policies," *New York Times*; "Trade Unionists Rally Against Textile Firm," *Los Angeles Times*; "Stevens Label Causes Stir: Tablecloths Fly Prior To Boycott Luncheon," *Indianapolis Star*; "State Labor Leaders Urge Textile Boycott," *Albany Times Union*; "Rally Supports Unionizing Effort," *Atlanta Constitution*; "Stevens Boycott Backers Meet," *Knoxville News-Sentinel*; David Kepple, "He Hopes to Put Heat on Business," *Birmingham News*; and, from December 7, 1978, "Hundreds Attend Detroit Rally in Support of Stevens Workers," *Michigan AFL-CIO News*.

For the "Don't Sleep with Stevens" slogan, see "Don't Sleep with Stevens Tonight," n.d., "Materials which accompanied Status Reports" folder, box 401, ACTWU-Cornell.

2. "Partial List of Endorsements of the J. P. Stevens Boycott," July 9, 1978, fiche 1 of 5, "J. P. Stevens Supporters and Resolutions" file, fiche box 7, Murray Finley Papers, held at the Kheel Center for Labor-Management Documentation and Archives, School of Industrial and Labor Relations, Cornell University (hereafter cited as "Finley Papers"; all sources cited here are in fiche box 7).

3. "Textile Mill Employment in the Southeast, 1969–73," July 11, 1973, box 7, Textile Workers Union of America Papers (MSS97–196), held at the State Historical Society of Wisconsin, Madison (hereafter cited as "TWUA Papers"). The figures refer to the states of Alabama, Florida, Georgia, Mississippi, North Carolina, South Carolina, Tennessee, and Virginia. Unless otherwise indicated, the MSS number for all the TWUA Papers cited here is MSS396.

4. Hodges, "Stevens and the Union," 56; Stetin quoted in 1976 TWUA Convention Proceedings, 12.

5. Hodges, "Stevens and the Union," 58.

6. *Decisions and Orders of the National Labor Relations Board*, vol. 220, case 34, p. 270 (hereafter cited in form 220 NLRB 34 at 270).

7. Daniel, *Culture of Misfortune*, 274–75; Hodges, "Stevens and the Union," 60–63.

8. Warren Brown, "Great Labor War Gains Tallied," *Washington Post*, October 26, 1980; Finley quoted in ACTWU General Executive Board Minutes, March 1–4, 1977, p. 9, "GEB March Meeting" folder, box 124, ACTWU-Cornell.

9. McIver memo, October 17, 1978, "J. P. Stevens IUD Harold McIver Campaign Co-Ordinator—Miscellaneous Correspondence" folder, box 366, ACTWU-Cornell; Sala quoted in David Leonhardt, "James Finley, Textile Executive, Dies at 86," *New York Times,* April 10, 2003.

10. The growth of southern labor history is summarized well in Zieger, *Organized Labor* and *Southern Labor in Transition,* and Eskew, *Labor in the Modern South.* The growth of the field has been particularly influenced by Hall et al., *Like a Family,* which effectively challenged the stereotype of the docile southern worker, showing instead how workers shaped the culture of the early southern mill villages. Studies of southern textile workers published since *Like a Family* include Flamming, *Creating the Modern South;* Simon, *Fabric of Defeat;* Brattain, *Politics of Whiteness;* Waldrep, *Southern Workers;* Clark, *Like Night and Day;* Minchin, *What Do We Need a Union For?;* Salmond, *Gastonia.* Two recent books have also explored the 1934 general textile strike, the biggest labor dispute in southern history: Irons, *Testing the New Deal,* and Salmond, *General Textile Strike.*

11. Conway, *Rise Gonna Rise.* Contemporary journalistic accounts include Guzzardi, "Upper Hand"; Kovler, "The South: Last Bastion"; McConville, "Southern Textile War"; Raskin, "Clenched Fist"; Tucker, "Struggle to Organize"; "Labor in the South: The Stonewall at Stevens"; "When a Union Goes All Out." National newspapers such as the *New York Times* covered the campaign extensively, particularly in the late 1970s. See, for example, A. H. Raskin, "J. P. Stevens: Labor's Big Domino," *New York Times,* August 15, 1976.

12. On Crystal Lee Sutton, see Hodges, "Real Norma Rae"; Toplin, "Norma Rae."

13. Hodges, "Stevens and the Union"; Daniel, *Culture of Misfortune.* This account draws chiefly on two collections of papers deposited by ACTWU. The collections, both recent additions that are unprocessed, are held at the Southern Labor Archives, Georgia State University, and at the Kheel Center for Labor-Management Documentation and Archives at Cornell University. Both contain a great deal of material on the union's efforts to organize Stevens that has not been utilized; the Cornell collection, in particular, comprises more than a thousand boxes, many of them dealing with the Stevens campaign. I have also used the papers of the TWUA, held at the State Historical Society of Wisconsin in Madison. This is a processed collection, and it has been well utilized by scholars, although the Stevens part of the collection has not been heavily mined.

14. The "new Stevens strategy" is detailed in Nick Builder, "J. P. Stevens: Walterboro, S.C. Campaign," February 1979, "J. P. Stevens Richard Rothstein 1978–1980" folder, box 331, ACTWU-Cornell. For the importance of black workers in convincing union leaders to continue with the campaign, see 1970 TWUA Convention Proceedings, 207.

15. Minchin, *Hiring the Black Worker,* 3; Raynor interview.

16. ACTWU General Executive Board Minutes, October 10, 1979, "10/10/79" folder, box 854, ACTWU-Cornell (Stetin quotation, 18).

17. Ross, "Weekly Organizing Activity Report," May 10, 1980, "Ross, Robert" folder, box 55, Papers of ACTWU's Southern Regional Office, held at the Southern Labor Archives, Georgia State University, Atlanta (hereafter cited as ACTWU-Atlanta).

18. Zieger and Gall, *American Workers, American Unions,* 208–9, 256 (quotation).

19. ACTWU General Executive Board Minutes, October 25–26, 1976, pp. 21, 23, "GEB October Meeting 1976" folder, box 124, ACTWU-Cornell.

20. *Heritage Foundation Backgrounder,* August 3, 1977, in "J. P. Stevens Newspaper Clippings" folder, box 34, ACTWU-Atlanta.

21. Gaventa and Smith, "Deindustrialization," 182–83; Charles Lunan, "Empty Mills Burden Carolinas," *Charlotte Observer,* July 22, 2002, and Irwin Speizer, "Crisis in Asia Costs N.C. Jobs in Textile Mills," *Raleigh News and Observer,* January 31, 1999, both in the North Carolina Collection Clipping File, held at the Wilson Library, University of North Carolina at Chapel Hill (hereafter cited as NCCCF), under "Textile Mills."

22. Norwood, *Strikebreaking and Intimidation,* 246–47 (quotations, 247); Geoghegan, *Which Side Are You On?* 253–54; Zieger and Gall, *American Workers, American Unions,* 240–70; M. Goldfield, *Decline of Organized Labor.*

23. Daniel, *Culture of Misfortune,* 278. For a summary of subsequent corporate campaigns, see Juravich and Bronfenbrenner, *Ravenswood,* 69–71. For Rogers's high-profile later involvement in the strike at the Hormel meatpacking company in Austin, Minnesota, see Rachleff, *Hard-Pressed in the Heartland.* On unions' recent efforts to exert international pressure on global firms, see Juravich and Bronfenbrenner, *Ravenswood,* 102–19, 156–69; Minchin, *Forging a Common Bond,* 51–57, 84–85, 99–100, 130–31.

Chapter 1. Selecting a Target

1. "Story of J. P. Stevens," 19; Whalen, "Durable Threads," 106–8 (quotation, 108).

2. Memo "Closed," June 1, 1966, and James G. McKnight to George Perkel, August 24, 1965, "J. P. Stevens (A + M Karagheusian, Freehold, New Jersey)" folder, box 680, ACTWU-Cornell; "Textile Mills Closed by J. P. Stevens and Co., Inc. in New England and Mid-Atlantic States, 1951 to date," October 1980, "J. P. Stevens Plant Closings 1951–" folder, box 628, ACTWU-Cornell.

3. Daniel, *Culture of Misfortune,* 157; TWUA Research Department Labor Relations Report no. 65, September 14, 1953, box 8, TWUA Papers (MSS 97–196).

4. Hodges, *New Deal Labor Policy,* 9–12; Hartford, *Where Is Our Responsibility?* 151; Hall et al., *Like a Family,* 197; Salmond, *General Textile Strike,* 2–3; George A. Kelly, "The J. P. Stevens Boycott: Is It Having An Effect?" May 14, 1979, p. 7, in "J. P. Stevens" folder, box 104, ACTWU-Cornell.

5. "Large TWUA Mills Liquidated Since 1954," November 1963, "Research Department 1963" folder, box 625, TWUA Papers; Minutes of the ACTWU General Executive Board, December 3–7, 1977, "GEB December 1977" folder, box 124, ACTWU-Cornell (Stetin quotation, 8); "TWUA Membership and Workers covered by TWUA Agreements, 1946–74," May 21, 1976, box 3, TWUA Papers (MSS97–196); Perkel interview, tape 5, side 1; Hartford, *Where Is Our Responsibility?* 152 (Barkin quotation).

6. "Total Production Worker Employment in the Textile Industry and Workers Covered by Union Agreements, by State," March 1964, "Political Notes, 1962–63" folder, box 661, TWUA Papers. For an insight into the relationship between the UTW and TWUA, see Minchin, *What Do We Need a Union For?* 168–76.

7. Hodges, *New Deal Labor Policy,* 61; Joseph Jacobs quoted in Irons, *Testing the New Deal,* 3. On the 1929 strikes, see Salmond, *Gastonia;* Hall et al., *Like a Family,* 212–36; Hall, "Disorderly Women." For the 1934 General Textile Strike, see Irons, *Testing the New Deal;* Salmond, *General Textile Strike.*

8. Irons, *Testing the New Deal,* 4; Conway, *Rise Gonna Rise,* 167 (Smith quote).

9. Griffith, *Crisis of American Labor,* 162; Minchin, *What Do We Need a Union For?* 26–47; Zieger, *CIO,* 231–41.

10. For the TWOC drive, see Hodges, *New Deal Labor Policy,* 157–79. For the 1951 strike, see Daniel, *Culture of Misfortune,* 205–28; Minchin, *What Do We Need a Union For?,* 99–176. For the Darlington case, see Daniel, *Culture of Misfortune,* 254–55; Gross, *Broken Promise,* 174–76; Arthur, "The Darlington Mills Case."

11. Clark, *Like Night and Day,* 168–98; Hodges, "Stevens and the Union," 55.

12. Stetin interview, tape 13, side 1.

13. "Background Report on J. P. Stevens and Company, Inc.: Patterson Plant," March 18, 1963; "Background Report on J. P. Stevens and Company, Inc.: Aragon Plant," March 13, 1963; "Labor Relations Report: Industrial Cotton Mills Division of J. P. Stevens and Company," March 12, 1963, all in "Stevens J. P. and Company General Labor, 1948–65" folder, box 678, ACTWU-Cornell.

14. "J. P. Stevens and Co. Inc.," July 21, 1972, "Stevens, J. P. and Company Inc., General Labor, 1972–74" folder, box 678, ACTWU-Cornell.

15. Marshall, *Labor in the South,* 308; "Profile of Personal Characteristics of American Textile Workers," November 24, 1967, "Department Reports—Executive Council Meeting, Bal Harbor, Florida, December 2–5, 1967" folder, box 595, TWUA Papers.

16. John Chupka to William Pollock, February 13, 1963, "Decision to Begin J. P. Stevens Campaign—1963" folder, box 627, ACTWU-Cornell; "Crystal Lee: The Plight of the Real Norma Rae," *Atlanta Journal and Constitution Magazine,* June 10, 1979 (quotation, 13).

17. Savory, "Forced off the Board," 28; Whalen, "Durable Threads," 106–8.

18. Campbell, "Head of the House," 21, 22.

19. Ibid., 41. For the history of J. P. Stevens, see also Overton et al., "Men at the Top."

20. "Story of J. P. Stevens," 22–23; "Predict Shuffle in Top Brass Won't Alter Stevens' Policy," *Daily News Record,* June 23, 1969, in "Stevens J. P. and Company General Labor, 1966–71" folder, box 678, ACTWU-Cornell.

21. Stevens 1973 Annual Report, 2, "J. P. Stevens and Co. Inc. Annual Reports—1967–1981" folder, box 677, ACTWU-Cornell.

22. "Remarks by James D. Finley, Chairman of the Board," to meeting of the New York Society of Security Analysts, October 10, 1972, same folder as n. 21.

23. Cobb, *Selling of the South,* 188; Freeman to Boyd E. Payton, October 30, 1959, "North and South Carolina Boyd Payton 1959" folder, box 620, TWUA Papers.

24. "Organizing Push Begins: TWUA Plans Role in Joint Labor Campaign," *Textile Labor,* February 1963, 20, 24; "Now It's Full Steam Ahead for IUD's Joint Labor Drive," *Textile Labor,* March 1963 (quotation, 24).

25. Appelbaum to Chupka, August 7, 1962, "IUD Greenville Spartanburg 1962" folder, box 625, TWUA Papers; Swaity interview, tape 3, side 1.

26. Rogin interview, tape 7, side 1; Hueter interview, tape 8, side 1; Cook interview, tape 5, side 1; McIver to J. P. Stevens Organizing Staff, n.d., fiche 1 of 7, "J. P. Stevens Correspondence" file, Finley Papers.

27. "Committee to Work on Selecting Target for IUD Organizing Drive," April 4, 1963, and Chupka to Pollock, February 13, 1963, "Decision to Begin J. P. Stevens Campaign—1963" folder, box 627, ACTWU-Cornell.

28. Perkel to Chupka, February 14, 1963, same folder as n. 13.

29. 125 NLRB 121 at 1359.

30. Pedigo to Pollock, May 3, 1959, "J. P. Stevens—Newspaper Clippings" folder, box 34, ACTWU-Atlanta; Chupka to Pollock, February 13, 1963 (see n. 27).

31. Pollock to Chupka, February 12, 1963, same folder as n. 27; Stetin interview, tape 9, side 1.

32. Daniel, *Culture of Misfortune*, 256–60 (Chupka quotation, 260); Stetin interview, tape 9, side 1; Swaity interview, tape 3, side 1.

33. Swaity interview, tape 3, side 1; Hoyman interview (author); Fiester interview, tape 7, side 2; Salmond, *General Textile Strike*, 202–7.

34. Hoyman interview (author); Whalen, "Durable Threads," 105. For the difficulties of organizing Cannon Mills, see Griffith, *Crisis of American Labor*, 53–56; Zieger, *CIO*, 237.

35. Swaity interview, tape 3, side 1; Stetin to TWUA Executive Council and Staff (U.S.)," February 11, 1976, "J. P. Stevens Roanoke Rapids North Carolina" folder, box 648, ACTWU- Cornell.

36. Labor Relations Report no. 65, September 14, 1953, "J. P. Stevens and Company, Inc. Migration from New England to South" folder, and Labor Relations Report no. 60–A, March 12, 1963, "Industrial Cotton Mills Division of J. P. Stevens and Company, Rock Hill, South Carolina" folder, box 8, TWUA Papers (MSS97–196); 125 NLRB 121 at 1354–55, 1358–59, 1376.

37. Hodges, *New Deal Labor Policy*, 193–94; Zieger, *CIO*, 78; Marshall, *Labor in the South*, 187–88, 191–92, 213–14.

38. "TWUA's Goals for Textile Workers in the South," June 11, 1969, box 3, TWUA Papers (MSS97–196); statement of Rev. G. W. Dennis, August 22, 1963, "J. P. Stevens and Company Inc. IUD Organizing Campaign—1963 (Dunean Plant)" folder, box 258, TWUA Papers; statement of Jimmy C. Riddle, August 4, 1965, "Jimmy Riddle" folder, box 258, TWUA Papers; "Stevens Ignores the Law," (quotation, 7).

39. Cribbs, "Day of Reckoning," 14; Helen Dewar, "Organizing the South: Labor Calls J. P. Stevens Key Barrier," *Washington Post*, June 7, 1977 (quotation, A9).

40. "Victory for Stuart Workers" (quotation, 9); Hall et al., *Like a Family*, 81; Conway, *Rise Gonna Rise*, esp. 20–23, 58–70, 96–99, 200–204; Glass, *Textile Industry*, 93–96.

41. "Profile of Personal Characteristics" (see n. 15); Hall et al., *Like a Family*, 67–70; McHugh, *Mill Family*.

42. Gretchen Donart, "Women Working at J. P. Stevens," *Labor Unity*, March 1979, 12–13, in "J. P. Stevens General Labor 1979" folder, box 677, ACTWU-Cornell (quotations); "J. P. Stevens and Company, Straightening Things Out," February 15, 1977, fiche 1 of 2, "Zensen Domei and Stevens Conference" file, Finley Papers.

43. Minchin, *Hiring the Black Worker*, 3; Hall et al., *Like a Family*, 66.

44. Purnell interview; Alston interview.

45. Moody interview; Minchin, *Hiring the Black Worker*, 17–23, 67–97.

46. Minchin, *Hiring the Black Worker*, 3; 1970 TWUA Convention Proceedings, 207; Alston interview.

47. "America's Stake in the South," 5; Fairclough, *Better Day Coming*, 279–81.

48. "America's Stake in the South," 4–5 (quotation, 5).

49. Ibid., 3–5 (quotation, 4); "Stepped-Up Organizing Called Key to Progressive Legislation," *Textile Labor*, March 1963, 19.

50. Zieger, *CIO*, 233.

Chapter 2. Persistent Unremedied Violations

1. Stetin quoted in Guzzardi, "Upper Hand," 87. For the union's recognition that the campaign would be lengthy, see TWUA Executive Council Minutes, November 11–13, 1963, pp. 327–28, box 598, TWUA Papers.

2. 157 NLRB 90 at 877; Hodges, "Stevens and the Union," 58 (Ricci quotation).

3. 1978 ACTWU Convention Proceedings, 200.

4. 157 NLRB 90 at 872.

5. See, for example, "Official Report of Proceedings before the National Labor Relations Board" (hereafter cited as "Proceedings before NLRB"), April 1, 1964, pp. 983, 1000, box 260, TWUA Papers.

6. 157 NLRB 90 at 943; 167 NLRB 38 at 294.

7. Leedom quoted in "Testimony of the Textile Workers Union of America, AFL-CIO Before the House of Representatives, Committee on Education and Labor, Subcommittee on Labor-Management Relations," March 15, 1976, "House Subcommittee" folder, box 390, ACTWU-Cornell (hereafter cited as "TWUA Testimony"), pp. 11–12.

8. Both quotations in Sharon Bond, "They're Trying To Improve Image," *Greensboro Daily News*, February 24, 1980, in NCCCF under "Stevens, J. P. and Co.—Unionization."

9. Hodges, "Stevens and the Union," 57.

10. "In the Name of 'Reform,' Union Leaders Now Reach for Unlimited Power," n.d., "J. P. Stevens Company's Letters to its Workers, 1977–78" folder, box 366, ACTWU-Cornell.

11. Si Lippa, "Stevens Looks on Union as Third-Party Intruder," *Daily News Record*, August 28, 1967, as in n. 20, chap. 1.

12. "J. P. Stevens Seen Still Moving Forward After 155 Years in Trade," *America's Textile Reporter*, March 7, 1968, in "Stevens, J. P. and Co. General Labor, 1966–71" folder, box 678, ACTWU-Cornell.

13. Guzzardi, "Upper Hand," 87; Beck quoted in Bond, "Image" (see n. 8).

14. Gore, "Report of Activities," June 15, 1963, "Gore, Lawrence" folder, box 682, TWUA Papers.

15. TWUA Executive Council Minutes, November 11–13, 1963, pp. 325–34, box 598, TWUA Papers (quotation, 324); 157 NLRB 90 at 872; Proceedings before NLRB, April 1, 1964, p. 981, box 260, TWUA Papers.

16. "Great Falls," n.d., and "Roanoke Rapids," n.d., "J. P. Stevens and Company Inc. IUD Organizing Campaign—1963 Plant-by-Plant" folder, box 258, TWUA Papers; TWUA Executive Council Minutes, November 11–13, 1963, p. 371, box 598, TWUA Papers.

17. Statements of Rosemond, September 12, 1963, and Powers, September 18, 1963, "J. P. Stevens and Company Inc. IUD Organizing Campaign—1963 Tufting Plant (Monaghan), Greenville, South Carolina" folder, box 258, TWUA Papers.

18. Proceedings before NLRB, April 27, 1966, pp. 353–60 (quotation, 358), box 260, TWUA Papers.

19. Proceedings before NLRB, June 13, 1966, pp. 2487, 2493, 2498, box 259, TWUA Papers; Proceedings before NLRB, March 31, 1964, pp. 813–18 (quotation, 818), box 260, TWUA Papers.

20. 380 F.2d 292 at 299; Proceedings before NLRB, April 29, 1964, pp. 2193–95, 2204,

2207 (quotation, 2204), box 260, TWUA Papers; Frank C. Porter, "The Press Reports on J. P. Stevens," *Textile Labor,* March 1968, 3.

21. 167 NLRB 338 at 291–94 (quotations, 292).

22. 157 NLRB 90 at 949.

23. Statement of Rev. G. W. Dennis (see n. 38, chap. 1).

24. Proceedings before NLRB, June 4, 1964, pp. 4849–50, 4883–90 (Williams quotation, 4886), box 261, TWUA Papers; Edward Wynne to Arnold F. Ordman, July 22, 1963, "J. P. Stevens and Company Inc. IUD Organizing Campaign—1963 Roanoke Rapids, North Carolina" folder, box 258, TWUA Papers.

25. 167 NLRB 38 at 274; 163 NLRB 24 at 240.

26. Proceedings before NLRB, March 24, 1964, p. 95, and April 1, 1964, pp. 964, 1023, box 260, TWUA Papers.

27. Proceedings before NLRB, April 27, 1964, p. 1848, box 260, TWUA Papers (Broughton quotation); Proceedings before NLRB, April 28, 1964, p. 2050, box 261, TWUA Papers (Lindsay quotation).

28. Proceedings before NLRB, June 13, 1966, pp. 2540, 2547, 2548, box 259, TWUA Papers.

29. Proceedings before NLRB, June 13, 1966, pp. 2599–2600, box 259, TWUA Papers; Proceedings before NLRB, June 4, 1964, pp. 4669–4681 (quotation, 4677–78), box 261, TWUA Papers.

30. Gore, "Report of Activities," June 8, 1963, "Gore, Lawrence" folder, box 682, TWUA Papers.

31. Gore, "Report of Activities," August 24, 1963, and February, 15, 1964, "Gore, Lawrence" folder, box 682, TWUA Papers.

32. Gore, "Report of Activities," March 7 and April 11, 1964, ibid.

33. Goad, "Report of Activities," July 23 and October 29, 1966, "Goad, Joel D." folder, box 681, TWUA Papers.

34. Hoyman, "Report of Activities," August 3, 1963, "Hoyman, Scott" folder, box 683, TWUA Papers; "Stevens Is Tagged Union-Buster, Price-Fixer in Two U.S. Actions," *Textile Labor,* September 1965, 24; Goad, "Report of Activities," December 14, 1963, and April 11, 1964, "Goad, Joel D." folder, box 681, TWUA Papers. For more examples of how much staff time was spent preparing NLRB charges and attending the hearings, see Hoyman's reports of August 24 and 31, 1963.

35. Wynne to Ordman, November 12, 1963, same folder as n. 24.

36. "J. P. Stevens Acts to Reinstate 69," *New York Times,* December 28, 1967; Perkel to Swaity, June 25, 1969, and "Remarks of Robert T. Stevens, President, J. P. Stevens and Co., Inc. Annual Meeting of Shareowners," March 4, 1969, same folder as n. 12; "High Court Leaves Standing NLRB Ruling Of Unfair Labor Dealings by J. P. Stevens," *Wall Street Journal,* December 12, 1967 (quotation).

37. Statements of Charles T. Knight, August 20, 1963, Bettex M. Beeco Jr., August 14, 1963, and William C. Aldridge, August 21, 1963, "J. P. Stevens and Company Incorporated IUD Organizing Campaign—1963 Great Falls, South Carolina Plant" folder; "Petitioner's Memorandum to Hearing Officer in Support of Objections to the Election," n.d., pp. 11–19, "J. P. Stevens and Company Incorporated Dunean Plant—Case Number 11-RC-2136" folder; "Decision and Order," June 29, 1964, "J. P. Stevens and Company Exposition Plant Case Number 10-CA-5428" folder, all in box 258, TWUA Papers.

38. Proceedings before NLRB, August 16, 1965, pp. 648–57, box 259, TWUA

Papers; "Request for Review of Second Supplemental Decision and Order," n.d., "Case Number 11-RC-2136" folder (see n. 37) (quotation, 2).

39. Statement of Betty Ann White, May 18, 1965, "Betty Ann White" folder, box 258, TWUA Papers.

40. Proceedings before NLRB, August 17, 1965, p. 600, box 259, TWUA Papers (Edwards quotation); statement of Phillips, May 1, 1965, "Gail Phillips" folder, box 258, TWUA Papers.

41. Statement of Aldridge, August 21, 1963, "Great Falls" folder (see n. 37); "Watts," n.d., "Plant-by-Plant" folder (see n. 16). For the way memories of the 1934 strike held back other subsequent organizing attempts, see Salmond, *General Textile Strike*, 239.

42. "To All Employees," August 28, 1963, "J. P. Stevens and Company Incorporated IUD Organizing Campaign—1963 (Slater Plant)" folder, box 258, TWUA Papers; Proceedings before NLRB, May 25, 1964, p. 3622, box 261, TWUA Papers.

43. Statements of Sanders, n.d., "J. P. Stevens and Company Inc. IUD Organizing Campaign—1963 (Dunean Plant)" folder, and of Lindsey, n.d., "J. P. Stevens and Company Inc. IUD Organizing Campaign 1963 Apalache Plant" folder, box 258, TWUA Papers.

44. Zieger and Gall, *American Workers, American Unions*, 197–98.

45. Statement of Robert Carsey, May 23, 1963, same folder as n. 24 (first quotation); statement of Ralph Moore, September 3, 1963, same folder as n. 17; statement of Ethel Blakely, August 11, 1965, "Jacky Holbrook" folder, box 258, TWUA Papers.

46. Fairclough, *Better Day Coming*, 227–93, provides a good overview of the upsurge in civil rights protest between 1955 and 1965. For the reaction of unions to the civil rights movement, see Draper, *Conflict of Interests*. For a detailed study of the Selma campaign, see Garrow, *Protest at Selma*.

47. 163 NLRB 24 at 237, 238; Proceedings before NLRB, August 16, 1965, p. 311 (Blakely quotation), and August 18, 1965, p. 792 (Du Bose quotation), box 259, TWUA Papers.

48. Proceedings before NLRB, August 18, 1965, pp. 785, 792, 818, box 259, TWUA Papers.

49. Proceedings before NLRB, August 17, 1965, pp. 667, 682, 683 (quotations, 682, 683), box 259, TWUA Papers.

50. "Supplemental Decision, Direction, and Notice of Hearing," July 16, 1965, p. 6, "J. P. Stevens and Company, Inc. Estes Plant—Case No. 11–RC-2137" folder, box 258, TWUA Papers; TWUA Testimony (see n. 7, chap. 2) (quotation, 8–9); Hoyman, "Report of Activities," May 15, 1965, "Hoyman, Scott" folder, box 683, TWUA Papers.

51. 157 NLRB 90 at 940–41, 965.

52. Statement of Sibley, August 13, 1963, "Great Falls" folder (see n. 37); Proceedings before NLRB, April 1, 1964, p. 981, box 260, TWUA Papers.

53. Statement of Collins, October 8, 1963, same folder as n. 42.

54. 163 NLRB 24 at 249; Bush interview; Hines interview.

55. Statements of Alfred D. Motley, September 6, 1963, Moore, September 3, 1963, and Foster, August 7, 1963, same folder as n. 17.

56. "Petitioner's Memorandum" (see n. 37), p. 1; TWUA testimony, p. 45; "NLRB Is Labeled Ally of Lawbreakers," *Textile Labor*, June 1965, 21 (Pollock quotation); 157 NLRB 90 at 943–60.

57. Stevens 1965 Annual Report, 5, and 1966 Annual Report, 6, "J. P. Stevens and Co. Inc. Annual Reports—1950–1966" folder, box 677, ACTWU-Cornell. For union

efforts to remain upbeat, see "Organizing—It's Still the No. 1 Job," *Textile Labor,* July 1964, 22.

58. Stevens 1967 Annual Report, 6, in "1967–1981" folder (see n. 21, chap. 1). For the strong economic performance of Stevens in these years, see 1963 Annual Report, 3; 1964 Annual Report, 4; 1965 Annual Report, 3, in "1950–1966" folder (see n. 57).

59. Murray Seeger, "N.L.R.B. Assailed By Textile Union," *New York Times,* May 16, 1965 (first quotation, 73); "Petitioner's Memorandum" (see n. 37), p. 2. For a good overview of positive national press coverage and the way it buoyed the spirits of union leaders, see "Nation's Press Tells the Story of Textile Workers Who Fight," *Textile Labor,* December 1965, 6–8.

Chapter 3. Changing Gears, 1966–1969

1. 1966 TWUA Executive Council Report, 19.

2. "Southern Region Staff Assignment as of May 15, 1967," and "Report on Organizing," May 22–27, 1967, "Department Reports—Executive Council Meeting, Montreal, Canada—May 22–26, 1967" folder, box 595, TWUA Papers.

3. Swaity interview, tape 3, side 1.

4. Swaity wrote in July 1969: "It is important that we free more of the southern staff from holding operations" (Swaity to John Kissack, July 3, 1969, "South-General-1969" folder, box 631, TWUA Papers).

5. Quotation from Swaity to Kissack; "For Mr. Pollock's Own Use," January 22, 1968, "South—General—1968" folder, box 630, TWUA Papers; "For Mr. Pollock's Own Use," April 11, 1967, "South—1967—General Correspondence" folder, box 629, TWUA Papers.

6. "Operation Focus," in "Montreal" folder (see n. 2).

7. "Report of the Publicity Department to the Executive Council," December 2, 1967, in "Bal Harbor 1967" folder (see n. 15, chap. 1). Both the "Hollow Promise" and the "Conspiracy in Southern Textiles" booklets are discussed extensively in this report.

8. William Pollock, "Conspiracy in Southern Textiles," *Textile Labor,* September 1967, 3–9; "Textile Union Annoyed by Linen It Is Served," *New York Times,* June 5, 1968 (quotation, 60); 1968 TWUA Convention Proceedings, 66–67.

9. Pollock, "Conspiracy" (see n. 8), 3–11 (quotations, 3, 4); Hodges, "Stevens and the Union," 55. For examples of firms that did establish a stable relationship with the union in the South, see Cross, *Dan River Runs Deep*; Flamming, *Creating the Modern South*; Brattain, *Politics of Whiteness.*

10. "IUD Greenville-Spartanburg Campaign," July 10, 1962, "IUD Greenville-Spartanburg 1962" folder, box 625; Swaity quoted in "Organizing Report," January 6, 1966, "Paul Swaity South 1965" folder, box 628; Pollock to Tom Barker, November 17, 1969, "South—General—1969" folder, box 631, all in TWUA Papers.

11. "Stevens Labels Union Action 'Retaliatory'" *America's Textile Reporter,* June 2, 1966, in "Stevens J. P. and Co., General Labor, 1966–71" folder, box 678, ACTWU-Cornell; "AFL- CIO Calls for Contract Ban on Stevens, Other Law-Breakers," *Textile Labor,* April 1967, 20; Sol Stetin to Nicholas Zonarich, September 4, 1974, same folder as n. 14, chap. 1.

12. "TWUA Raps Apologists for Stevens," *Textile Labor,* May 1966, 21; Rivers quoted in "Stevens Labels Union Action 'Retaliatory'" (see n. 11).

13. James Blackwell to Pollock, March 23, 1967, "South—1967—General Correspondence" folder, box 629, TWUA Papers.

14. Frank Thompson Jr., "No Hunting License For Union-Busters," *Textile Labor*, July 1966, 3–4 (quotation, 4); "Stevens Case Sparks Probe of Union-Busters by House," *Textile Labor*, June 1967, 24.

15. Quotations in "The Salt of the Earth," *Textile Labor*, September 1967, 10.

16. Ruth Stack, "From Tears to Triumph: The Story of 2 Stevens' Workers," *Textile Labor*, December 1968 (quotation, 3); "Mill Workers' Refusal to Unionize," *New York Times*, August 28, 1967.

17. Proceedings before NLRB, June 14, 1966, box 259, TWUA Papers (quotations, 2614, 2645).

18. Lee quoted in Proceedings before NLRB, August 18, 1965, pp. 817–18, box 259, TWUA Papers; Proceedings before NLRB, May 25, 1964, p. 3622, box 261, TWUA Papers.

19. Statement of Jimmy C. Riddle (see n. 38, chap. 1).

20. "The Conscience of the Community: A New Force Joining Battle For Textile Workers' Rights," *Textile Labor*, June 1967, 3–4.

21. "J. P. Stevens Cancels Special Board Events in Face of Protests," *Wall Street Journal*, April 7, 1967.

22. "Stevens' N.Y. Office Picketed in Support of Unionization Bid," *Daily News Record*, December 15, 1967, and "S.C. Mills Feel Union Ire in Hospital Case," *Daily News Record*, June 26, 1969; "'We'll Organize J. P. Stevens, No Matter What It Takes,'" *Textile Labor*, February 1968, 18, 24.

23. Walter Rugaber, "Union Drive at Stevens Has Wide Import for South," *New York Times*, August 19, 1967; "Labor's Unwon Wars," *New York Times*, August 19, 1967.

24. "Mill Workers' Refusal to Unionize," *New York Times*, August 28, 1967.

25. Pollock to John P. Stevens, March 22, 1967, and "Stevens Answers the Union in 'Open Letter,'" *America's Textile Reporter*, May 4, 1967, in same folder as n. 11.

26. 177 NLRB 120 at 947.

27. Ibid., pp. 945, 953. For complaints of racial hiring in the 1970s, see Harold W. Bagwell, "Weekly Organizing Activity Report," April 7, 1979, "Harold Bagwell" folder, box 48, ACTWU-Atlanta.

28. 171 NLRB 163 at 1207.

29. Ibid. at 1207–8, 1223–24 (quotation, 1208).

30. 183 NLRB 5 at 27, 29.

31. "National Labor Relations Board Weekly Summary of Cases," June 1–5, 1970, same folder as n. 11.

32. "Brief for the National Labor Relations Board in Opposition," October Term 1972, Supreme Court Case 72–740, "J. P. Stevens 1973" folder, box 647, ACTWU-Cornell.

33. 179 NLRB 47 at 257, 258, 265.

34. Cribbs, "Day of Reckoning," 14.

35. Ibid.; 179 NLRB 47 at 259.

36. 179 NLRB 47 at 266, 269, 284.

37. NLRB decision quoted in TWUA Testimony (see n. 7, chap. 2), p. 25.

38. "National Labor Relations Board," November 4, 1970, same folder as n. 11; Patricia E. Eames to Peter G. Nash, October 31, 1972, same folder as n. 14, chap. 1.

39. Eames to Nash.

40. B. H. Pelham to Pollock, March 24, 1968, and Pollock to James Pierce, March 28, 1968, "South—General—1968" folder, box 630, TWUA Papers.

41. Johnson to Pollock, October 14, 1969, "South—General—1969" folder, box 631, TWUA Papers. The way such letters buoyed TWUA leaders' confidence is shown in "We'll Organize" (see n. 22), 18, 24.

42. Ruth Stack, "The Press Reports on J. P. Stevens," *Textile Labor,* March 1968, 3.

43. Quotation in Rugaber, "Union Drive" (see n. 23), 13. For similar sentiments, see the interview with Janie Hawkins in *MacNeill/Lehrer Report,* "J. P. Stevens."

44. 1968 TWUA Executive Council Report, 20.

45. Cobb, *Selling of the South,* 188; Bartley, *New South,* 259–60; 1966 TWUA Executive Council Report, 18 (quotation).

46. "We'll Organize" (see n. 22), 18, 24 (quotations, 24).

47. "Stetin Urges Massive Drive in South," *Textile Labor,* July 1968, 31; Hoyman quoted in David Gelsanliter, "He Predicts Union Surge in 5 Years," *Charlotte Observer,* January 18, 1970, p. 19A, in "South—General—1970" folder, box 632, TWUA Papers; 1968 TWUA Convention Proceedings, 239.

Chapter 4. Saving the Campaign, 1970–1974

1. Perkel interview, tape 2, side 2; Swaity interview, tape 3, side 1.

2. Minchin, *Hiring the Black Worker,* 3; Frederickson, "Four Decades of Change," 62.

3. Moody interview; Swaity interview, tape 3, side 1; Minchin, *Hiring the Black Worker,* 3; "The Potential for Union Organization in the South," November 22, 1972, "The Potential for Union Organization in the South" folder, box 3, TWUA Papers (MSS97–196).

4. Hoyman to Billy R. Smith, July 22, 1975, "J. P. Stevens Statesboro, Georgia" folder, box 648, ACTWU-Cornell; "Statement of J. P. Stevens and Co., Inc. to the Labor Subcommittee, Committee on Human Resources, United States Senate," November 7, 1977, p. 13, "History of J. P. Stevens Campaign up to 1977" folder, box 366, ACTWU-Cornell. For a summary of the union's case that the plant was closed to avoid unionization, see "The Unfair Labor Practices of the J. P. Stevens Company in the Closing of the Statesboro Plant," June 18, 1975, "J. P. Stevens Roanoke Rapids North Carolina" folder, box 648, ACTWU-Cornell.

5. "Unfair Labor Practices"; W. H. Gray to all employees, n.d., same folder.

6. Affidavit of McIver, August 28, 1975, "J. P. Stevens July-December 1975" folder, box 647, ACTWU-Cornell. For the use of the Statesboro situation in other campaigns, see Hoyman to Henry Woicik, July 8, 1975, and Harston Fuller et al. to All Employees, August 17, 1974, "J. P. Stevens Roanoke Rapids North Carolina" folder, box 648, ACTWU-Cornell.

7. Weiser to Swaity, January 3, 1974, same folder as n. 14, chap. 1; "Walterboro Captive Audience Speech—Jack McGill Speaker," n.d., "J. P. Stevens Roanoke Rapids, North Carolina" folder, box 648, ACTWU-Cornell.

8. "Supplemental Decision and Certification of Results of Election," May 23, 1974, "J. P. Stevens and Company Inc. 1974" folder, box 647, ACTWU-Cornell (quotation, 5).

9. "Brief to the Administrative Law Judge on Behalf of the Charging Party," November 13, 1974, pp. 2–4, same folder.

10. NLRB Decision, *J. P. Stevens v. Textile Workers Union of America,* November

22, 1974, same folder (quotation, 9). For the Wallace firings, see also "Brief" (see n. 9), 18–19; "Remarks of Senator Edward M. Kennedy," October 4, 1973, *Congressional Record,* in same folder as n. 14, chap. 1.

11. "Remarks of Senator Edward M. Kennedy."

12. Ed McConville to Sol Stetin, July 21, 1978, pp. 71–74, "McConville, Ed: Story of J. P. Stevens Outline and Chapters" folder, box 370, ACTWU-Cornell (quotation, 74); "J. P. Stevens Is Sued by Union for Allegedly Bugging Officers," *New York Times,* August 16, 1973.

13. McConville to Stetin, July 21, 1978, pp. 75–76.

14. Ibid. (quotations, 75, 76).

15. TWUA Testimony (see n. 7, chap. 2), pp. 35–37.

16. "Department of Organization: Report to Executive Council on Organizing," February 1971, p. 31, "AFL-CIO Executive Council February 15, 1971—Bal Harbor, Fla" folder, box 659, TWUA Papers.

17. "Statement by the AFL-CIO Executive Council," February 23, 1973, same folder as n. 14, chap. 1.

18. "Predict Shuffle in Top Brass" (see n. 20, chap. 1); Savory, "Forced off the Board," 28.

19. Macioce quoted in Bill Somplatsky-Jarman to Mileski, July 6, 1979, "Allied" folder, box 400, ACTWU-Cornell.

20. Leonhardt, "James Finley" (see n. 9, intro.); James D. Finley to All Stevens Employees, September 20, 1979, "J. P. Stevens Company Letters to its Workers, 1977–78" folder, box 366, ACTWU-Cornell.

21. Swaity interview, tape 3, side 1; Perkel interview, tape 2, side 2.

22. Swaity interview, tape 3, side 1.

23. "Draft for JS," attached to Jacob Sheinkman to Charles Kligman, September 26, 1979, "February Minutes" folder, box 104, ACTWU-Cornell.

24. "Sol Stetin address to TWUA International Staff Conference," January 29–30, 1973, pp. 3, 4, 13, "J. P. Stevens Richard Rothstein, 1978–79" folder, box 331, ACTWU-Cornell.

25. Ibid., pp. 4, 8, 9.

26. 1970 TWUA Convention Proceedings, 207; "The Potential for Union Organization in the South," November 22, 1972, p. 3, box 3, TWUA Papers (MSS97–196).

27. Raynor interview.

28. Todd interview, tape 4, side 1.

29. 1987 ACTWU General Executive Board Report (quotation, 2); Raynor interview.

30. "Remarks of Robert T. Stevens" (see n. 36, chap. 2); "Pentagon Weighs Textile Contract," *New York Times,* February 1, 1969; "8 House Negroes Write President," *New York Times,* April 4, 1969.

31. Perkel to Woicik, August 5, 1975, "J. P. Stevens July-December 1975" folder, box 647, ACTWU-Cornell; Stevens Annual Report 1972, 4, in "1967–1981" folder (see n. 21, chap. 1). The Title VII litigation against Stevens is explored in Minchin, *Hiring the Black Worker,* 71–75, 135–37.

32. "Stevens Workers Vote Tie to Union," *New York Times,* September 1, 1974; Swaity interview, tape 3, side 1.

33. "Introduction," n.d., "J. P. Stevens Roanoke Rapids, North Carolina" folder, box 648, ACTWU-Cornell.

34. Ibid.

35. "J. P. Stevens, Roanoke Rapids Mtg. of Org. Committee," August 15, 1974, same folder as n. 14, chap. 1; "The Company's Reports to the U.S. Equal Employment Opportunity Commission," plaintiff's exhibit 90 in *Sledge et al. v. J. P. Stevens*, 30; Findings of Fact and Conclusions of Law, December 22, 1975, *Sledge*, 23; "Comparison of Pay Rates of Hourly and Incentive Male Employees by Race and Education Level at J. P. Stevens Plants in Roanoke Rapids, N.C.," exhibit data, December 28, 1980, *Sledge*; Alston interview.

36. Charge of Discrimination of Cromwell Faulcon Jr. and Charge of Discrimination of Mable Moody Miles, September 18, 1970, "J. P. Stevens Miscellaneous Through 1972" folder, box 648, ACTWU-Cornell.

37. Swaity interview, tape 3, side 2; Boone interview.

38. J. P. Stevens and Co. Inc., to All Employees, April 25, 1973, and Swaity to Hoyman, May 9, 1973, same folder as n. 14, chap. 1.

39. Stevens to All Employees (see n. 38); McConville to Stetin, May 3, 1978, p. 42, "McConville, Ed: Story of J. P. Stevens: Outline and Chapters" folder, box 370, ACTWU-Cornell; B. Taylor interview; Boone interview.

40. Boyer et al., *Enduring Vision*, 695–96; Woicik to Stetin, February 26, 1975, "J. P. Stevens January-June 1975" folder, box 647, ACTWU-Cornell; Bush interview.

41. B. Taylor interview.

42. Swaity interview, tape 3, side 1; Hodges, "Real Norma Rae," 254–55.

43. "Stevens Workers Vote Tie to Union," *New York Times*, September 1, 1974; 1976 TWUA Executive Council Report, 21.

Chapter 5. Planning a Boycott

1. "Union Breakthroughs," *New York Times*, September 2, 1974; Perkel to Stetin, December 24, 1974, same folder as n. 14, chap. 1.

2. Perkel to Stetin, December 24, 1974, January 24, 1974, September 28, 1972, August 4, 1975, April 14, 1975, and March 5, 1975, same folder.

3. Swaity interview, tape 3, side 2.

4. Stetin to I. W. Abel, March 11, 1975, "J. P. Stevens January-June 1975" folder, box 647, ACTWU-Cornell (first quotation); Stetin interview, tape 10, side 2.

5. G. Gordon Walker and Milton Southerland to All Employees, February 8, 1975, and Harold McIver to Reed Johnston, February 25, 1975, "J. P. Stevens January-June 1975" folder, box 647, ACTWU-Cornell.

6. Stetin to Abel (see n. 4).

7. Swaity interview, tape 3, side 2; *National Observer*, October 6, 1973, in same folder as n. 14, chap. 1.

8. Woicik to Stetin, February 26, 1975, "J. P. Stevens January-June 1975" folder, box 647, ACTWU-Cornell.

9. Perkel to William DuChessi, November 20, 1974, and Swaity to DuChessi, October 28, 1974, "J. P. Stevens and Co. Inc. 1974" folder, box 647, ACTWU-Cornell.

10. "Testimony of Sol Stetin before the Oversight Hearings on the National Labor Relations Act Procedures and Remedies," March 15, 1976, p. 31, "House Subcommittee" folder, box 390, ACTWU-Cornell.

11. Bob Dennis, "How J. P. Stevens and the Union Reached a Truce," *Charlotte Observer*, October 25, 1980, in NCCCF under "Stevens, J. P. and Co.—Unionization."

12. Quotation in Swaity to DuChessi (see n. 9); *MacNeill/Lehrer Report,* "J. P. Stevens."

13. ACTWU General Executive Board Minutes, June 13–16, 1977, pp. 15–16, "GEB June Meeting" folder, box 124, ACTWU-Cornell.

14. Swaity to Executive Council and Staff, September 19, 1975, "J. P. Stevens July-December 1975" folder, box 647, ACTWU-Cornell; Swaity, "Activity Report—Southern Region,". March 9, 1965, "Paul Swaity South 1965" folder, box 628, TWUA Papers (quotation).

15. "For Mr. Pollock's Own Use," January 22, 1968, "South—General—1968" folder, box 630, TWUA Papers; "Percentage Membership in TWUA Locals in the South," January 25, 1973, box 3, TWUA Papers (MSS 97–196).

16. Swaity to Kissack, June 23, 1969, "South—General 1969" folder, box 631, TWUA Papers; "Southern Plants Where TWUA is Technically the Bargaining Agent but where Labor Agreements have never been signed," January 5, 1955, box 2, TWUA Papers (MSS97–196).

17. "For Mr. Pollock's Own Use," April 11, 1967, "South—1967—General Correspondence" folder, box 629, TWUA Papers. On strikes in the southern textile industry immediately after World War II, see Minchin, *What Do We Need a Union For?,* 69–98.

18. Patterson to Jack Bradshaw, March 17, 1975, "J. P. Stevens January-June 1975" folder, box 647, ACTWU-Cornell.

19. Swaity interview, tape 3, side 2; Bush interview; Swaity to DuChessi (see n. 9).

20. Both quotations in *MacNeill/Lehrer Report,* "J. P. Stevens."

21. Ibid (Blackwell quote).

22. Ibid (Bloom quote).

23. Perkel to Stetin, December 24, 1974 (see n. 1).

24. Swaity to Executive Council and Staff (see n. 14); Joel Ronald Ax to Swaity, October 13, 1972, "J. P. Stevens Misc. Through 1972" folder, box 648, ACTWU-Cornell.

25. Perkel to Stetin, September 28, 1972, and July 20, 1972, same folder as n. 14, chap. 1.

26. Perkel to Stetin, December 30, 1974, and March 5, 1975, same folder.

27. Perkel to Stetin, December 24, 1974. In the same folder, see also Perkel to Swaity, August 4, 1975.

28. Haberland, "Women's Work," 144–50 (quotation, 145); DeMoss, *Apparel Manufacturing in Texas,* 174–76.

29. "Report of Activities on J. P. Stevens Publicity Campaign Weeks of December 22, 1975–January 18, 1976, "J. P. Stevens 1976" folder, box 647, ACTWU-Cornell.

30. Zieger and Gall, *American Workers, American Unions,* 215; L. Pope interview; Stetin interview, tape 10, side 2.

31. Perkel to Swaity, January 24, 1974, same folder as n. 14, chap. 1.

32. Perkel to Stetin, December 24, 1974; Hoyman interview (author). For examples of previous TWUA strike defeats in the South, see Daniel, *Culture of Misfortune,* 159–61, 251–53.

33. "Report to the IUD Executive Committee on the J. P. Stevens Campaign," October 1977, p. 7, "History of J. P. Stevens Campaign up to 1977" folder, box 366, ACTWU-Cornell.

34. Stetin to Edward T. Hanley, March 3, 1976, fiche 5 of 6, "J. P. Stevens" file, Finley Papers.

35. Howard D. Samuel to Murray H. Finley, March 6, 1975, fiche 1 of 7, "J. P. Stevens Correspondence" file, Finley Papers.

36. Hoyman to Stetin, July 9, 1975, "J. P. Stevens July–December 1975" folder, box 647, ACTWU-Cornell.

37. Arthur M. Goldberg and Irving J. Alter, "Legal Implications Incident to the Stevens Boycott," September 17, 1976, "J. P. Stevens 1976" folder, box 647, ACTWU-Cornell.

38. Hoyman to Stetin, July 9, 1975; "Pressure Program to Get Contracts at J. P. Stevens, Roanoke Rapids, N.C.," August 4, 1975, "J. P. Stevens July–December 1975" folder, box 647, ACTWU-Cornell.

39. Swaity interview, tape 3, side 2; quotation in Goldberg and Alter, "Legal Implications" (see n. 37).

40. Moore to Swaity et al., November 19, 1975, pp. 27–28, "J. P. Stevens July–December 1975" folder, box 647, ACTWU-Cornell; Hoyman quoted in Wayne King, "Southern Leaders Form Group to Support Stevens Textile Workers," *New York Times*, December 18, 1976.

41. ACTWU General Executive Board Minutes, October 25–26, 1976, pp. 24–25, "GEB October Meeting 1976" folder, box 124, ACTWU-Cornell.

42. 1976 TWUA Executive Council Report, 21, 22.

43. "Statement by the AFL-CIO Executive Council," February 23, 1976, fiche 5 of 6, "J. P. Stevens" file; George Meany to Sir and Brother, June 16, 1976, fiche 2 of 7, "J. P. Stevens Correspondence" file, Finley Papers. For a good summary of Meany's background and views, see Zieger and Gall, *American Workers, American Unions*, 204–5, 208–9.

44. Donahue quoted in Stetin to Donahue, February 10, 1976, untitled folder, box 58, ACTWU-Atlanta; McIver to J. P. Stevens Organizing Staff (see n. 26, chap. 1).

45. Raynor interview; Daniel, *Culture of Misfortune*, 274.

46. Stetin and DuChessi to Murray Finley, March 12, 1976, "3/16/76" folder, box 854, ACTWU-Cornell; 1976 ACTWU Convention Proceedings, 9.

47. Burt Beck, "Manuscript: A History of the Amalgamated Clothing and Textile Workers Union," pp. 236–38, "Burt Beck Manuscript pp. 201–316" folder, box 8, TWUA Papers (MSS 97–196); Swaity interview, tape 3, side 2. For the early history of the ACWA, see Fraser, *Labor Will Rule*.

48. Stetin interview, tape 13, side 1; Daniel, *Culture of Misfortune*, 273. Sheinkman died in January 2004. A good overview of his career is provided by Steven Greenhouse, "Jack Sheinkman, 77, Lawyer; Led Clothing Workers' Union," *New York Times*, January 30, 2004.

49. ACTWU General Executive Board Minutes, September 18–29, 1978, p. 4, "9/18/78" folder (Finley quotation), and May 30–June 1, 1979, p. 9, "5/30/79" folder, box 854, ACTWU-Cornell.

50. ACTWU General Executive Board Minutes, February 26, 1979, p. 10, "2/26/79" folder, box 854, ACTWU-Cornell; Damon Stetson, "Textile Unions to Merge and Plan Drive in South," *New York Times*, June 2, 1976.

51. Vera Miller to Beck, February 17, 1978, "ACTWU Boycott on the Financial Condition of the J. P. Stevens Company, February 17, 1978" folder, box 456, ACTWU-Cornell; Samuel to Murray H. Finley et al., September 8, 1976, "Status Reports I" folder, box 401, ACTWU-Cornell.

52. James D. Finley to All Stevens Employees, January 31, 1977, untitled folder, box

33, ACTWU-Atlanta; "Report to the IUD Executive Committee on the J. P. Stevens Campaign," October 1977, "History of J. P. Stevens Campaign up to 1977" folder, box 366, ACTWU-Cornell.

53. ACTWU GEB Minutes, March 1977 (see n. 8, intro.), 2, 4 (quotations), and October 1976 (see n. 19, intro.), 34; Zieger and Gall, *American Workers, American Unions*, 247–48.

Chapter 6. Stirring the Nation's Conscience

1. Sheinkman to William Schallert, April 11, 1980, fiche 1 of 4, "Kleeper—Public Relations J. P. Stevens" file, Finley Papers; Guzzardi, "Upper Hand," 94.

2. "Partial List of Endorsements of the J. P. Stevens Boycott" (see n. 2, intro.); ACTWU GEB Minutes, March 1977 (see n. 8, intro.), 23; Marvin Klapper, "New Era Looms for Stevens," *Daily News Record*, October 8, 1980, in "J. P. Stevens and Company Inc., General Labor, 1980–81" folder, box 677, ACTWU-Cornell.

3. Hodges, "Real Norma Rae," 265–68; "Partial List of Endorsements" (see n. 2, intro.).

4. Abel and Stetin to Representative, February 4, 1976, untitled folder, box 58, ACTWU-Atlanta.

5. "J. P. Stevens and Occupational Safety and Health," fiche 2 of 9, "J. P. Stevens Progress Reports" file; "Fight Racial Discrimination at J. P. Stevens!" fiche 3 of 8, "J. P. Stevens Citizens' Committee" file, Finley Papers.

6. Stetin to TWUA Executive Council and Staff, February 11, 1976, untitled folder, box 58, ACTWU-Atlanta. For "Don't Sleep with Stevens" slogan, see n. 1, intro.

7. Samuel to General Officers and Leadership, November 1, 1976, fiche 8 of 9, and "For Immediate Release," n.d. (quotation), fiche 7 of 9, "J. P. Stevens Progress Reports" file, Finley Papers.

8. "J. P. Stevens Workers Need Your Support!"n.d.; "Summary of Meeting," March 30, 1977; Ann Meyerson and Oliver Rosengart to NYU Faculty, April 5, 1977; "J. P. Stevens Frontlash Support Activities," January 1–March 31, 1977, all on same fiche. The quotation is in "Report on J. P. Stevens Boycott Campus Program," n.d., fiche 4 of 8, "J. P. Stevens Citizens' Committee" file, Finley Papers.

9. "Boycott of Textile Company Supported at 75 Colleges," *Chronicle of Higher Education*, November 6, 1978 (quotation); "Report on J. P. Stevens Boycott Campus Program" (see n. 8).

10. Nancy Nappo, "Princeton: Activism is Reborn," *New York Times*, December 25, 1977; "Boycott of Textile Company" (see n. 9).

11. Paul Minkoff to Del Mileski, June 11, 1979, "Status Reports III" folder (quotation), and Mileski to General Officers and Leadership, January 8, 1979, "Status Reports II" folder, box 401, ACTWU-Cornell.

12. Isadore Barmash, "Stevens: Amid Boycott, Rising Profits," *New York Times*, March 3, 1980.

13. News release, March 15, 1978, fiche 2 of 5, "J. P. Stevens Clergy" file, Finley Papers.

14. Mileski quoted in ACTWU GEB Minutes, February 1979 (see n. 50, chap. 5), 13. For the importance of religious backing to the union, see also Mileski, "Status Report on the J. P. Stevens Boycott," June 5, 1978, fiche 1 of 9, "J. P. Stevens Progress Reports" file, Finley Papers.

15. Quotations from "Southerners for Economic Justice," n.d., fiche 3 of 9, same file. See also Samuel to General Officers and Leadership (see n. 7) and King, "Southern Leaders Form Group" (see n. 40, chap. 5).

16. 1978 ACTWU Convention Proceedings, 121; Coretta Scott King to Employees of J. P. Stevens Company, October 18, 1984, untitled folder, box 26, ACTWU-Atlanta. For her address to the 1977 Stevens stockholders' meeting, see Conway, *Rise Gonna Rise*, 136.

17. "From a Famous Rights Sit-in 20 Years Ago to Hub Counter," *Boston Globe*, May 25, 1980.

18. "Fight Racial Discrimination" (see n. 5). For the union's broader efforts to mobilize support from civil rights groups, see Mileski to General Officers and Leadership, March 24, 1977, "Status Reports I" folder, box 401, ACTWU-Cornell.

19. "Straightening Things Out" (see n. 42, chap. 1), 13–14.

20. "Women's Division, Board of Global Ministries, United Methodist Church," April 9, 1978; "National Assembly of Women Religious," n.d.; and "Statement of the Board of Directors of the National Coalition of American Nuns," March 1977, all in "Materials which accompanied Status Reports" folder, box 401, ACTWU-Cornell.

21. "NOW Protest Against J. P. Stevens," July 19, 1977 (quotations), and "National Organization for Women," n.d., same folder. For an overview of NOW's founding, see Chafe, *Paradox of Change*, 199, 202–4; Evans, *Born for Liberty*, 275–78.

22. "Resolution in Support of the Boycott of J. P. Stevens Products," April 29, 1977, same folder as n. 20.

23. "Action Alert," n.d., and "NOW Protest Against J. P. Stevens," July 19, 1977, same folder. Quotations in Carol Somplatsky-Jarman to Mileski, August 20, 1979, "Status Reports III" folder, box 401, ACTWU-Cornell.

24. Smeal quoted in James M. Shevis, "Women's Coalition Joins Stevens Fight," *AFL-CIO News*, March 25, 1978, in same folder as n. 20. For the organization of the National Women's Committee, see also "National Women's Committee to Support J. P. Stevens Workers: Founding Meeting," March 17, 1978, and "NOW Boycotts J. P. Stevens: Update," n.d., same folder.

25. Shevis, "Women's Coalition Joins Stevens Fight" (quotation); "NOW Boycotts J. P. Stevens: Update."

26. Smeal et al. to Gibbons, March 13, 1980, "Woolworth/Woolco" folder, box 401, ACTWU-Cornell.

27. Mary C. Steele to Ralph Lazarus, April 6, 1979, and Joy Chute to Lazarus, April 13, 1979, "Letters to Lazarus" folder, box 400, ACTWU-Cornell. For similar examples, see also Emma I. Darnell to Lazarus, May 16, 1979, same folder, and Cheryl R. Huff to Allen Questrom, November 16, 1979, "Rich's" folder, box 400, ACTWU-Cornell.

28. Mileski to General Officers and Leadership, January 8, 1979 (see n. 1, intro., with partial list of clippings on Justice Day protests across the country).

29. "Unionists Take Factory Boycott to Center Square," *Allentown Morning Call*, and "Rev. Graham Recalls Days Building Union," *Cincinnati Enquirer*, December 1, 1978, in Mileski to General Officers and Leadership, as above.

30. "Don't Buy J. P. Stevens Textile Products," *Oregon Labor Press*, December 8, 1978, and "Protest Staged at Mall," *New Haven Journal-Courier*, December 1, 1978, in same folder.

31. "State Labor Leaders Urge Textile Boycott" (see n. 1, intro.).

32. Mileski to General Officers and Leadership, January 8, 1979; "News from Stevens," November 30, 1978, "Status Reports II" folder, box 401, ACTWU-Cornell.

33. Minkoff to Mileski (see n. 11); Manfred Ohrenstein et al. to Marvin Traub, August 1, 1978, "Gimbels" folder, box 401, ACTWU-Cornell.

34. Examples of northern press coverage that mention the runaway shop theme are "Protest Staged At Mall" (see n. 30) and "Unionists March for Boycott," *Philadelphia Daily News*, December 1, 1978, in Mileski to General Officers and Leadership, as above. For the way union strategists exploited this issue, see ACTWU flyer "Why Did J. P. Stevens Close 21 Mills and Put 11,700 People Out of Work?" in fiche 3 of 8, "J. P. Stevens Citizens' Committee" file, Finley Papers.

35. "Partial List of Endorsements" (see n. 2, intro.).

36. Mileski to General Executive Board, October 7, 1977, fiche 4 of 9, "J. P. Stevens Progress Reports" file, Finley Papers; Sister Jeannine Maynard, C.P., "A Report on the Women's Constituency," September 1978, "Status Report I" folder, box 401, ACTWU-Cornell.

37. "Unionists Take Factory Boycott to Center Square" (see n. 29). For the growth of the southern automobile industry, see Hulsemann, "Greenfields."

38. Mileski to General Officers and Leadership, August 16, 1978, and Stetin to Herb Butler, May 23, 1979, "Stevens Boycott 1978" folder, box 33, ACTWU-Atlanta.

39. Schaufenbil interview, tape 2, side 1; Guzzardi, "Upper Hand," 98 (Aaron quotation); "Stevens Label Causes Stir," *Indianapolis Star*, December 1, 1978 (see n. 1, intro.).

40. Hall et al., *Like a Family*, 81–82; "Dust Standards"; "Brown Lung Isn't Beautiful," n.d., "Bloomingdale's" folder, box 400, ACTWU-Cornell; Darnell to Lazarus (see n. 27).

41. "Dust Standards," 31–32, 34.

42. "Please Don't Buy J. P. Stevens Products Sold at Bloomingdale's," n.d., "Bloomingdale's" folder, box 400, ACTWU-Cornell; Gloria Emerson, "Organizing the Plantation: The Union vs. J. P. Stevens," *Village Voice*, July 16, 1979, in "J. P. Stevens General Labor 1979" folder, box 677, ACTWU-Cornell.

43. "The Struggle for Economic Justice at J. P. Stevens," fiche 8 of 9, "J. P. Stevens Progress Reports" file, Finley Papers.

44. Ramona Ripston to Lazarus, April 11, 1979, and Darnell to Lazarus (see n. 27).

45. Report, October 9, 1979, "Status Reports II" folder, box 401, ACTWU-Cornell.

46. Hodges, "Real Norma Rae," 251–56; Buck interview.

47. Sheinkman to Field, April 11, 1980, same fiche as n. 1; "'Norma Rae' 1, J. P. Stevens 0," *Washington Post*, October 24, 1980. For Hollywood's depiction of unions in other films, see Walsh, "Films We Never Saw"; Zieger and Zieger, "Silver Screen."

48. Interoffice memo, August 29, 1979 (first quotation), and Sutton to Stetin, August 30, 1979, "J. P. Stevens/Crystal Lee Jordan/Sutton Unemployment Case" folder, box 367, ACTWU-Cornell.

49. Mileski to Sheinkman and Stetin, September 14, 1979, same folder; Hodges, "Real Norma Rae," 264–65.

50. Jeffords to Murray Finley et al., June 30, 1980, same fiche as n. 1; Hodges, "Real Norma Rae," 267.

51. Hodges, "Real Norma Rae," 253; "Struggle for Economic Justice" (see n. 43). For a broader perspective on the middle-class background of most feminists, see Chafe, *Paradox of Change*, 212–13; Woloch, *Women and the American Experience*, 348–49.

52. Jackson quoted in Sarah Blue, "Statesboro: Two Years Later: The Union Helps

Workers Survive As the J. P. Stevens Plant Lies Idle," *Labor Unity*, July 1977, in "J. P. Stevens and Company Statesboro, Georgia: Closing—J—General" folder, box 680, ACTWU-Cornell; "Illegally Fired Worker Reinstated" (quotation, 27).

53. Emerson, "Organizing the Plantation" (see n. 42), 11–15 (quotations, 11, 13); McConville, "Southern Textile War."

54. Conway, *Rise Gonna Rise*, 10–12, 191–96; *New York Times* quoted in Emerson, "Organizing the Plantation," 13; Mileski to General Officers and Leadership, March 24, 1977 (see n. 18).

55. ACTWU General Executive Board Minutes, March 28, 1978, p. 9, "3/28/78" folder, box 854; "Report to the IUD Executive Committee on the J. P. Stevens Campaign," October 1977, "History of J. P. Stevens Campaign up to 1977" folder, box 366; Hilda Howland M. Mason to Woodward and Lothrop Executive, March 3, 1980, "Woodward and Lothrop" folder, box 401, all in ACTWU-Cornell.

56. ACTWU GEB Minutes, March 1977 (see n. 8, intro.), 23, and June 1977 (see n. 13, chap. 5), 17.

Chapter 7. Corporate Campaigns and Boycotts

1. Swaity interview, tape 3, side 2.

2. Kelly, "Stevens Boycott" (see n. 4, chap. 1), 1, 23–25; "The Boycott Hasn't Hurt Us: Stevens," *Daily News Record*, November 6, 1978, in "J. P. Stevens Company Statements (Various)" folder, box 366, ACTWU-Cornell.

3. J. F. Carroll to Rev. William Troy, February 5, 1980, "Woolworth/Woolco" folder, and Rexford C. Simpson to Peter Goldstein, September 2, 1980, "J. C. Penney" folder, box 401, ACTWU-Cornell.

4. B. Somplatsky-Jarman to Allied Stores Interreligious Delegation Participants, April 7, 1980, "Allied" folder, box 400, ACTWU-Cornell; "Stevens Agent in Japan Said to Bar Imports," *Daily News Record*, November 29, 1977, in "International Japan" folder, box 390, ACTWU-Cornell; *Sixty Minutes*, "Target J. P. Stevens."

5. Kelly, "Stevens Boycott," 23–24; Miller to Beck (see n. 51, chap. 5).

6. Kelly, "Stevens Boycott," 5; Stevens 1978 Annual Report, 2, in "1967–1981" folder (see n. 21, chap. 1).

7. Kelly, "Stevens Boycott," 26–27; Stevens 1979 Annual Report, 2, and 1980 Annual Report, 2, in "1967–81" folder.

8. Henrietta Dabney to General Officers, February 22, 1980, pp. 1, 8, 9 (quotation, 1), "J. P. Stevens Boycott, February 22, 1980" folder, box 456, ACTWU-Cornell.

9. Kelly, "Stevens Boycott," 28–29 (Finley quotation, 29); "Gathering Momentum" (quotations, 147).

10. *Sixty Minutes*, "Target J. P. Stevens"; Patterson quoted in *MacNeill/Lehrer Report*, "J. P. Stevens."

11. Gay to Mileski, March 21 (first quotation) and July 31, 1979, and W. J. Ford to Allen Questrom, n.d., "Rich's" folder, box 400, ACTWU-Cornell.

12. "Report on the Women's Committee and Jordan Marsh," September 20, 1979, "Allied" folder, box 400, ACTWU-Cornell; B. Somplatsky-Jarman to Delegation (see n. 4).

13. Mileski to General Officers and Leadership, March 24, 1977, "Status Reports I" folder, box 401, ACTWU-Cornell; Mike Szpak to All Interested Parties, February 4, 1978, "Stevens Boycott 1978" folder, box 33, ACTWU-Atlanta.

14. "Questions and Notes—Delegation," June 24, 1980, "Woolworth/Woolco" folder, and Mileski Status Report, March 1979, "Status Reports II" folder, box 401, ACTWU-Cornell.

15. Goldstein to Mileski, December 19, 1978, "Sears" folder, box 401, ACTWU-Cornell; Artha Adair to Friend, n.d., and John Rizzo to David Dyson, August 4, 1980, "J. C. Penney" folder, same box.

16. Scheidt to Rev. Robert T. Strommen, February 14, 1979, "Montgomery Ward" folder; B. Somplatsky-Jarman to Mileski, June 18, 1979, "Status Reports III" folder; Bacon to Donald W. McIlvane, June 6, 1979, "Sears" folder, all in box 401, ACTWU-Cornell.

17. Carroll to Troy; Simpson to Goldstein, "J. C. Penney" folder, box 401, ACTWU-Cornell.

18. Scheidt to Strommen (see n. 16); Copeland to William K. Conrad, January 9, 1979, "Strawbridge and Clothier" folder, and C. Somplatsky-Jarman to Mileski, May 19, 1980, "Woolworth/Woolco" folder, box 401, ACTWU-Cornell.

19. ACTWU General Executive Board Minutes, December 3–7, 1977, pp. 15, 24 (quotation, 15), "GEB December 1977" folder, box 124, ACTWU-Cornell; "J. P. Stevens International Meeting," September 7, 1977, "International Japan" folder, box 390, ACTWU-Cornell.

20. "Zensen Action Programme Supporting Boycott Against J. P. Stevens," n.d., "International Japan" folder, and Janet Salaff to Beck, November 28, 1978, "International Japan" folder, same box.

21. Salaff to Beck; "Stevens Agent" (see n. 4).

22. K. Boeykens to Sir, May 13, 1980, and Charles Ford to Sheinkman, May 21, 1980, "International Ford Correspondence" folder, same box.

23. Ford to Mileski, July 11, 1977, "International ACTWU Correspondence" folder; Finley to Tadashi Miura, February 22, 1978, "International Japan" folder, both in box 390, ACTWU-Cornell.

24. Lionel Murray to Ford, October 15, 1979, same folder as n. 22.

25. Christophersen to Samuel, January 16, 1977, "International Labor Support" folder, box 367, ACTWU-Cornell.

26. Irving Brown to Sheinkman, March 28, 1980, "France—International" folder, and J. Macgougan to M. H. Finley, September 21, 1977, "International Japan" folder, box 390, ACTWU-Cornell.

27. Fred Dyson to Mileski, May 27, 1977, "International Japan" folder, same box; Ford to Sheinkman, October 12, 1976, and Mileski to Ford, October 22, 1976, "International Belgium" folder, same box.

28. "J. P. Stevens International Meeting" (see n. 19); quotation in Helen Dewar, "Foreign Aid Pledged in Textile Fight," *Washington Post,* September 3, 1977.

29. Hughes to Ford, November 16, 1976, "International—Australia" folder, box 390, ACTWU-Cornell.

30. Steve Hendrickson to Harriet Teller, May 5, 1977, "International Meeting Washington" folder, and Mileski to Sheinkman, January 23, 1979, "International Ford Correspondence" folder, box 390, ACTWU-Cornell.

31. Whalen, "Durable Threads" (quotation, 105); Hendrickson to Teller.

32. Macgougan to Finley (see n. 26); "Stevens Boycott in Japan," *Newsweek,* November 14, 1977, 39.

33. HB to SS, December 11, 1978, and Thompson to Finley, Sheinkman, and Stetin,

December 11, 1978, "J. P. Stevens Reports to Jack Sheinkman" folder, box 331, ACTWU-Cornell.

34. Si Kahn to ACTWU/IUD, May 22, 1978, "Si Kahn Services 10/25/76–1977–78" folder, box 367, ACTWU-Cornell.

35. Dennis, "Truce" (see n. 11, chap. 5); Michael C. Jensen, "Union Strategist on Wall Street," *New York Times,* March 26, 1978.

36. Savory, "Forced off the Board" (quotation, 17).

37. Ibid., 18; Wayne King, "Stevens Head Leaving Bank Under Pressure," *New York Times,* March 8, 1978.

38. "Gathering Momentum," 148; King, "Stevens Head Leaving" (Finley and Beck quotations, D1).

39. King, "Stevens Head Leaving"; "Unions: Labor's New Muscle," 58.

40. C. Somplatsky-Jarman to Chapter President, May 13, 1980, "Woolworth/ Woolco" folder, box 401, ACTWU-Cornell.

41. Michael C. Jensen, "Chairman of Avon Leaves Stevens on Union Pressure," *New York Times,* March 22, 1978 (first quotation); Savory, "Forced off the Board" (quotation, 25).

42. Savory, "Forced off the Board" (quotation, 17).

43. "People," *New York Times,* March 11, 1979 (quotation, C7); Damon Stetson, "Unions Stage J. P. Stevens Protest," *New York Times,* October 12, 1979, B3.

44. Rogers quoted in Derickson to Stetin, February 17, 1978, "J. P. Stevens Corporate Campaign 1977–78–79" folder, box 366, ACTWU-Cornell.

45. "Gathering Momentum," 148.

Chapter 8. The Backlash

1. "Stevens Employee Group Seeks Decert," *Labor Analysis and Forecast* 21:7 (April 1, 1977), in "J. P. Stevens—Newspaper Clippings," box 34, ACTWU-Atlanta.

2. James D. Finley to Stevens Employees, September 9, 1977, untitled folder, box 33, ACTWU-Atlanta; "Statement by J. P. Stevens and Company, Inc. Concerning the Union Boycott," June 1976, "J. P. Stevens 1976" folder, box 647, ACTWU-Cornell; *MacNeill/Lehrer Report,* "J. P. Stevens."

3. "News from Stevens," June 1976, untitled folder, box 58, ACTWU-Atlanta.

4. James D. Finley to All Stevens Employees, January 31, 1977, untitled folder, box 33, ACTWU-Atlanta. Similar letters are Finley to Stevens Employees and "Statement" (see n. 2).

5. Stefanie Weiss, "J. P. Stevens Administrator Defends Textile Company Against Union Accusations," *Cornell Daily Sun,* April 19, 1978, in "J. P. Stevens Company's Statements (Various)" folder, box 366, ACTWU-Cornell.

6. "Presentation to Presbyterian Church Group," November 9, 1976, pp. 3–4, fiche 1 of 5, "J. P. Stevens Clergy" file, Finley Papers (quotation); Palmer, "A National Boycott: The Most Unfair Labor Practice of All," November 9, 1977, "J. P. Stevens Company's Letters to its Workers, 1977–78" folder, box 366, ACTWU-Cornell; Mileski to General Officers and Leadership, January 8, 1979 (see n. 11, chap. 6), 8.

7. Barmash, "Stevens" (see n. 12, chap. 6).

8. Palmer, "National Boycott" (see n. 6).

9. "Boycotts Are Evil," *Greenville News-Piedmont,* June 13, 1976, and "Stevens Union Tiff Desperate Measure," *Greenville Piedmont,* August 15, 1976, in "J. P.

Stevens 1976" folder, box 647, ACTWU-Cornell. For the negative impact of this press opposition on the union's organizing campaign in the South, particularly in the Greenville area, see Michael Krivosh to McIver, June 18, 1976, same folder.

10. "No—Thank You!" *Hendersonville Times-News,* September 7, 1977, in "J. P. Stevens—Newspaper Clippings" folder, box 34, ACTWU-Atlanta.

11. Palmer, "National Boycott" (see n. 6).

12. "J. P. Stevens film—White Horse 1/10/78," "J. P. Stevens—Company Film—The Issue—The Right to Choose 1978" folder, box 366, ACTWU-Cornell.

13. Weiss, "Administrator Defends Textile Company" (see n. 5).

14. "Statement of J. P. Stevens" (see n. 4, chap. 4) (quotations, 3, 17, 22, 25).

15. Raskin, "Labor's Big Domino" (see n. 11, intro.) (quotations, C11); *MacNeill/ Lehrer Report,* "J. P. Stevens."

16. "Interview with anti-union 'consultant' George Hood," August 13, 1979, p. 20, "Richard Rothstein, 4/2/79–5/25/79" folder, box 331, ACTWU-Cornell; "Stevens Employee Group Seeks Decert" (see n. 1).

17. "Stevens Employee Group Seeks Decert" (see n. 1); "Watch Out for 'Stevens Bill' and Attack on R-T-W Laws," *Labor Analysis and Forecast* 21:9 (May 1, 1977), in "J. P. Stevens—Newspaper Clippings," box 34, ACTWU-Atlanta.

18. Savory, "Forced off the Board," 33; Robinson, *George Meany,* 372.

19. Institute for Southern Studies to Interested Parties, October 31, 1976, "J. P. Stevens Anti Union Committee (Work Folder)" folder, box 649, ACTWU-Cornell.

20. Jack F. Hankins to Helms, August 4, 1978, "Marshall v. J. P. Stevens Education Committee" folder, and NCFIR press release, November 17, 1978, "North Carolina Fund for Individual Rights" folder, box 648, ACTWU-Cornell.

21. NCFIR press release; Bryan quoted in Tony Dunbar to McIver, May 21, 1979, same folder.

22. Affidavit of Lambert, April 30, 1980, and Memorandum of Decision and Order, July 15, 1980, pp. 1, 10, 16 (quotations, 10), "Marshall v. J. P. Stevens Education Committee" folder, box 648, ACTWU-Cornell.

23. "Help Us Save Our Jobs: Buy Stevens Products," n.d., "Company Supporters—Stevens Employees Educational Committee" folder, box 366, ACTWU-Cornell.

24. *MacNeill/Lehrer Report,* "J. P. Stevens."

25. Ibid.

26. "Stevens Employes Hear Talk on Decertification," *Roanoke Rapids Daily Herald,* October 4, 1976, and Bush to Goldberg, October 4, 1976, same folder as n. 19.

27. Swaity interview, tape 3, side 2; NCFIR press release (see n. 20).

28. Goldberg to Larry Gold, November 6, 1980, same folder as n. 20; Rothstein note, same folder as n. 16. For the wider pioneering use of direct mail by New Right groups in the 1970s, see Chafe, *Unfinished Journey,* 463–64.

29. "If You Never Read Another Handout—Read This One"; "Don't Jump on a Sinking Ship"; "Ask J. P.—What Will Happen When Most Textile Workers Go Union?" all undated in "Leaflets and Labels" folder, box 29, ACTWU-Atlanta.

30. "Dear Fellow J. P. Stevens Worker," August 1979, "Wagram 1980" folder, box 29, ACTWU-Atlanta.

31. Ibid.; "5 Long Years," July 16, 1979, same folder.

32. "Buyer Beware," n.d., "Leaflets and Labels" folder, box 29, ACTWU-Atlanta.

33. "Everybody Is A Liar But The Union," n.d., and "Question—Would the Union Close Your Plant?" n.d., same folder.

34. "Caution: Don't Let <u>Anyone</u> talk <u>you</u> into <u>signing</u> your name on the <u>Union Blue</u>

Card," n.d., same folder; "No Raise," May 25, 1979, "Wagram" folder, box 29, ACTWU-Atlanta.

35. "Caution" (first quotation); "Special to Tifton Employees"; "Non-Union Meetings," all undated in "Leaflets and Labels" folder, box 29, ACTWU-Atlanta.

36. Ramsey to "Henry," January 4, 1977, "J. P. Stevens Educational Committee" folder, box 649, ACTWU-Cornell.

37. Brenda Paschal, "Stevens Backers Armed with Cards," *Greenville Piedmont*, December 13, 1977, in "ACW—J. P. Stevens Employees Education Committee" folder, box 649, ACTWU-Cornell.

38. Ramsey to Sir, n.d. (first quotation); Ramsey to Henry (see n. 36).

39. Hoyman interview (author); Lambert quoted in *Sixty Minutes*, "Target J. P. Stevens"; Smith quoted in *MacNeill/Lehrer Report*, "J. P. Stevens"; Purnell interview.

40. Institute for Southern Studies to Interested Parties, October 31, 1976, "J. P. Stevens Anti Union Committee (Work Folder) folder, box 649, ACTWU-Cornell.

Chapter 9. The New Stevens Strategy

1. 1978 ACTWU Convention Proceedings, 202.

2. Robinson, *George Meany*, 377–78; "Progress Report J. P. Stevens Organizing," November 3, 1977, fiche 1 of 8, "J. P. Stevens Citizens' Committee" file, Finley Papers.

3. "The Campaign to Organize J. P. Stevens," February 10, 1977, untitled folder, box 33, ACTWU-Atlanta; ACTWU GEB Minutes, February 1979 (see n. 50, chap. 5), 13; Kahn to ACTWU/IUD (see n. 34, chap. 7).

4. "Gathering Momentum" (quotation, 148); "Campaign" (see n. 3).

5. "Gathering Momentum"; McIver to J. P. Stevens Organizing Staff (see n. 26, chap. 1); "Progress Report" (see n. 2).

6. "J. P. Stevens and Co. Inc Position Paper," June 1, 1979, untitled folder, box 58, ACTWU-Atlanta; Stevens 1979 Annual Report, 20, in "1967–81" folder (see n. 21, chap. 1).

7. "AFL-CIO Meeting on J. P. Stevens," June 14, 1976, fiche 2 of 7, "J. P. Stevens Correspondence" file, Finley Papers.

8. "Watch Out for 'Stevens Bill'" (see n. 17, chap. 8).

9. Gordon interview, tape 5, side 1; Robinson, *George Meany*, 377; ACTWU GEB Minutes, June 1977 (see n. 13, chap. 5), 15.

10. "In the Name of 'Reform,' Union Leaders Now Reach for Unlimited Power," "J. P. Stevens Company's Letters to its Workers, 1977–78" folder, box 366, ACTWU-Cornell.

11. Robinson, *George Meany*, 377–78.

12. Ibid., 373–74; Zieger and Gall, *American Workers, American Unions*, 247–48.

13. The Weekly Organizing Activity Reports (hereafter cited as Weekly Reports) are in folders labeled with the organizer's name in boxes 48–50 and 56–58 of ACTWU-Atlanta. For the introduction of the new reports, and leaders' complaints that some organizers were not filling them in accurately, see McIver to All Stevens Staff, August 11, 1977, same folder as n. 9, intro.

14. Weekly Reports by Hamilton, August 18, 1979, box 48; Spencer, January 5, 1980, box 50; Nichols, July 28 and December 8, 1979, box 49.

15. Weekly Report by Mann, August 25, 1979, box 49. Mann further details these fears in reports of September 15, 22, and 30. For the Darlington case, see Daniel, *Culture of Misfortune*, 254–55.

16. J. P. Stevens Report, n.d., fiches 1 and 2 of 9, "J. P. Stevens Progress Reports" file, Finley Papers.

17. Jackson quoted in Sarah Blue, "Statesboro: Two Years Later," *Labor Unity,* July 1977; "Factory Opens in Statesboro," *Savannah Morning News,* October 17, 1978; Keir Jorgensen to Hoyman, October 19, 1979, all in "J. P. Stevens and Company, Statesboro, Georgia Closing—J—General" folder, box 680, ACTWU-Cornell.

18. Rothstein to Stetin, March 12, 1979, "J. P. Stevens Richard Rothstein 1980" folder, box 331, ACTWU-Cornell. For the union's typical focus on the company's lawlessness, see "J. P. Stevens 1979: 'Further Harm Is Done': A Report on J. P. Stevens and Company From Stevens Workers and The Amalgamated Clothing and Textile Workers Union," "J. P. Stevens and Company, Inc. Labor—General 1980–81" folder, box 677, and "The J. P. Stevens Company: Human Rights in 1977," "J. P. Stevens Human Rights Report 1978—Si Kahn" folder, box 366, ACTWU-Cornell.

19. Weekly Reports by Melvin Burris, September 1, 1979, box 48; Hamilton, August 18, 1979, box 48; John Barry, January 27, 1979, box 48; Kathleen Hope Curry, February 27, 1977, box 57.

20. Weekly Reports by Phillip R. Pope, October 15, 1977, box 57, and Pitt, September 22, 1979, box 49; Stevens 1977 Annual Report, 9, and 1979 Annual Report, 1, in "1967–81" folder (see n. 21, chap. 1).

21. Tedder quoted in Mary Bishop, "The Organizer: This Priest Has a Union Mission," *Charlotte Observer,* November 6, 1977, in NCCCF under "Stevens, J. P. and Co.—Unionization"; Weekly Report by Nichols, July 7, 1979, box 49. For the unevenness of economic growth in the Sun Belt era and the continuing dominance of low-wage industries such as textiles, see Cobb, *Selling of the South,* esp. 255–56; Schulman, *Cotton Belt to Sunbelt,* 180–82, 202–3; D. Goldfield, *Black, White, and Southern,* 204–5.

22. Weekly Report by Cumbee, December 22, 1979, box 48; "J. P. Stevens and Co., Inc.—Facts," June 13, 1977, "J. P. Stevens, Roanoke Rapids, Leaflets" folder, box 9; "ACTWU Facts," July 19, 1979, "Wagram—1980" folder, box 29, all in ACTWU-Atlanta.

23. "Position Paper" (see n. 6); Rothstein to Hoyman, June 15, 1978, "J. P. Stevens Richard Rothstein, 1978–79" folder, box 331, ACTWU-Cornell.

24. "Position Paper" (see n. 6); Nethery quoted in *MacNeill/Lehrer Report,* "J. P. Stevens."

25. Interview with Hood (see n. 16, chap. 8), 22–23.

26. Weekly Reports by Sachen, September 1 and October 6, 1979, box 49.

27. Builder, "J. P. Stevens: Walterboro, S.C. Campaign," February 1979, "J. P. Stevens Richard Rothstein 1978–1980" folder, box 331, ACTWU-Cornell.

28. Guzzardi, "Upper Hand" (quotation, 98).

29. ACTWU GEB Minutes, February 1979 (see n. 50, chap. 5), 10; Swaity interview, tape 3, side 2.

30. Stu Campbell, "Stevens Sees an End to Epic Labor Battles," *Daily News Record,* September 15, 1981, in "J. P. Stevens Magazine Articles, 1978–79" folder, box 366, ACTWU-Cornell; "Stevens Company: Human Rights in 1977" (see n. 18); 268 NLRB 25 at 93–96; 246 NLRB 133 at 1166–68; 240 NLRB 35 at 135.

31. "Is the J. P. Stevens War Over?" 85–87.

32. 243 NLRB 159 at 1004; 268 NLRB 20 at 31.

33. McIver to All J. P. Stevens Staff, May 26, 1977, same folder as n. 9, intro.; J. P. Stevens Report (see n. 16).

34. J. P. Stevens Report (see n. 16); "The NLRB Lands on Stevens," *New York Times,* January 1, 1978.

35. "NLRB Lands on Stevens"; ACTWU General Executive Board Minutes, June 12, 1978, "6/12/78" folder, box 854, ACTWU-Cornell.

36. "Stevens Plant Votes 68–48 to Unionize," *Raleigh News and Observer,* October 6, 1979, in NCCCF under "Stevens, J. P. and Company—Unionization"; "Is the J. P. Stevens War Over?" 85–87; "J. P. Stevens Workers Go Heavily for Union," *High Point Enterprise,* October 5, 1979, and "Union Officials Say Stevens Win No Turning Point," *Winston-Salem Journal,* October 6, 1979, in "J. P. Stevens High Point, North Carolina plant—Election 10–4–79" folder, box 366, ACTWU-Cornell.

37. Swaity, "J. P. Stevens Organizing Campaign: An Analysis and Recommendations," August 9, 1978, fiche 5 of 6, "J. P. Stevens" file, Finley Papers.

Chapter 10. We Need More White Involvement

1. Minchin, *Hiring the Black Worker,* 3.

2. Stevens 1977 Annual Report, 10, in "1967–81" folder (see n. 21, chap. 1).

3. Hoyman interview (TWUA), tape 3, side 2.

4. Hines interview.

5. Hines interview. The literature on the civil rights movement is vast, but for an effective summary of the movement's success in abolishing Jim Crow and inspiring blacks across the South, see Cook, *Sweet Land of Liberty?* 112–49; Fairclough, *Better Day Coming,* 249–71.

6. Hoyman interview (author).

7. Weekly Reports by Agre, September 30 and November 11, 1978, box 58. For similar problems, see also Agre's report dated December 4, 1978.

8. Weekly Reports by Tate, October 27, 1977, box 57, and Smith, September 1, 1979, box 49. See also similar reports by Smith dated August 25 and December 15, 1979.

9. Weekly Report by Sachen, May 12, 1979, box 49. Sachen detailed similar problems in several other reports; see report of August 11, 1979.

10. Weekly Report by Pope, October 22, 1977, box 57; Rothstein memo, March 5, 1979, "JPS—Richard Rothstein 1978–1980" folder, box 331, ACTWU-Cornell.

11. Rothstein to McIver, April 10, 1979, "Richard Rothstein, 4/2/79–5/25/79" folder, box 331, ACTWU-Cornell.

12. Weekly Report by Krenik, October 27, 1979, box 49; Rothstein, "Current Campaign Status," November 6, 1978, "J. P. Stevens, Richard Rothstein, 1978–79" folder, box 331, ACTWU-Cornell.

13. Minchin, *Hiring the Black Worker,* 36–37, 111–12; "Stevens Company: Human Rights in 1977" (see n. 18, chap. 9).

14. "Comparison of Pay Rates" (see n. 35, chap. 4).

15. Brown to Goldberg, August 23, 1976, "J. P. Stevens Milledgeville, Georgia" folder, box 22, ACTWU-Atlanta.

16. Weekly Report by Agre, December 4, 1978, box 58. For similar complaints, see report by Curry, August 21, 1977, box 57.

17. Weekly Report by Bagwell, April 7, 1979, box 48; Raynor interview.

18. "WHO AM I?" in "Wagram 1980" folder, and "WHY PAY <u>HARD EARNED MONEY TO THE UNION</u>?" in "Leaflets and Labels" folder, box 29, ACTWU-Atlanta.

19. John Barry, "Report on Film," January 20, 1978, "J. P. Stevens Education Committee" folder, box 649, ACTWU-Cornell.

20. "Stevens film—White Horse" (see n. 12, chap. 8), 10.

21. Brown to Goldberg (see n. 15); Hodges, "Stevens and the Union," 60. For an overview of the Montgomery bus boycott, see Williams, *Eyes on the Prize*, 59–89.

22. Weekly Reports by Cumbee, August 4, 1979, and Barry, June 9, 1979, box 48.

23. Barry, "Report on J. P. Stevens—Wagram, NC," March 18, 1981, "John Barry" folder, box 48, ACTWU-Atlanta.

24. "Report on J. P. Stevens Organizing Progress," May 16, 1977, fiche 6 of 9, "J. P. Stevens Progress Reports" file, Finley Papers.

25. Bishop, "The Organizer" (see n. 21, chap. 9); Stetin to William Roger Dove, May 23, 1980, "J. P. Stevens Richard Rothstein 1978–1980" folder, box 331, ACTWU-Cornell; McIver and Rothstein to Stetin, July 12, 1978, "J. P. Stevens Richard Rothstein, 1978–79" folder, same box.

26. Marsh to Rothstein, May 1, 1979, "Charles Marsh" folder, box 49; Fred Nye to Jack Goldstein, February 7, 1978, "Fred Nye" folder, box 56; Heller to Rothstein, August 15, 1979, "Jonathan Heller" folder, box 48, all in ACTWU-Atlanta.

27. Howard Brown to Stetin, December 19, 1979, "J. P. Stevens Richard Rothstein, 1978–79" folder, box 331, ACTWU-Cornell; "Progress Report on Organizing J. P. Stevens Plants," January 17, 1977, fiche 8 of 9, "J. P. Stevens Progress Reports" file, Finley Papers; Weekly Reports by Nye, May 27, 1978, box 56, and Tate, June 11, 1977, box 57.

28. ACTWU GEB Minutes, February 1979 (see n. 50, chap. 5), 12; Rothstein to Sheinkman, February 19, 1979, same folder as n. 11.

29. Rothstein to McIver, October 1979, same folder.

30. "Statement by J. P. Stevens and Company, Inc. Concerning the Union Boycott," June 1976, "J. P. Stevens 1976" folder, box 647, ACTWU-Cornell; "AFL-CIO Meeting on J. P. Stevens," June 14, 1976, fiche 2 of 7, "J. P. Stevens Correspondence" file, Finley Papers.

31. Rothstein to Stetin, August 1, 1978, "J. P. Stevens Richard Rothstein, 1978–79" folder, box 331, ACTWU-Cornell.

32. Reynolds to All Employees, June 26, 1978, and Rothstein to Swaity et al., July 14, 1978, "J. P. Stevens Company Letters to Its Workers" folder, box 366, ACTWU-Cornell. For another example of Stevens using the boycott against the union, see Jim Wellons to Bernice, June 28, 1978, same folder.

33. "Boycotts Are Evil," *Greenville News Piedmont*, June 13, 1976; "Stevens Union Tiff Desperate Measure," *Greenville Piedmont*, August 15, 1976; Krivosh to McIver, June 18, 1976, all in "J. P. Stevens 1976" folder, box 647, ACTWU-Cornell.

34. ACTWU GEB Minutes, December 1977 (see n. 19, chap. 7), 23; Dave Goldberg, "Southern Strategy: Textile-Union Dispute Pits Friend Against Friend," *Winston-Salem Journal*, November 6, 1977, in NCCCF under "Stevens, J. P. and Co.—Unionization."

35. Weekly Reports by Tate, February 5 and 12, 1977, box 57; Rothstein to Debbie Tyson, November 19, 1980, "Statesboro, Georgia" folder, box 29, ACTWU-Atlanta.

36. Deposition of Rice, April 25, 1979, pp. 9–58, *Amalgamated Clothing and Textile Workers Union, AFL-CIO v. Robert Rice et al.*, in fiche 2 of 3, "J. P. Stevens Milledgeville, Georgia" file, Finley Papers (quotations, 9, 10, 11).

37. Ibid., 11; "Statement of Facts," n.d., "J. P. Stevens Milledgeville" folder, box 628,

ACTWU-Cornell; affidavit of Miller, January 23, 1979, p. 2A, fiche 1 of 3, same file as n. 36.

38. Affidavit of Alston, July 29, 1978, pp. 1–4, same fiche (quotations, 3). For examples of the press coverage generated by the Milledgeville case, see Anne Adams and Peggy Marion, "Town vs. Union: The Trouble in Milledgeville," *Daily News Record,* July 23, 1979, and Steve Twomey, "A Ga. Town's Covert War against Unionism," *Philadelphia Inquirer,* August 26, 1979, in "J. P. Stevens Milledgeville" folder, box 628, ACTWU-Cornell; Urban C. Lehrer, "As Union Organizers Get to Milledgeville, Ga., The Mayor Holds an Unusual Welcoming Party," *Wall Street Journal,* February 29, 1980.

39. Twomey, "Ga. Town's Covert War" (see n. 38), 2A.

40. Alston quoted in Lehner, "Union Organizers" (see note 38); Tate quoted in Adams and Marion, "Town vs. Union" (see n. 38); "ACTWU News," December 13, 1979, "J. P. Stevens Milledgeville" folder, box 628, ACTWU-Cornell; "Concord Dropped From Suit; Will Pay ACTW $18,000," *Daily News Record,* December 14, 1979, in same folder.

41. ACTWU General Executive Board Minutes, February 25–29, 1980, p. 4, "GEB Minutes 8/25/80; 5/5/80; 2/25/80" folder, box 1005, ACTWU-Cornell; ACTWU General Executive Board Minutes, July 27–30, 1982, pp. 5–6, "GEB Minutes 7/27/82; 5/20/82" folder, box 1005, ACTWU-Cornell; "Elections and Recognitions (Other Than J. P. Stevens: ACTWU Textile Division)," January 1–December 31, 1978, folder 3, box 523, ACTWU-Cornell; "Recommendations to Improve Our Organizing Progress," September 21, 1981, pp. 9, 17, "GEB Minutes 10/26/81; 5/25/81; 4/14/81" folder, box 1005, ACTWU-Cornell.

Chapter 11. Settlement

1. "Press Conference—Stevens Settlement: Remarks of J. Sheinkman," October 19, 1980, "J. P. Stevens 1980–" folder, box 104, ACTWU-Cornell.

2. "Labor Takes Notice of Tactics by Organizer of J. P. Stevens Workers," *New York Times,* November 30, 1980 (quotation, 68); Contract Agreement, October 19, 1980, "J. P. Stevens Contract Agreement 1980" folder, box 104, ACTWU-Cornell.

3. Doug McInnis, "Stevens May Have Felt Pressure Put on Insurer," *Raleigh News Observer,* October 21, 1980, in NCCCF under "Stevens, J. P. and Co.—Unionization"; Dennis, "Truce" (see n. 11, chap. 5).

4. Franklin quoted in Savory, "Forced off the Board," 39; S. Campbell, "Epic Labor Battles" (see n. 30, chap. 9).

5. "Stevens Accord"; "Ripples Spreading," 108; Jensen, "Chairman of Avon Leaves Stevens" (see n. 41, chap. 7); "J. P. Stevens: A Beginning or an End?" *Economist,* October 25, 1980, clipping in "J. P. Stevens and Company Inc. General Labor, 1980–81" folder, box 677, ACTWU-Cornell.

6. Hoyman interview (author); Shabecoff, "J. P. Stevens Pact: Breakthrough, but War Goes On," *New York Times,* October 21, 1980.

7. ACTWU GEB Minutes, March 1978 (see n. 55, chap. 6), 10 (first quotation), and February 1979 (see n. 50, chap. 5), 10.

8. McInnis, "Pressure Put on Insurer" (see n. 3); "Is the J. P. Stevens War Over?" 85, 87 (quotation, 85).

9. James D. Finley to All Stevens Employees, September 20, 1979 (see n. 20, chap.

4); B. Somplatsky-Jarman to Mileski, July 6, 1979 (see n. 19, chap. 4). For Finley's unhappiness with any softening in the firm's antiunionism, see Guzzardi, "Upper Hand," 98.

10. Dennis, "Truce" (see n. 11, chap. 5).

11. ACTWU General Executive Board Minutes, October 19, 1980, p. 2, "GEB Minutes 2/23/81; 1/7/81; 10/19/80" folder, box 1005, ACTWU-Cornell; Dennis, "Truce."

12. Dennis, "Truce."

13. ACTWU GEB Minutes, October 1980 (see n. 11), 2, 3.

14. ACTWU General Executive Board Minutes, January 7, 1981, p. 4, same folder as n. 11.

15. "Devil's Advocate Questions," n.d., "J. P. Stevens 1980–" folder, box 104, ACTWU-Cornell; Shabecoff, "Stevens Pact Is Ratified, Encouraging Unions in South," New York Times, October 20, 1980 (quotations, A16).

16. Bob Hiles, "Will Town Live Happily Ever After?" Greensboro Daily News, October 23, 1980, in NCCCF under "Stevens, J. P. and Co.—Unionization."

17. Ibid.

18. Moynihan to Sheinkman, October 22, 1980; Harrington to Murray Finley, October 21, 1980; Metzgar to Sheinkman, October 22, 1980; Mitchell and Arnold Aronson to Finley, October 22, 1980, all in "J. P. Stevens 1980–" folder, box 104, ACTWU-Cornell.

19. Gene Upshaw and Ed Garvey to Murray Finley, October 22, 1980, and statement by Kirkland, October 19, 1980, same folder.

20. 1981 ACTWU Convention Proceedings, 33.

21. Shabecoff, "Stevens Pact Is Ratified" (see n. 15) (quotation, A16); Bernstein, "The Fall of J. P. Stevens and Co.: A Triumph for Labor's Southern Strategy," Los Angeles Times, October 26, 1980, pt. 7 (quotation, 1).

22. Warren Brown, "Great Labor War Gains Tallied," Washington Post, October 26, 1980; 1982 ACTWU Executive Board Report, 64; "Fact Sheet: ACTWU-J. P. Stevens Roanoke Rapids Contract," n.d., "J. P. Stevens 1980–" folder, box 104, ACTWU-Cornell.

23. 1982 ACTWU Executive Board Report (quotations, 64); "Fact Sheet."

24. "Ripples Spreading," 107; "Devil's Advocate Questions" (see n. 15).

25. Kugler to Murray Finley, October 21, 1980, and Chaikin to Finley, October 20, 1980, "J. P. Stevens 1980–" folder, box 104, ACTWU-Cornell.

26. ACTWU GEB Minutes, October 1980 (see n. 11), 2.

27. Hal Taylor, "Stevens-ACTWU Shape Up Comprehensive Agreement," Daily News Record, July 31, 1980, in "J. P. Stevens 1980–" folder, box 104, ACTWU-Cornell.

28. Judith Schoolman, "Stevens' Pact Irks Some Dixie Mill Men," Daily News Record, October 21, 1980.

29. John Barry, "Report on J. P. Stevens—Wagram, NC," March 18, 1981, "Wagram" folder, box 29, ACTWU-Atlanta.

30. "Recommendations" (see n. 41, chap. 10), 2.

31. McInnis, "J. P. Stevens Pact Silences Union Blitz," Raleigh News and Observer, February 8, 1981, in NCCCF under "Stevens, J. P. and Co.—Unionization."

32. McInnis, "Pressure Put on Insurer" (see n. 3).

33. Brown, "War Gains Tallied" (see n. 22) (quotation, A14); ACTWU General Executive Board Minutes, March 5–8, 1984, p. 16, "GEB Minutes 9/29–30/83; 3/5–8/84; 5/1–3/84; 6/4/84–6/6/84" folder, box 1005, ACTWU-Cornell; ACTWU GEB Minutes, June 1977 (see n. 13, chap. 5), 34.

34. "Stevens Announces Sixth Plant Closing," *Textile Week,* January 4, 1982, in "Stevens Clippings—1983" folder, box 628, ACTWU-Cornell; Harold E. Addis to Hoyman, December 3, 1982, "J. P. Stevens West Boylston Plant" folder, same box.

35. "Agreement Ends Bitter Struggle," *Hickory Daily Record,* October 26, 1981, in NCCCF under "Stevens, J. P. and Co.—Unionization"; ACTWU General Executive Board Minutes, February 23–27, 1981, same folder as n. 11 (quotations, 4, 7).

36. ACTWU GEB Minutes, March 1984 (see n. 33), 8, and July 1982 (see n. 41, chap. 10), 3.

37. ACTWU GEB Minutes, June 1977 (see n. 13, chap. 5), 3.

38. ACTWU GEB Minutes, January 1981 (see n. 14), 6; Stetin to Sheinkman, January 23, 1981, and Sheinkman to Stetin, January 23, 1981, "ACTWU Jack Sheinkman" folder, box 51, ACTWU-Cornell.

39. ACTWU General Executive Board Minutes, May 20–21, 1982, p. 4, "GEB Minutes 7/27/82; 5/20/82" folder, box 1005, ACTWU-Cornell; Stetin quoted in Hodges, "Stevens and the Union," 63.

40. "Agreement Ends Bitter Struggle" (see n. 35); "Recommendations" (see n. 41, chap. 10), 4, 9 (quotation, 4).

41. ACTWU GEB Minutes, July 1982 (see n. 41, chap. 10), 7.

42. "The Stevens Settlement," *Southern Textile News,* November 17, 1980, in "J. P. Stevens and Co. Inc., General Labor, 1980–81" folder, box 677, ACTWU-Cornell.

43. "Stevens Accord"; Daniel, *Culture of Misfortune,* 279.

44. Hiles, "Will Town Live Happily Ever After?" (see n. 16).

45. McInnis, "Pact Silences Union Blitz" (see n. 31); "Agreement Ends Bitter Struggle" (see n. 35).

46. 1987 ACTWU General Executive Board Report, 4; Hoyman interview (author).

47. "Robert T. Stevens Dies at 83: Rites Wednesday," *Daily News Record,* February 1, 1983, in "Stevens Clippings 1983" folder, box 628, ACTWU-Cornell; ACTWU GEB Minutes, March 1984 (see n. 33), 17.

48. "NLRB Clears Settlement of J. P. Stevens Charges," *Daily Labor Report* no. 204 (October 20, 1983), "J. P. Stevens ACTWU Press Release 10/83 NLRB Settlement after Twenty Years" folder, box 628, ACTWU-Cornell.

49. Joann S. Lublin, "J. P. Stevens Agrees to Spend $1.2 Million to End 20–Year War with Clothing Union," *Wall Street Journal,* October 21, 1983 (Stevens quotation); "Stevens' Settlement With Union Approved," *Winston-Salem Journal,* October 21, 1983, in same folder.

Epilogue

1. Stevens 1977 Annual Report, in "1967–1981" folder (see n. 21, chap. 1); Stevens 1987 Annual Report, "J. P. Stevens and Company Inc. Annual Reports, 1982–1988" folder, box 677, ACTWU-Cornell; Hodges, "Stevens and the Union," 62; Zingraff, "Facing Extinction?" 199–200, 209–16; Zieger and Gall, *American Workers, American Unions,* 244.

2. Gaventa and Smith, "Deindustrialization," 182–83; Speizer, "Crisis in Asia" (see n. 21, intro.).

3. John Holusha, "Squeezing the Textile Workers: Trade and Technology Force a New Wave of Job Cuts," *New York Times,* February 21, 1996 (statistic, D1).

4. 1987 ACTWU General Executive Board Report, 6–7.

5. Ibid., 24–25.

6. ACTWU GEB Minutes, March 1984 (see n. 33, chap. 11), 7 (quotation); Glass, *Textile Industry*, 96–100.

7. Stevens 1987 Annual Report, in "1982–1988" folder (see n. 1); Hodges, "Stevens and the Union," 62.

8. Leslie Wayne, "Buyout Bid Is Received by Stevens," *New York Times*, February 9, 1988 (quotation, D1).

9. Peter Applebome, "Reminders of Its Old Poverty Hit South in Recession's Grip," *New York Times*, September 10, 1991 (quotation, D19).

10. Zieger and Gall, *American Workers, American Unions*, 263–64; *Where Do You Stand?*; Lunan, "Empty Mills Burden Carolinas" (see n. 21, intro.).

11. "Pulling J. P. Stevens, and Labor, into 1980," *New York Times*, October 21, 1980; David Firestone, "Union Victory at Plant in South Is Labor Milestone," *New York Times*, June 25, 1999; *Where Do You Stand?*; Tony Mecia, "Pillowtex Judge OKs Sale," *Charlotte Observer*, October 8, 2003; Sara Leitch, "Unemployed Residents Can Get Free Food," *Charlotte Observer*, October 3, 2003.

12. Boyer et al., *Enduring Vision*, 705 (quotation); "Boycott of Textile Company Supported at 75 Colleges" (see n. 9, chap. 6). For the way civil rights historians have focused mainly on the major protests of the 1955–65 era, see Norrell, "One Thing We Did Right"; Wright, "Economic Consequences"; Williams, *Eyes on the Prize*. For an overview of the New Right's emergence in the late 1970s, see Chafe, *Unfinished Journey*, 461–66; Berman, *America's Right Turn*, 28–29, 60–63; Morgan, *Beyond the Liberal Consensus*, 179–83.

13. As Robert Zieger and Gilbert Gall have noted (*American Workers, American Unions*, 248), "by the time of conservative icon Reagan's victory over Carter in 1980, the outlines of the precipitous decline of labor's political, and eventually organizational, fortunes were clear."

14. Meany quoted in Robinson, *George Meany*, 372; Swaity to All ACTWU Vice Presidents, Regional and Industry Directors, January 3, 1979, untitled folder, box 58, ACTWU-Atlanta.

15. Zieger and Gall, *American Workers, American Unions*, 243; Norwood, *Strikebreaking and Intimidation*, 246–47.

16. *MacNeill/Lehrer Report*, "J. P. Stevens"; quotation in TWUA Testimony (see n. 7, chap. 2), 47.

17. Donald C. Carroll, dean of Wharton School, University of Pennsylvania, quoted in Jensen, "Chairman of Avon Leaves Stevens" (see n. 41, chap. 7).

18. For an overview of other corporate campaigns and how they were influenced by the Stevens struggle, see Juravich and Bronfenbrenner, *Ravenswood*, 69–72; Minchin, *Forging a Common Bond*, 172–73. On the Hormel strike, see Rachleff, *Hard-Pressed in the Heartland*. On the IP dispute, see Getman, *Betrayal of Local 14*.

19. Juravich and Bronfenbrenner, *Ravenswood*, 110–19, 156–69 (quotation, 169); Minchin, *Forging a Common Bond*, 84–85, 99–100, 130–31.

20. Dewar, "Foreign Aid Pledged" (see n. 28, chap. 7); "Filibusters Have Thwarted Labor Law Reform Over the Years," *Paperworker*, September 1994, 8.

21. Hodges, "Stevens and the Union" (quotation, 63); Raynor interview; Zieger and Gall, *American Workers, American Unions*, 244–46, 252–56, 261–62, 267–69.

BIBLIOGRAPHY

ACTWU (Amalgamated Clothing and Textile Workers Union) Papers. Kheel Center for Labor-Management Documentation and Archives, School of Industrial and Labor Relations, Cornell University, Ithaca, N.Y.

ACTWU (Amalgamated Clothing and Textile Workers Union) Southern Regional Office Papers. Southern Labor Archives, Pullen Library—South, Georgia State University, Atlanta.

Alston, Sammy. Interview with author. Roanoke Rapids, N.C., February 9, 1996.

"America's Stake in the South." *Textile Labor,* July 1963, 3–5.

Arthur, Bill. "The Darlington Mills Case; or, 17 Years Before the Courts." *New South* 28 (summer 1973): 40–47.

Bartley, Numan V. *The New South, 1945–1980: The Story of the South's Modernization.* Baton Rouge: Louisiana State University Press, 1995.

Berman, William C. *America's Right Turn: From Nixon to Bush.* Baltimore: Johns Hopkins University Press, 1994.

Boone, James. Interview with author. Roanoke Rapids, N.C., February 9, 1996.

Boyer, Paul S., Clifford E. Clark Jr., Sandra McNair Hawley, Joseph F. Kett, Neal Salisbury, Harvard Sitkoff, and Nancy Woloch. *The Enduring Vision: A History of the American People.* Concise 3rd ed. Boston: Houghton Mifflin, 1998.

Brattain, Michelle. *The Politics of Whiteness: Race, Workers, and Culture in the Modern South.* Princeton, N.J.: Princeton University Press, 2001.

Buck, Billy. Interview with author. Opelika, Ala., January 26, 1996.

Bush, Clyde. Interview with author. Roanoke Rapids, N.C., February 9, 1996.

Campbell, Jerome. "The Head of the House of J. P. Stevens." *Modern Textiles Magazine,* January 1960, 21–22, 41.

Chafe, William H. *The Paradox of Change: American Women in the 20th Century.* New York: Oxford University Press, 1991.

———. *The Unfinished Journey: America Since World War II.* 3rd ed. New York: Oxford University Press, 1995.

Clark, Daniel J. *Like Night and Day: Unionization in a Southern Mill Town.* Chapel Hill: University of North Carolina Press, 1997.

Cobb, James C. *The Selling of the South: The Southern Crusade for Industrial Development, 1936–1980.* Baton Rouge: Louisiana State University Press, 1982.

Conway, Mimi. *Rise Gonna Rise: A Portrait of Southern Textile Workers.* Garden City, N.Y.: Anchor Press, 1979.

Cook, Robert. *Sweet Land of Liberty? The African-American Struggle for Civil Rights in the Twentieth Century.* London: Longman, 1998.

Cook, Wesley W. Interview. TWUA Oral History Project, April 6–7, 1978.

Cribbs, Myrtle. "I Think the Day of Reckoning Is Coming." *Mountain Life and Work,* September 1978, 14–15.

Cross, Malcolm A. *Dan River Runs Deep: An Informal History of a Major Textile Company, 1950–1981.* New York: Total Book, 1982.

Daniel, Clete. *Culture of Misfortune: An Interpretative History of Textile Unionism in the United States.* Ithaca, N.Y.: ILR Press, 2001.

DeMoss, Dorothy. *The History of Apparel Manufacturing in Texas, 1897–1981.* New York: Garland, 1989.

Draper, Alan. *Conflict of Interests: Organized Labor and the Civil Rights Movement in the South, 1954–1968.* Ithaca, N.Y.: ILR Press, 1994.

"Dust Standards." *Mountain Life and Work,* September 1978, 30–43.

Eskew, Glenn T., ed. *Labor in the Modern South.* Athens: University of Georgia Press, 2001.

Evans, Sara M. *Born for Liberty: A History of Women in America.* New York: Free Press, 1989.

Fairclough, Adam. *Better Day Coming: Blacks and Equality, 1890–2000.* New York: Viking, 2001.

Fiester, Kenneth. Interview. TWUA Oral History Project, April 10–11, 1978.

Flamming, Douglas. *Creating the Modern South: Millhands and Managers in Dalton, Georgia, 1884–1984.* Chapel Hill: University of North Carolina Press, 1992.

Fraser, Steve. *Labor Will Rule: Sidney Hillman and the Rise of American Labor.* New York: Free Press, 1991.

Garrow, David J. *Protest at Selma: Martin Luther King, Jr., and the Voting Rights Act of 1965.* New Haven, Conn.: Yale University Press, 1978.

"A Gathering Momentum against J. P. Stevens." *Business Week,* March 20, 1978, 147–48.

Gaventa, John, and Barbara Ellen Smith. "The Deindustrialization of the Textile South: A Case Study." In Leiter, Schulman, and Zingraff, *Hanging by a Thread,* 181–96.

Geoghegan, Thomas. *Which Side Are You On? Trying to Be for Labor When It's Flat on Its Back.* New York: Farrar, Straus and Giroux, 1991.

Getman, Julius. *The Betrayal of Local 14: Paperworkers, Politics, and Permanent Replacements.* Ithaca, N.Y.: ILR Press, 1998.

Glass, Brent D. *The Textile Industry in North Carolina: A History.* Raleigh: North Carolina Department of Cultural Resources, 1992.

Goldfield, David R. *Black, White, and Southern: Race Relations and Southern Culture, 1940 to the Present.* Baton Rouge: Louisiana State University Press, 1990.

Goldfield, Michael. *The Decline of Organized Labor in the United States.* Chicago: University of Chicago Press, 1987.

Gordon, William. Interview. TWUA Oral History Project, November 10, 1977; July 19, 1978.

Griffith, Barbara S. *The Crisis of American Labor: Operation Dixie and the Defeat of the CIO.* Philadelphia: Temple University Press, 1988.

Gross, James A. *Broken Promise: The Subversion of U.S. Labor Relations Policy, 1947–1994.* Philadelphia: Temple University Press, 1995.

Guzzardi, Walter, Jr. "How the Union Got the Upper Hand on J. P. Stevens." *Fortune,* June 19, 1978.

Haberland, Michelle. "Women's Work: The Apparel Industry in the United States South, 1937–1980." Ph.D. diss., Tulane University, 2001.

Hall, Jacquelyn Dowd. "Disorderly Women: Gender and Labor Militancy in the Appalachian South." *Journal of American History* 73 (September 1986): 354–82.

Hall, Jacquelyn Dowd, James Leloudis, Robert Korstad, Mary Murphy, Lu Ann Jones, and Christopher B. Daly. *Like A Family: The Making of a Southern Cotton Mill World*. Chapel Hill: University of North Carolina Press, 1987.

Hartford, William F. *Where Is Our Responsibility? Unions and Economic Change in the New England Textile Industry, 1870–1960*. Amherst: University of Massachusetts Press, 1996.

Hines, Vonnie. Interview with author. Chapel Hill, N.C., February 20, 1996.

Hodges, James A. *New Deal Labor Policy and the Southern Cotton Textile Industry, 1933–1941*. Knoxville: University of Tennessee Press, 1986.

———. "The Real Norma Rae." In Zieger, *Southern Labor in Transition*, 251–72.

———. "J. P. Stevens and the Union: Struggle for the South." In *Race, Class, and Community in Southern Labor History*, edited by Gary M. Fink and Merl E. Reed, 53–64. Tuscaloosa: University of Alabama Press, 1994.

Hoyman, Scott. Interview. TWUA Oral History Project, May 1985.

———. Interview with author. Summerville, S.C., November 6, 1995.

Hueter, Joseph. Interview. TWUA Oral History Project, April 18–19, 1977; July 20 and 22, 1977; July 23, 1978.

Hulsemann, Karsten. "Greenfields in the Heart of Dixie: How the American Auto Industry Discovered the South." In *The Second Wave: Southern Industrialization from the 1940s to the 1970s*, ed. Philip Scranton, 219–54. Athens: University of Georgia Press, 2001.

"Illegally Fired Worker Reinstated." *Mountain Life and Work*, September 1978, 26–27.

Irons, Janet. *Testing the New Deal: The General Textile Strike of 1934 in the American South*. Urbana: University of Illinois Press, 2000.

"Is the J. P. Stevens War Over?" *Business Week,* June 9, 1980, 85–87.

Juravich, Tom, and Kate Bronfenbrenner. *Ravenswood: The Steelworkers' Victory and the Revival of American Labor.* Ithaca, N.Y.: ILR Press, 1999.

Kovler, Peter. "The South: Last Bastion of the Open Shop." *Politics Today,* March-April 1979, 26–31.

"Labor in the South: The Stonewall at Stevens." *Commonweal,* March 31, 1978, 196–98.

Leiter, Jeffrey, Michael D. Schulman, and Rhonda Zingraff, eds. *Hanging by a Thread: Social Change in Southern Textiles*. Ithaca, N.Y.: Cornell University Press, 1991.

MacNeill/Lehrer Report. "J. P. Stevens." Videotape. PBS, December 22, 1976. Transcript in untitled folder, box 58, ACTWU-Atlanta.

Marshall, F. Ray. *Labor in the South*. Cambridge, Mass.: Harvard University Press, 1967.

McConville, Ed. "The Southern Textile War." *Nation,* 2 October 1976, 294–99.

McHugh, Cathy L. *Mill Family: The Labor System in the Southern Cotton Textile Industry, 1880–1915.* New York: Oxford University Press, 1988.

Minchin, Timothy J. *Forging a Common Bond: Labor and Environmental Activism during the BASF Lockout*. Gainesville: University Press of Florida, 2003.

———. *Hiring the Black Worker: The Racial Integration of the Southern Textile Industry, 1960–1980*. Chapel Hill: University of North Carolina Press, 1999.

———. *What Do We Need a Union For? The TWUA in the South, 1945–1955*. Chapel Hill: University of North Carolina Press, 1997.

Moody, Joe P. Interview with author. Roanoke Rapids, N.C., March 12, 1996.

Morgan, Iwan W. *Beyond the Liberal Consensus: A Political History of the United States since 1965.* New York: St. Martin's Press, 1994.

Mountain Life and Work. "Special Issue: Southern Textile Workers," September 1978. Copy in "J. P. Stevens Magazine Articles, 1978–79" folder, box 366, ACTWU-Cornell.

Norrell, Robert J. "One Thing We Did Right: Reflections on the Movement." In Robinson and Sullivan, *New Directions in Civil Rights Studies,* 65–80.

Norwood, Stephen H. *Strikebreaking and Intimidation: Mercenaries and Masculinity in Twentieth-Century America.* Chapel Hill: University of North Carolina Press, 2002.

Overton, Jim, et al. "The Men at the Top: The Story of J. P. Stevens" *Southern Exposure* 6 (spring 1978): 52–63.

Perkel, George. Interview. TWUA Oral History Project, September 25 and 28, 1978; November 16, 1978.

Pope, Laura Ann. Interview with author. Andrews, S.C., April 1, 1996.

Purnell, Jettie. Interview with author. Roanoke Rapids, N.C., February 9, 1996.

Rachleff, Peter. *Hard-Pressed in the Heartland: The Hormel Strike and the Future of the Labor Movement.* Boston: South End Press, 1993.

Raskin, A. H. "Show 'Em the Clenched Fist." *Forbes,* October 2, 1978, 31–32.

Raynor, Bruce. Interview with author. Greensboro, N.C., July 28, 1995.

"The Ripples Spreading from the Stevens Pact." *Business Week,* November 3, 1980, 107–10.

Robinson, Archie. *George Meany and His Times: A Biography.* New York: Simon and Schuster, 1981.

Robinson, Armstead L., and Patricia Sullivan, eds. *New Directions in Civil Rights Studies.* Charlottesville: University Press of Virginia, 1991.

Rogin, Lawrence. Interview. TWUA Oral History Project, May 2, 1978.

Rosenblum, Jonathan D. *Copper Crucible: How the Arizona Miners' Strike of 1983 Recast Labor-Management Relations in America.* Ithaca, N.Y.: ILR Press, 1995.

Salmond, John A. *Gastonia, 1929: The Story of the Loray Mill Strike.* Chapel Hill: University of North Carolina Press, 1995.

———. *The General Textile Strike of 1934: From Maine to Alabama.* Columbia: University of Missouri Press, 2002.

Savory, Laina. "Forced off the Board: The ACTWU Corporate Campaign against J. P. Stevens." *Directors and Boards,* summer 1979, 16–43. Copy in folder "J. P. Stevens and Company Inc. General Labor 1979," box 677, ACTWU-Cornell.

Schaufenbil, Francis. Interview. TWUA Oral History Project, December 5, 1978.

Schulman, Bruce J. *From Cotton Belt to Sunbelt: Federal Policy, Economic Development, and the Transformation of the South, 1938–1980.* New York: Oxford University Press, 1991.

Simon, Bryant. *A Fabric of Defeat: The Politics of South Carolina Millhands, 1910–1948.* Chapel Hill: University of North Carolina Press, 1998.

Sixty Minutes. "Target J. P. Stevens." Videotape. CBS, March 13, 1977. Copy in ACTWU-Cornell.

Sledge et al. v. J. P. Stevens. Case 1201, United States District Court, Eastern District of North Carolina, 1970. Records held at the court.

Stetin, Sol. Interview. TWUA Oral History Project, July 18, 1977; March 13–14, 1978; July 25, 1978; November 16, 1978.

"Stevens Accord: Semi-Cease-Fire in the South." *Time,* November 3, 1980, 83.

"Stevens Boycott in Japan." *Newsweek,* November 14, 1977, 39.

"Stevens Ignores the Law." *Mountain Life and Work,* September 1978, 5–7.

"The Story of J. P. Stevens." *Mountain Life and Work,* September 1978, 17–23.

Swaity, Paul. Interview. TWUA Oral History Project, November 15, 1978.

Taylor, Bennett. Interview with author. Roanoke Rapids, N.C., February 9, 1996.

Todd, Edward. Interview. TWUA Oral History Project, September 28, 1978.

Toplin, Robert Brent. "Norma Rae: Unionism in an Age of Feminism." *Labor History* 36 (spring 1995): 282–98.

Tucker, George. "The Struggle to Organize J. P. Stevens." *Political Affairs* 57 (May 1978): 2–9.

TWUA (Textile Workers Union of America) Papers. State Historical Society of Wisconsin, Madison.

"Unions: Labor's New Muscle." *Newsweek,* April 3, 1978, 58–59.

"A Victory for Stuart Workers." *Mountain Life and Work,* September 1978, 8–10.

Waldrep, G. C., III. *Southern Workers and the Search for Community: Spartanburg County, South Carolina.* Urbana: University of Illinois Press, 2000.

Walsh, Francis R. "The Films We Never Saw: American Movies View Organized Labor, 1934–1954." *Labor History* 27 (fall 1986): 564–80.

Whalen, Richard J. "The Durable Threads of J. P. Stevens." *Fortune,* April 1963.

"When a Union Goes All Out in a Boycott Drive." *U.S. News and World Report,* June 20, 1977, 71–72.

Where Do You Stand? 25 Years in a Southern Textile Mill. Videotape. Nyack, N.Y.: Mighty Fine Films, 2003.

Williams, Juan. *Eyes on the Prize: America's Civil Rights Years, 1954–1965.* New York: Viking, 1987.

Woloch, Nancy. *Women and the American Experience: A Concise History.* New York: McGraw-Hill, 1995.

Wright, Gavin. "Economic Consequences of the Southern Protest Movement." In Robinson and Sullivan, *New Directions in Civil Rights Studies,* 175–83.

Zieger, Gay P., and Robert H. Zieger. "Unions on the Silver Screen: A Review Essay." *Labor History* 23 (winter 1982): 67–78.

Zieger, Robert H. *The CIO, 1935–1955.* Chapel Hill: University of North Carolina Press, 1995.

———, ed. *Organized Labor in the Twentieth-Century South.* Knoxville: University of Tennessee Press, 1991.

———, ed. *Southern Labor in Transition, 1940–1995.* Knoxville: University of Tennessee Press, 1997.

Zieger, Robert H., and Gilbert J. Gall. *American Workers, American Unions.* 3rd ed. Baltimore: Johns Hopkins University Press, 2002.

Zingraff, Rhonda. "Facing Extinction?" In Leiter, Schulman, and Zingraff, *Hanging by a Thread,* 199–216.

INDEX

Aaron, Benjamin, 102
ABC (American Broadcasting Companies), 91, 105
Aberdeen, N.C., 60, 62, 67, 68, 147
Abraham & Strauss (retail chain), 97
ACLU. *See* American Civil Liberties Union (ACLU)
ACTWU. *See* Amalgamated Clothing and Textile Workers Union (ACTWU)
ACWA. *See* Amalgamated Clothing Workers of America (ACWA)
Addis, Hal, 28–29, 150, 167
AFL (American Federation of Labor), 11, 16
AFL-CIO: and authorization cards, 141; creation of, 16; on employer intimidation, 7; and increased resistance to unionization, 65; Industrial Union Department (IUD) of, 15–16, 19, 36, 46, 47–48, 51, 58; and Jimmy Carter, 89; and labor law reform, 5, 7, 66, 141, 143, 183–84; mentioned, 62; and NAFTA, 181; North Carolina local of, 74; and organizing drives, 6, 16, 86, 143; predecessors of, 11, 12, 16, 17; and Selma-Montgomery march, 40; and Stevens campaign, 4, 48, 65–66, 76, 86, 90, 171, 174; and TWUA, 48, 86, 87
African Americans: twenty-first-century unions and, 184; churches of, 162; and civil rights movement, 5, 39, 68, 154, 155, 159; and class-action suits, 70, 156–57; as clergy, 155, 163–64; and credit, 158; and EEOC, 70; and job discrimination, 5, 23–24, 71, 83, 95–96, 154, 155, 156–57, 159; in Milledgeville, Ga., city government, 164; mill occupations of, 23–24, 25, 39, 52, 60, 61, 71, 76, 96, 155, 157, 159; number of, at Stevens plants,

5, 154; and Oneita Knitting Mills, 83; and Southerners for Economic Justice, 94, 102; and southern textile industry, 23, 60–61, 68; and TWUA, 32, 69; as union opponents, 158–59, 163–64; as union organizers, 160; as union supporters, 5–6, 24, 52, 61, 68, 70, 71, 76, 80–81, 138–39, 153, 154, 155, 157–58, 159, 164; wages of, 94, 96, 154, 157
Agre, Louis, 155, 157
Air traffic controllers, 176
Alabama, 185n3. *See also* specific locations
Albany, N.Y., 1
Albemarle Paper Company, 74, 135
Aldridge, William C., 38
Allendale, S.C., 145, 152
Allentown, Pa., 99, 101–2
Allied Stores (retail chain), 114
Alston, C. Wayman, 163–64
Alston, Sammy, 23–24
Amalgamated Clothing and Textile Workers Union (ACTWU): after 1980 settlement, 176; and AFL-CIO, 76; and apparel industry, 88; and authorization cards, 141, 152–53; and bargaining rights, 4, 141–42, 152–53; and benefits, 148; and changes in Stevens's tactics, 140–41, 151, 152; civil rights record of, 69–70, 160; community opposition to, 151; conflict within, 153, 154, 160–61; on Congress and free trade, 180; and continuation of Stevens campaign, 45; court decisions favoring, 151; creation of, 3, 76, 87, 141; and Crystal Lee Sutton, 106–8; damages paid to, 164, 178; and difficulties obtaining office space, 162; and elections, 141, 143, 152, 165, 176; and

Black Hawk cotton warehouse
(Greenville, S.C.), 52–53
Blacklisting, 11–12, 49–50, 137
Blackwell, Danny, 81
Blakely, Ethel, 39, 40
Blakeney, Whiteford, 38, 151
Bloom, Howard, 81
Bob Jones University, 42
Bond, Julian, 94
Bon Marché (retail chain), 118
Boone, James, 72, 80
Boston, Mass., 20, 95, 97
Botelho, Mike, 30
Bowen, William, 54
Boyce, Timmons, 157–58
Boycott, against Stevens: ACTWU and,
87–89, 122, 141; adoption of, 76;
American unions and, 86, 101–2, 110; as
antiunion issue, 112, 113–14, 133, 140,
143, 151, 153, 154, 158, 161, 162; and
appeals to retailers, 85; benefits of, 85–
86; celebrity support for, 91, 104–5;
church groups and, 90, 93–94, 110, 114,
128–29; civil rights groups and, 90, 94–
95, 114; clergy on, 129; committees for,
88; communities and, 88, 110, 162;
consumers and, 113; costs of, 85, 174;
Employee Education Committees
on, 4; end of, 3, 166, 175, 176; in
Europe, 119–20; impact of, 111–12, 113,
139, 140, 168; international unions and,
112, 117–19, 121–22; and Justice for J. P.
Stevens' Workers Day, 1–2; launch of,
2, 3, 61, 88–89, 90, 131, 141; and letter-
writing campaigns, 114; literature
related to, 85, 88, 91–92, 93, 95, 103,
105, 118, 120; media coverage of, 108–
10, 113, 162; minority support for, 110;
and NLRA, 85; in North, 115; obstacles
to, 111, 119; offices of, 88; petitions for,
88; political support for, 2, 90–91, 99–
100, 101; and profitability, 147; publicity
for, 85, 90, 118; and public relations, 2;
and racial discrimination, 95; retail
stores and, 88, 111–12, 113, 114–17; risks
of, 76, 84–85; Roanoke Rapids, N.C.,
and, 81, 134; senior citizens' groups
and, 90; Southerners for Economic
Justice and, 94; Stevens People and
Friends for Freedom and, 138;

Stevens's response to, 112–13, 114–15,
127–29, 130–31, 147, 158, 161, 162;
students and, 90, 92–93; TWUA
consideration of, 82–87; women and,
90, 96–98, 114
Boycotts: ACWA and, 83; AFL-CIO
support for, 66; costs of, 87; against
Farah Manufacturing Company, 76, 83,
85, 87, 94, 110, 112, 137; in France, 120;
illegal, 87, 112, 120, 162; against Oneita
Knitting Mills, 83; success of, 82–83;
United Farm Workers and, 83, 94
Boyd, Lloyd A., 50
British American Tobacco, 119
British National Union of Dyers,
Bleachers, and Textile Workers, 120
British Tobacco Workers' Union, 119
Britton, Joseph Carlton, 35
Broughton, William, 34
Brown, John, 3
Brown, Ralph Manning, Jr., 92, 125
Brown, Robert Tim, 157, 159
Brown lung disease, 22, 83, 102–4, 130
Brussels, Belgium, 118
Bryan, Richard J., 133
Bryan, Wilson, 133
Buckner, Nadine, 23
Buffalo, N.Y., 129, 130
Builder, Nick, 149
Burlington, N.C., 12
Burlington Industries: and affirmative
action, 70; and government contracts,
19, 70; industry position of, 15;
nonunionized plants of, 177; and plant
distribution, 17; TWUA assessment of,
18, 19, 20; and unionization, 17, 18, 21, 88
Burns, Leland, 33–34, 41–42
Burroughs, Larry Emerson, 65
Bush, Clyde, 73, 80, 169, 177
Bush, Joyce, 170
Business Week, 113, 167
Byssinosis. *See* Brown lung disease

Campbell, Randy, 181
Canada, 117
Cannon, Lundee, 22
Cannon Mills, 20, 21, 77, 176, 177, 181
Capitol Hill, 170. *See also* Congress, U.S.;
Washington, D.C.
Carey, Hugh L., 1, 100

of, 7; results of, 112, 140; Stevens executives on, 167

Costanza, Midge, 98

Cotton dust, 80, 96–99, 102–4, 130; standards for limiting, 102, 103

Council of Labor Union Women, 2

Court of Appeals, U.S., 3, 49, 55–56, 145–46, 151

Courts, 2–3, 4, 35, 36, 107, 117, 134

Crafted with Pride in the USA program, 180

Cribbs, Myrtle, 22, 54–55, 108

Crown Mills, 47

Cudd, Jess, 31–32, 36

Cudd, Mrs. Jess, 31–32

Culture of Misfortune (Daniels), 4

Cumbee, Verney L., 147

Cuomo, Mario, 1

Daily News Record, 15, 29, 66, 173

Daily Tar Heel, 133

Daniel, Clete, 4, 177

Dan River Mills, 47, 70

Danville, Va., 12

Darlington, S.C., 12, 21, 38, 49, 145

Darnell, Emma L., 104

Deauthorizations, 182

Decatur, Ga., 114

Decertifications, 133, 134, 182

Deering Milliken, 12, 21, 38, 49, 133, 177

Defense, Department of, U.S., 48, 70

Delaware, 11

Democrats, 49, 89, 100, 143, 181, 184

Dennis, G. W., 32–33

Derickson, Alan, 125–26

Detroit, Mich., 99, 129, 130

Detroit Free Press, 108

District Court, U.S., 65, 134. *See also* Courts

Donahue, Thomas R., 86

Dorn, William Jennings Bryan, 49

Downing, Rudolph, 161

Drug and Hospital Workers Union, 51

Dublin, Ga., 53, 162

Du Bose, Harold, 40

Dues, union: automatic checkoff of, 3, 78–79, 120, 137, 172

Dunean plants (Greenville, S.C.): African Americans at, 39; antiunion propaganda at, 37–38, 39; elections at,
39, 40–41, 43, 50; and firing of union members, 31, 32–33; and integration, 39–40; products of, 17; threat of closing, 38; union opponents at, 138; union supporters at, 50

Dupree, Franklin T., 134

Durham, N.C., 12

Dyers Federation, 67

Dyson, Fred, 120

Economist, 167

Economy, 73, 84, 117, 129

Edwards, Lonnie, 37–38

EEC. *See* Employee Education Committees (EECs)

EEOC (Equal Employment Opportunity Commission), 70, 71

Elections, union: in 1980, 176; in Aberdeen, N.C., 60, 62, 67, 68; ACTWU and, 141, 143, 165, 176; in Allendale, S.C., 152; at Aragon Mill (Rock Hill, S.C.), 13; at Black Hawk cotton warehouse (Greenville, S.C.), 52–53; at Cannon Mills (Kannapolis, N.C.), 77; at Dunean plants (Greenville, S.C.), 39, 40–41, 43, 50; at Estes plant (Piedmont, S.C.), 40–41; Harold McIver on, 142; in High Point, N.C., 152; in Kannapolis, N.C., 77, 181–82; and Labor Reform Act of 1977, 143; at Linn-Corriher Corporation (N.C.), 176; in Montgomery, Ala., 159; Murray Finley on, 141; NLRB and, 43, 63, 77, 141, 182; at Oneita Knitting Mills, 83; proportion won by unions, 182; in Roanoke Rapids, N.C. (1948), 13; in Roanoke Rapids, N.C. (1959), 18; in Roanoke Rapids, N.C. (1965), 43, 46, 70, 72; in Roanoke Rapids, N.C. (1974), 61, 68, 73, 74, 75–76, 77, 84, 86, 108, 134, 142–43; in Rock Hill, S.C., 13, 175; in Shelby, N.C., 60; in South (1978), 165; in Statesboro, Ga., 54–55, 61; Stevens on, 142–43; and Stevens boycott, 143; in Turnersburg, N.C., 60, 62, 67; unsuccessful, 45, 46, 56, 59, 60, 136; in Wallace, N.C., 76–77; in Wallace, S.C., 63, 64, 67; in Walterboro, S.C., 60, 62–63, 67, 68, 149

El Paso, Tex., 137

Emerson, Gloria, 108–9

Employee Education Committees (EECs): arguments of, 136–38, 140; and decertification, 133; and direct mail, 136; financing of, 127, 133; organization of, 131; and race, 138–39, 157; in Roanoke Rapids, N.C., 114, 133–35; in Slater, S.C., 135; Stevens and, 151; and Stevens boycott, 4, 112, 127, 139, 140; success of, 4–5, 136; supporters of, 136, 138–39; in Tifton, Ga., 135, 136, 137; in Wagram, N.C., 135–36, 137–38

England. *See* United Kingdom
Episcopal Diocese of Massachusetts, 95
Equal Rights Amendment, 97–98
Ervin, Sam, 49
Estes plant (Piedmont, S.C.), 40–41, 42
Europe, 117, 118, 119–20, 121, 183
Evans, David L., 151

"Fall of J. P. Stevens, The" (Bernstein), 171
Farah Manufacturing Company: boycott of, 76, 83, 85, 87, 94, 110, 112, 137; brand names of, 112; Ray Rogers and, 122; and retail market, 112
Faulcon, Cromwell, 71
Federal Bureau of Investigation (FBI), 65
Federated Department Stores, 98, 104
Feinstein, Frederic, 132
Fendley, Amos E., 32
Field, Sally, 106, 109
Fifth Circuit Court. *See* Court of Appeals, U.S.
Fine Arts (Stevens brand name), 112
Finley, James D.: as antiunion symbol, 169; assessments of, 66; biography of, 66–67; on labor movement, 128; on labor relations, 66; and letters to company workers, 128; management style of, 66, 67; and Manufacturers Hanover Trust Company, 123, 124; and Murray Finley, 169; and New York Life Insurance board, 125; replacement of, 168–69; and Robert T. Stevens, 66, 67; and settlement, 168–69; as Stevens board member, 169; as Stevens CEO, 15, 66, 67; and Textile Manufacturers' Institute, 131; on underpricing products, 113

Finley, Murray H.: on 1980 settlement, 169–70; on ACTWU budget, 175; on ACTWU image, 109; as ACWA head, 88; and apparel industry, 88; biography of, 88; on Burlington Mills, 88; on elections, 141; on imports, 175; interviews by, 88; and James D. Finley, 169; on organization efforts, 173, 175, 176; on secret negotiations with Stevens, 168, 169; on Stevens boycott, 91, 119; on Stevens campaign, 3, 88; and Whitney Stevens, 169
Firings, of union supporters: in Anderson, S.C., 16, 48; causes given for, 31, 32–34; Crystal Lee Sutton and, 105; in Dublin, Ga., 53; in Great Falls, S.C., 30, 35; in Greenville, S.C., 31, 32–33, 35, 42, 51; in Hickory, N.C., 54; mentioned, 2, 27, 45, 145, 182; in Milledgeville, Ga., 164; and NLRB hearings, 21, 32, 33, 34, 35, 36, 42, 145, 150; number of, 150; and reinstatement, 36–37, 75, 178, 183; in Roanoke Rapids, N.C., 21, 30, 31, 32, 33–35, 49–50, 80, 105; in Rock Hill, S.C., 34, 50; in Statesboro, Ga., 55; Stevens on, 33–35, 36–37, 50; in Taylorsville, N.C., 48; at Victor plant, 31; in Wallace, S.C., 63, 64; in Walterboro, S.C., 63; in Whitmire, S.C., 31–32, 36
Florida, 185n3
Fonda, Jane, 91, 105
Ford, Gerald, 89
Ford, W. J., 114
Fortune, 9, 20, 29, 90, 121, 149
Foster, Roger D. 42
Fowler, Melvin, 50
Foxton, New Zealand, 120
France, 117, 120, 121
Franklin, James R., 167
Freehold, N.J., 9
Freeman, Robert, 15
Froeber, Robert, 53–54
Fruit of the Loom (brand name), 120
F. W. Woolworth (retail chain), 95, 98, 111, 115, 116, 117

Galbraith, John Kenneth, 91
Gall, Gilbert J., 6, 214n13
Garfield, N.J., 9
Gay, Joel, 114

Mondale, Walter, 89
Montgomery, Ala., 39, 40, 56, 159, 172, 175
Montgomery Ward (retail chain), 115–16
Moody, Joseph P., 24
Moore, Philip W., 85–86
Moore, Ralph, 42–43
Motley, Al, 36, 64, 65
Moynihan, Daniel Patrick, 170
M. T. Stevens, 14, 20
Murray, Lionel, 119
"My Hometown" (Springsteen), 9–10

NAACP. *See* National Association for the Advancement of Colored People (NAACP)
NAFTA. *See* North American Free Trade Agreement (NAFTA)
Nagoya, Japan, 118
Nash, Peter, 85
Nation, 109
National Association for the Advancement of Colored People (NAACP), 2, 39, 90, 94
National Association of Manufacturers, 144
National Coalition of American Nuns, 96
National Consumer League, 97
National Council of Catholic Women, 96, 97
National Council of the Churches of Christ, 93–94
National Football League Players Association, 171
National Industrial Recovery Act (NIRA), 11
National Labor Relations Act (NLRA), 21, 58, 85, 100
National Labor Relations Board (NLRB): and ACTWU, 141, 142; and ACWA, 85; AFL-CIO on, 66; and back pay awards, 7, 58; on Black Hawk cotton warehouse layoffs, 52–53; charges before, 145; Crystal Lee Sutton and, 106; and decisions against Stevens, 2–3, 21, 48, 51, 53, 54, 57, 58–59, 91; and decisions for Stevens, 150; and decisions against TWUA, 63, 65; and decisions against Wellington Mills, 48; and Department of Defense, 48; and Dublin, Ga., 53; and

elections, 43, 55, 63, 77, 136, 141, 182; on firings of union supporters, 27, 54, 55; on harassment of union supporters, 34; hearings by, 36, 42; and Hickory, N.C., 54; Jerold Lehlman and, 149; and Labor Reform Act of 1977, 143; Lawrence Gore on, 35; media and, 51; mentioned, 143; pace of, 7, 130; preparation of cases for, 36; recognition by, 152; and reinstatement of fired workers, 7, 35, 53, 58, 106, 182–83; Richard Scheidt on, 117; and Roanoke Rapids, N.C., 43, 75, 134, 151; and Shelby, N.C., 53; staffing levels of, 183; and Statesboro, Ga., 55, 61; Stevens and, 27, 28, 33, 130, 149, 150, 166; Stevens supporters on, 138; and Tifton, Ga., 150–51; TWUA and, 44, 55, 82; on union's rights to address workers in plants, 172; on use of company resources to cause union withdrawals, 41; and Wallace, N.C., 77; and Wallace, S.C., 63; Whitney Stevens and, 178. *See also* specific networks; specific publications
National Organization for Women (NOW), 2, 96–98, 99
National Right to Work Committee, 106
National War Labor Board, 12
National Women's Committee to Support J. P. Stevens Workers, 97–98
National Women's Party, 97
Negro College Fund, 157
Nethery, Opal, 148
New Deal, 11
New England, 6, 9–11, 20, 114, 122
New Haven, Conn., 100, 115
New Jersey, 11, 49, 67, 143, 146
New Right, 136, 182
New South Wales, Australia, 120
Newsweek, 121
New York, N.Y.: corporate campaign against Stevens in, 125, 126; Justice for J. P. Stevens' Workers Day in, 1, 99, 100; Manufacturers Hanover Trust Company in, 123; mentioned, 81, 98; secret negotiations in, 168; and Stevens boycott, 1, 88, 97, 99, 100, 101; Stevens executives in, 51; Stevens headquarters in, 1; taxes in, 129, 130;

New York, N.Y. (cont.):
unemployment in, 130; wages in, 129,
130
New York City Central Labor Council,
168
New York Daily News, 108
New York Life Insurance, 125
New York Times: on 1968 TWUA
convention, 47; on 1980 settlement,
168, 171, 181; and ACTWU, 109; A. H.
Raskin column in, 131; on Great Falls,
S.C., 181; on Roanoke Rapids, N.C.,
victory (1974), 75; and Robert T.
Stevens, 51–52; on Stevens, 75, 171; and
Stevens campaign, 51, 75, 186n11; on
student activism, 93
New York Times Magazine, 105
New York University, 92
New Zealand, 117, 120
Nichols, Eddie, 145, 147
NIRA. *See* National Industrial Recovery
Act (NIRA)
Nixon, Richard M., 89, 102–3
NLRA. *See* National Labor Relations Act
(NLRA)
NLRB. *See* National Labor Relations
Board (NLRB)
Norma Rae (film): Crystal Lee Sutton on,
107; impact of, 91, 105, 106; inspiration
for, 2, 4, 105, 109; and Stevens boycott,
2; synopsis of, 106; viewings of, 121, 170
North: ACTWU support in, 100; brown
lung issue in, 103; deindustrialization
of, 88, 91, 100, 130; economy of, 100;
liberals in, 91; media coverage in, 100;
politicians in, 100; public opinion in,
102; and Stevens boycott, 91; taxes in,
129–30; unemployment in, 129–30;
unionization in, 130; wages in, 129–30
North American Free Trade Agreement
(NAFTA), 7, 181
North Carolina: AFL-CIO local in, 74;
Indians in, 159–60; mentioned, 125;
NLRB staff in, 150; regions of, 61, 76,
129, 159; senators from, 49, 133; state
line of, 64; textile employment in, 11,
179, 185n3; unemployment in, 84, 182;
union membership in, 11, 79. *See also*
specific locations
North Carolina Conservative Union, 133

North Carolina District Court, 134. *See
also* Courts
North Carolina Fund for Individual
Rights, 133
North Carolina Textile Manufacturers'
Association, 177
Northwestern University, 88
Norwood, Stephen H., 7, 182
NOW. *See* National Organization for
Women (NOW)
Nye, Fred, 161

Occupational Safety and Health Act, 82
Ogletree, J. Frank, 149
Ohio, 11, 99
Ohmikenshi Cotton Shipping Factory,
118
Oil, Chemical & Atomic Workers Union,
183
Oneita Knitting Mills, 83
Opelika, Ala., 106
Opelika Manufacturing Company, 106
Operation Dixie, 12, 26, 173
Operation Focus, 46
Organizers, union, 160–61
Osaka, Japan, 118
Osborne, Charles, 163
OSHA (Occupational Safety and Health
Administration), 103
Oswald, Rudolph, 174

Pacific Mills (Columbia, S.C.), 147
Palmer, E. Marshall, 128–29, 130
Pamplico, S.C., 156
Paris, France, 121
PATCO. *See* Professional Air Traffic
Controllers Organization (PATCO)
Patterson, Gene, 114, 136
Patterson, Henry, Jr., 79–80
Patterson Mill (Roanoke Rapids, N.C.),
13
PBS (Public Broadcasting Service), 80–
81, 109
Peanuts (Stevens brand name), 112
Pedigo, Joe, 18
Penney, J. C. *See* J. C. Penney (retail
chain)
Pennsylvania, 11. *See also* specific
locations
Pentagon, 48, 98

Stepto, Bob, 54
Stetin, Sol: on 1980 settlement, 170; on
ACTWU layoffs, 175; and AFL-CIO,
87; on African Americans, 5, 68; on
arbitration, 78; biography of, 67–68;
and Crystal Lee Sutton, 106–7;
mentioned, 81; on merging with
another union, 68, 87, 170; on northern
textile industry, 86; on Oneita Knitting
Mills boycott, 83; on organizing South,
86; photos of, 104, 107; on post-
settlement organization efforts, 175; on
Reagan administration, 176; and
Roanoke Rapids, N.C., 68, 70; on
runaway shops, 10–11; on southern
textile workers, 77; and Stevens
campaign, 2, 20, 58, 67, 68, 84, 86, 92,
102; on Stevens's response to organization, 27; on strikes, 12–13, 78, 84; on
UAW, 102; and Wallace, N.C., 76, 77;
on William Pollock, 19
Stevens, John (ancestor), 14
Stevens, John P. (descendant), 14
Stevens, J. P. (company). *See* J. P. Stevens
Stevens, Moses, 14
Stevens, M. T. (company). *See* M. T.
Stevens
Stevens, Nathaniel, 14
Stevens, Robert Ten Broeck: ACTW
assessment of, 2; biography of, 14–15;
continuing influence of, 67; death of,
178; as head of J. P. Stevens, 15; and
James D. Finley, 66, 67; management
style of, 66, 67; media and, 20, 29, 51–
52; response of, to union, 29, 52;
retirement of, 178; as secretary of the
army, 14–15, 20; and Stevens's labor
policies, 178; and World War II, 66
Stevens, Whitney, 92, 167, 168, 169, 178,
180
Stevens bill. *See* Labor Reform Act of
1977
Stevens-Bremner (Australia), 121
Stevens-Bremner (New Zealand), 120
Stevens I (NLRB cases), 28
Stevens People and Friends for Freedom
(SPFF), 138
Stevens Tower (New York, N.Y.), 15, 51,
99
Straub, Bob, 99–100

Strawbridge and Clothier (retail chain),
117
Strikebreaking and Intimidation
(Norwood), 182
Strikes: by air traffic controllers, 176; as
antiunion issue, 12, 37–38, 62, 76, 134,
137, 138; by auto workers, 3; chances
for success of, 78, 83–84, 183; community opposition to, 84; general textile,
11–12, 13, 38; in Henderson, N.C., 12,
18–19, 37–38, 62; media and, 12; against
Oneita Knitting Mills, 83; in Piedmont
region, 11; in Rock Hill, S.C., 13, 21, 38;
in Rockville, Conn., 9; by steelworkers, 3; Stevens on, 53, 76, 78, 84; and
strikebreakers, 12, 13, 84; as traditional
tactic, 8; TWUA and, 62, 76, 78, 79, 84
Students: activism of, 93, 95; Roanoke
Rapids EEC on, 134; and Stevens
boycott, 90, 92–93, 95, 128; as union
supporters, 45, 50–51, 90, 92–93, 95,
128, 182
Supreme Court, U.S., 36, 107. *See also*
Courts
Sutton, Crystal Lee, 4, 74, 91, 105–8, 109
Swaity, Paul: on AFL-CIO campaigns, 16;
on African American support, 68; on
Burlington Industries, 20; on continuation of Stevens campaign, 67; on
failure to obtain contracts, 79; on need
for economic impact on Stevens, 111;
on non-dues-paying workers, 79; and
non-Stevens drives, 161; on organizing
strategy, 152; on other businesses'
adoption of Stevens's tactics, 182; on
post-1965 organization efforts, 46; on
resources assigned to Stevens
campaign, 46, 193n4; and Roanoke
Rapids, N.C., 46, 70, 72, 78, 135, 150; on
Schneider Mills, 48; and staff
shortages, 46; and Statesboro, Ga., 78;
on Stevens's strategies, 20, 150; and
targeting of Stevens, 20; on Wallace,
N.C., election, 77
Synagogue Council of America, 94
Szpak, Mike, 115

Tariff Schedule, U.S., 180
Tastemaker (Stevens brand name), 112
Tate, Mel, 156, 161, 163, 164

Taxes, 7, 15, 129–30, 183
Taylor, Bennett, 72, 73–74
Taylor, Lucy, 21–22
Taylorsville, N.C., 48
Teamsters, 39, 102
Tedder, Debbie, 147
Tennessee, 99, 185n3
Texas, 83, 93, 124, 137
Textile industry: and 1980 settlement, 171, 177; African Americans in, 5; decline of, 178, 179, 181; employment levels in, 179; and imports, 7, 175, 179; Lane Kirkland on, 171; and layoffs, 146–47; migration of, to South, 6; and NAFTA, 7, 181; in New England, 6; and plant locations, 13; and plant size, 13; profitability of, 113; union forecast for, 181; unionization of, 2, 3; wages in, 172
Textile industry, northern, 6, 38, 67, 68, 86, 130
Textile industry, southern: African Americans and, 5, 23; and benefits, 25–26; and blacklists, 137; and brown lung disease, 22; and civil rights movement, 24–25; and class, 23; competition in, 137; and cotton-dust standards, 102–3; and economy, 2, 6–7, 147; and imports, 137; and labor shortage, 60; leaders of, 131, 133, 177; and other industries, 147; and plant closings, 180; and plant locations, 13, 147; post-Civil War, 23; privileges in, 37; and race, 23, 24, 39, 60–61, 68; Roanoke Rapids, N.C., EEC on, 134; scholarship on, 4; Stevens on, 131; and support for Stevens, 131; unionization efforts in, 67, 131; and wages, 25–27, 37, 57, 69, 148; women and, 23; worker migration from, 57; working conditions in, 69
Textile Labor, 16, 51, 58
Textile Manufacturers' Institute, 131
Textile Workers Organizing Committee (TWOC), 12
Textile Workers Union of America (TWUA): in 1930s and 1940s, 6; on 1965 campaign, 44; and ACWA, 83; and AFL-CIO, 16, 48, 86; and African Americans, 60, 61, 68, 158; and arbitration, 56, 78; and automatic checkoff of union dues, 56, 77–79; and

Black Hawk cotton warehouse (Greenville, S.C.), 52–53; and boycott against Stevens, 82–87; and Burlington Industries, 20; and Cannon Mills, 20, 77; changing tactics of, 45, 46, 75–76, 81–82; civil rights groups and, 83; and civil rights movement, 24–25; civil rights record of, 69–70, 158; civil suit by, 65; and collapse of first Stevens campaign, 36; and Congress, 47, 49; and continuation of Stevens campaign, 45, 56, 58–59, 60, 67, 68; conventions of, 19, 47, 58–59, 68; on court rulings, 55–56, 58–59; and deindustrialization of North, 10–11, 87; in Dublin, Ga., 53; and elections, 43, 45, 46, 56, 59, 60; establishment of, 12; factions within, 19; feminist-group support for, 83; and finances of, 3, 6, 174; and fired workers, 35–36, 58; on government contracts to Stevens, 45; in Hickory, N.C., 54; and Hilton hotels, 47; "holding operations" of, 46; image of, 19; on importance of Stevens campaign, 47; and imports, 87; and industrial migration to South, 6, 88; on integration of textile industry, 69; and IUD, 19, 58; and labor law reform, 26, 45, 46–47, 57; and labor leaders' support, 45; and media, 47; membership of, 6, 11, 68, 79, 87; and merger with ACWA, 3, 76, 87, 122, 170; NLRB decisions against, 63, 65; in North, 10–11, 38; and Oneita Knitting Mills boycott, 83; oral history project of, 69; and organizing drives, 2–3, 45, 46; papers of, 186n13; political support for, 45; and preparation of NLRB cases, 36; publications of, 46–47; and publicity, 45, 46–47, 57, 67, 90; rallies of, 58; and religious leaders, 47; and reporting of members' names to management, 35; and Roanoke Rapids, N.C., 13, 18, 43, 61, 68, 70–74, 77–79, 80; and Rock Hill, S.C., 13; and Schneider Mills (Taylorsville, N.C.), 48; in South, 11; on "southern anti-union conspiracy," 45, 47; and Statesboro, Ga., 54–55, 56, 59, 145; and Stevens campaign, 2, 3, 16–21, 26, 43, 45, 52, 56, 57–59, 60, 67, 68, 86; on

Tim Minchin is a senior lecturer in North American history at La Trobe University in Melbourne, Australia. He has authored five books on the topic of labor as well as several articles and pamphlets. He was awarded the Richard A. Lester Prize for the Outstanding Book in Labor Economics and Industrial Relations in 1999 for his *Hiring the Black Worker: The Racial Integration of the Southern Textile Industry, 1960–1980.*